BEING EURASIAN

MW00982321

Hong Kong University Press thanks Xu Bing for writing the Press's name in his Square Word Calligraphy for the covers of its books. For further information, see p. iv.

BEING EURASIAN
Memories Across Racial Divides

VICKY LEE

香港大學出版社

HONG KONG UNIVERSITY PRESS

Hong Kong University Press
14/F Hing Wai Centre
7 Tin Wan Praya Road
Aberdeen
Hong Kong

ISBN 962 209 670 0 (Hardback)
ISBN 962 209 671 9 (Paperback)

Secure On-line Ordering
http://www.hkupress.org

British Library Cataloguing-in-Publication Data
A catalogue record for this book is available
from the British Library.

Printed and bound by Kings Time Printing Press Ltd., in Hong Kong, China

Hong Kong University Press is honoured that Xu Bing, whose art explores
the complex themes of language across cultures, has written the Press's
name in his Square Word Calligraphy. This signals our commitment to
cross-cultural thinking and the distinctive nature of our English-language
books published in China.

"At first glance, Square Word Calligraphy appears to be nothing more
unusual than Chinese characters, but in fact it is a new way of rendering
English words in the format of a square so they resemble Chinese
characters. Chinese viewers expect to be able to read Square Word
Calligraphy but cannot. Western viewers, however are surprised to find
they can read it. Delight erupts when meaning is unexpectedly revealed."

— Britta Erickson, *The Art of Xu Bing*

Contents

Preface

Both my parents originally came from Zhongshan. On the paternal side of my family, I have five Eurasian uncles and one Eurasian aunt from my grandfather's first marriage in Cairns, Australia. These Eurasian uncles and aunts were raised by my Chinese grandmother in Zhongshan. I remember as a young child, I loved to hear them switch from their heavy Cairns English to the Lundo dialect as they told us their childhood adventures in Shekki. In Hong Kong during the late 1950s and 1960s, there were still traces of the Hong Kong Eurasian community in my father's workplace, in our neighbourhood as well as in the French Convent school which I attended for 15 years. One of my mother's mahjong buddies was a Eurasian lady, Mrs Waites (whom we called *chat gu neuhng*). *Chat gu neuhng*'s British husband was a ship captain and was often away. Her mother was a self-taught Chinese herbalist from Macau, and friends and neighbours often sought her advice and remedies for their little ailments. I used to spend long afternoons at the Waites' home after school playing with the youngest of the Waites girls, while the adults shuffled their tiles energetically on the mahjong table amid occasional outbursts of Cantonese and English exclamations. It was in the late 1960s and early 1970s that old Eurasian neighbours and school friends gradually disappeared from our lives. Many migrated to Australia, others to Canada and England, and with them their Eurasian charm and eccentricity.

Acknowledgements

This book is a revised doctoral thesis. I would like to thank my supervisor Dr Douglas Kerr for his guidance and continuous support. I would also like to thank Dr Staci Ford, Professor Gerald Horne, Professor Shirley Lim, Veronica Needa, Dr Elizabeth Sinn, and Reverend Carl Smith for their advice and encouragement. In particular, I would like to extend my special thanks to Anne Ozorio for all the suggestions and ideas that she has given me on my manuscript.

Every effort has been made to contact copyright holders of the photographs in this book before publication. However, in some cases, this has been impossible. If contacted, the author and the publisher will ensure that full credit is given at the earliest opportunity.

Introduction

Race is something which we utilized to provide clues about who a person is. The fact is made painfully obvious when we encounter someone whom we cannot conveniently racially categorize — someone who is, for example, racially 'mixed' or of an ethnic-racial group with which we are not familiar. Such an encounter becomes a source of discomfort and momentarily a crisis of racial meaning. Without a racial identity, one is in danger of having no identity.

(Omi, 62)

The term 'Eurasian' could elicit very different responses at different times and in different places in history. Oftentimes, it has the power as Michael Omi suggests, of arousing momentarily a crisis of racial meaning — of suddenly undoing all our fixed and secured conditioned ideas about race. Yet it is precisely this power of Eurasianness, I believe, which could make us re-think and re-examine all those fixed and clearly defined boundaries about races.

Interracial marriages have become quite a common phenomenon in Hong Kong. Looking back half a century ago, a European was often thought to be ideologically liberal and progressive if he or she married a Chinese. Similarly, a Chinese was often associated with a lack of Chinese cultural and racial sensitivity if he or she married a European. But that was something belonging to the past, interracial marriage in contemporary Hong Kong no longer evokes that sense of ethnic tension and ideological implications it once suggested. Eurasian children can be seen quite often in parks and playgrounds. A visit to any of the international schools in Hong Kong would quickly confirm the large number of Eurasian children growing up in the community. Yet, probably not many of the contemporary offspring of these Hong Kong mixed marriages realize that they are in fact living in a community whose attitudes towards them are very different from what they used to be seventy or eighty years ago.

The term 'Eurasian'[1] has generally been understood to refer to someone of mixed European and Asiatic parentage and/or ancestry since the nineteenth century — a term invented by Marquis of Hastings, the Governor-General of India in the early 1800s, as embracing all the progeny of white fathers and native Indian mothers. In the pre-war generation in Hong Kong, members of this community usually accepted the term 'Eurasian' to describe themselves and they were often distinguished from the Hong Kong Portuguese community or the Hong Kong Portuguese Eurasian community (whose 'mesticos' heritage arose from very different historical circumstances). The Hong Kong Eurasian community, which this book looks into, is the mixed-raced community in Hong Kong whose members are descendants of mainly European and Chinese (sometimes Parsee or Middle-eastern) residents. And it is the *memory* of this metis community as expressed in the Eurasian autobiographies that this book is most interested in.

'Eurasian community' when used in this book will mean the community referred to by the Eurasian authors as the community in which they belonged. However, it must be noted that their views and memories of this community do not always agree. One Eurasian author might remember the community as very westernized and often quite *apart* from the Chinese community. Another Eurasian author might remember it as a small community, which was itself *a part of* the Chinese community. There were, of course, Eurasians in different segments and stratum of the Hong Kong community during the periods referred to by the authors. But, as shall be seen, the Eurasian community as recalled by the memoirists is one, which focuses more on the middle and upper-middle class.

I must state that this book is *not* a historical study of Hong Kong Eurasians. It is simply a reading of the memoirs written by different Hong Kong Eurasians and their articulation of Eurasianness in their memory. The methodologies adopted by this book in looking at Hong Kong life histories are essentially inter-disciplinary, coalescing literary, historical and cultural studies approaches. And I must apologize for it not being able to fit neatly into the boundaries prescribed by each of these disciplines.

The three memoirists to be introduced are Joyce Symons, Jean Gittins and Irene Cheng. They are all second and third (sometimes fourth) generation Eurasians in Hong Kong via both paternal and maternal sides. They are in fact all related within the network of the Eurasian community (a community where endogamous practices were quite common). Joyce Symons's paternal aunt was married to the cousin of Jean Gittins and Irene Cheng. As for Jean Gittins and Irene Cheng, they are sisters from the large Ho Tung family, which consists of more than ten children. In exploring the memories of the two Ho Tung sisters, I shall also occasionally be looking at the memoir of another younger Ho Tung sister, Florence Yeo, for purposes of seeing how the extended Ho Tung Eurasian family was being remembered. I have not included a separate chapter of Florence Yeo but discussion of her memoir will be found in the section titled 'Weighing Loyalties' of the Irene Cheng chapter where I shall be juxtaposing the different mnemonic inflections and cultural orientations of the three Ho Tung sisters.

In my research of Hong Kong memoirs, I realize that the small corpus of Hong Kong Eurasian memoirs had been written mainly by Eurasian women. Perhaps this phenomenon could be explained by the fact that women had always been vessels of cultural memory. As B. J. Reagon says, women have always been 'carriers of cultural traditions, key to the formation and continuance of culture' (quoted in Friedman, 43).

As shall be seen in the Eurasian memoirs, the desire to add meaning and to make sense of their cultural diversities and heritage remains strong throughout. The consideration of numerous 'versions' of Eurasianness conceptualized by various communities, individuals, as well as Eurasian autobiographers themselves shall be the main foci of this book.

Historically, in the context of western colonial discourse and biological race theories, 'Eurasians' had often been interpreted as a form of degeneration, transgression, adulteration, impurity, regression, and moral laxity.[2] Within the framework of traditional Chinese race-thinking though, Eurasians were not perceived in such moral and biological terms. They were often seen as a living betrayal of one's racial loyalty — a loyalty that in effect is a crucial extension of one's lineage loyalty as well as national loyalty. Yet co-existing with these attitudes of fear, anxiety and betrayal concerning Eurasianness, there were also beliefs, in both the Eastern and Western worlds, that Eurasians were in fact the ideal hybrid race, the specimen race, bringing together the best of both worlds, amalgamating two great civilizations of the human race.

Set against these widely differed perceptions of Eurasianness, what was it like to be a Eurasian living in a British Colony populated predominantly with Cantonese in the twentieth century during those inter-war years, the Occupation, and the post-war decades before the signing of the Sino-British Joint Declaration — a defining moment in history where the city of Hong Kong was told that it shall be returned to China?

For those who like the memoirists discussed in this book, who think of themselves as being Eurasians, Eurasianness can be an issue, which consciously or unconsciously shapes a life, defines or problematizes an identity. In the writings of these Eurasian authors, we will see how each of them had chosen to interpret and define Eurasianness in her own way, yet remained highly conscious of how their interracial heritage was being perceived under different contexts. Eurasianness vacillates between being a privilege, an asset at one moment but a social stigma or personal albatross at another. Articulating Eurasianness becomes a lifelong process of self-definition and redefinition. These memoirs are both a *record* of their self-defining process as well as a *continuation* of that process.

Part I

Historical & Generic Considerations

1

The Vanishing Community?

They do not realize that, after all, there is no gulf between a Chan and a Smith amongst us and that underlying superficial differences in names and outlook, the spirit of kinship and brotherhood burns brightly. We Eurasians ... with the blood of Old China mixed with that of Europe in us, we show the world that this fusion, to put it no higher, is not detrimental to good citizenship.

(Eric Ho, 9)

It is true that the Eurasian community was (and still is) only a very minute segment of the Hong Kong society. Yet its presence in this city could hardly be ignored. Numerous attempts by the Hong Kong Census, between 1897 and 1931, reflect a gross under-estimation of the size of the Eurasian community. The figures that appeared in these reports strongly point to the fact that a great number of Eurasians often declared themselves as Chinese and, in some cases, Europeans. As a result of the fluid collective identity of the Hong Kong-Eurasian community, they were often perceived as not being truly and authentically representative of Hong Kong — a city which has always had a dominating majority of Cantonese.

Partly because of their ambiguous and often unstable identity, the writings of Hong Kong-Eurasians could be said to suffer from the 'traumata of insignificance', a phrase that Patrick Bellegard-Smith applied to Haitian writers (quoted in Lionnet, 6). This fateful marginality of Hong Kong-Eurasian autobiographers can be explained in several ways. First, memoirs had never been taken as a very serious genre, and had never been popular in Hong Kong until the memoir boom in the mid-1990s.[1] Second, the vibrant bourgeois community invoked in these autobiographical writings, that had so much influenced Hong Kong, was already something of the past at the time they were written. Since the Second World War, the Eurasian community had joined the diaspora to England, Australia and America. The loss of Hong Kong as their 'home' is poignantly represented in these writings. Even during the pre-war period, the community had never been more than a small-insulated minority, belonging to a small British colony nestling next to a vast Chinese nation. It is the belief of many Eurasians of the pre-war generation that they should not be beguiled into thinking that they could represent anyone other than themselves.

Whether in Hong Kong or other European colonies in the East, Eurasians had often been perceived as the living embodiment of colonial encounters. They belonged to a marginalized and isolated colonial category that straddled racial, ethnic and sometimes national boundaries. Racial crossings can be extremely worrying, 'because it threatened both to destabilize national identity and the Manichean categories of the ruler and the ruled' (Stoler, 1997, 226). In Hong Kong, the isolation of the community was much less obvious and discrimination less consistent than elsewhere in Asia, e.g. India (Gaikward), Indonesia (Wittermans) and Malaya (Crabb).[2] (One obvious reason for this was undoubtedly the Eurasians' economic and political influence within the colony.) But on a subterranean level, their sense of marginalization and isolation was perhaps much more acute and insidious in its own way, compared to that of Eurasians in other parts of Asia, as they found themselves stranded between two mutually aloof, at times mutually contemptuous, cultural worlds. In Hong Kong, they were often forced to celebrate and enhance their native side at certain moments in order to play the perfect native for the European rulers.

Precisely because of the marginalized and perhaps forgotten status of this now dispersed community, Eurasian autobiographical writings can be seen as the focalizing literature which offers, to borrow Olney's description of the importance of autobiography for African American and women's studies in America, 'a privileged access to an experience ... that no other variety of writing can offer. ... [A]utobiography renders in a peculiarly direct and faithful way the experience and the vision of a people. ...' (1980, 13).

It is as the voice of a vanished cultural experience that these texts have their primary value.

Apart from the access they offer to a privileged minority experience, another reason for my interest in these memoirs is the ambiguous ethnic identities expressed in them, which provide a fertile site for an exploration of the shifting boundaries of racial and ethnic identities. The Eurasian authors here, in their respective autobiographical acts, have reconstructed and retranslated their lifelong process of identity formation and reformation and their memoirs are both a record of that process of identity (or identity as process) and a crucial part of the process itself. Their protean and nebulous social and ethnic identities, as I shall show, not only challenge the essentialist assumption of a stable, immutable, unified sense of self and identity, but they also subvert the notion of closed and rigid boundaries between socially constructed categories of race, ethnicity and other divides. The works examined in this book foreground and privilege the intermediary spaces where boundaries are rendered porous and binary modes of division collapse into each other.

The three memoirists, Joyce Symons, Jean Gittins, and Irene Cheng, all belonged to important branches of the Hong Kong Eurasian families. The first to be considered is the memoir of Joyce Symons (1918–2004), a Hong Kong educationalist, who retired to Walton-on Thames, England in 1985. Symons was principal of the Diocesan Girls' School for more than three decades. She prided herself as a member of the Hong Kong Eurasian community and was a committee member of the charitable organization for Eurasians called The Welfare League. Her views on Eurasian identity formulation depend to a large extent on class and economic factors. She sees the China Coast Eurasian communities as intricately bound to compradorism and the history of European traders in China.

The second memoirist to be discussed is Jean Gittins (1908–1995) who left Hong Kong for Australia right after the Second World War. Her notion of Eurasianness is less distinct, less clearly delineated. It is an identity that is often based on undecidability and indeterminacy. 'Ethnic Indeterminacy' of the Gittins chapter deals with her positioning of the subject within the Confucian-Victorian worlds in her family. The second section of the chapter, 'Ethnic Options', is devoted to examining her experience as a Eurasian internee in the infamous Stanley Camp during the Japanese occupation of

Hong Kong. Comparisons will also be made between Gittins's narrative of life in the camp as a Eurasian and other camp narratives by European internees.

The last of the three Eurasian authors to be considered is Irene Cheng. The older sister of Jean Gittins, she was born in 1904 and left Hong Kong in 1967 for San Diego, USA. As an educationalist, Cheng was a school inspector and later principal of the Confucian Tai Shing School. The notion of Eurasianness is an issue that is more often expressed through silence and precariously handled through passing allusion. One purpose of this chapter is to juxtapose the autobiographical works of these two Ho Tung sisters, their very different representations of the Ho Tung family, and their commonly shared events and experiences. The work of Florence Yeo, the youngest of the Ho Tung girls, will also be referred to in this chapter. Particular attention will be paid to the contrasting cultural identification and political orientation expressed in the respective memoirs and the way these ideological factors produce a radically different modality in the sisters' memoirs, even when they are recalling the same event or people. The omissions and silences in some of the sisters' narratives will be shown to be often particularly eloquent. Certain passages of memory occluded by one sibling are frequently expressed and celebrated by the other. It is sometimes the unsaid, untold and the deafening silences concerning their own Eurasianness that constitute the poignant autobiographical ethos in these memoirs.

Eurasian as an ethnic category or sub-category had never been recognized officially or unofficially by the Chinese or British communities in pre-war or post-war Hong Kong. The sense of Eurasian culture and that of a Eurasian ethnic community have been gradually effaced and forgotten by the process of immigration abroad and assimilation into the dominating Chinese ethnicity. These memoirs have helped to redeem and preserve through language the identity of Eurasians as an ethnic group, a political power and a privileged and exclusive social clan in pre-war Hong Kong. In asserting personal memory, the memoirs serve as resisting voices to the collective amnesia of the post-war, post-colonial and post-compradore capitalist Hong Kong. These memoirs are, to a certain degree, a revenge on history[3] — a history that threatens to consign them, individually and tribally to imminent oblivion.

These autobiographers wrote not for lofty introspective, philosophical or aesthetic purposes. Their works contrast markedly in terms of aesthetics with canonical autobiographies. But in their own prosaic form, these memoirs are fascinating in their rhetoric and manifest valuable pluralistic modes of thoughts from the cultural margins of Hong Kong.

2

The Birth of a Eurasian Community

Little Edith Eaton says to herself, 'Why are we what we are? I and my brothers and sisters. Why did God make us to be hooted and stared at? Papa is English, mamma is Chinese. Why couldn't we have been either one thing or the other? Why is my mother's race despised? ... I believe that some day a great part of the world will be Eurasian. I cheer myself with the thought that I am but a pioneer. A pioneer should glory in suffering.'

(Sui Sin Far [Edith Eaton] ,
'Leaves From the Mental Portfolio of a Eurasian', 222)

The person of mixed blood is one whom fate has condemned to live in two societies and in two, not merely different but antagonistic cultures.

(Park, [1937] 1961, xiii)

Unlike their Portuguese counterparts in Macau, the British colonial attitude towards miscegenation had never embraced the kind of free liberalism promoted by its neighbour. Under the Portuguese colonial ideology, miscegenation was officially hailed as a positive step towards social harmony and a form of the 'benign consummation of Portuguese panracialism' (C. Cheng, 156). As C. Cheng says, extensive miscegenation becomes the distinctive pattern of Portuguese presence in Africa and Asia. Affonso de Albuquerque, who Braga describes as being the greatest of Portugal's governors of India and an important figure in the building of the Portuguese empire in Asia, had already in the 1500s advocated his policy of inducing his countrymen to settle down and produce a loyal population through mixed marriages with native women (Braga, 85–88). Intermarriages, as Braga suggests, became one important strategy of successful colonization.

The British colonial leaders in Hong Kong, on the other hand, had quite an opposite view of marriages or unions with native women. The troubling question of racial mixture in colonial encounters was not only seen as a colonial transgression, but the idea of racial mixture often fed the colonial imagination with phantoms of degeneration, abnormality, as well as moral and intellectual regression. It was government policy to insist on demarcating a safe distance from the indigenous elements in the colony. Their attitudes towards the products of miscegenation could shift from abominations, contemptuousness, suspicion, and avoidance to trust, hope, reliance and dependence.

From the time when Hong Kong was ceded to Britain in 1842 up until the Japanese invasion in 1941, Hong Kong was a society based on segregation. Early colonial anxieties about the intermixing of Europeans and Chinese were reflected in a letter to the Duke of Newcastle in 1861 by Sir John Bowring (Governor, 1859–65), as he fretted over the rapid increase in the Chinese population.

> My constant thought has been how best to prevent a large Chinese population establishing themselves [sic] at Kowloon, and as some native population is indispensable, how best to keep them to themselves and preserve the European and American community from the injury and inconvenience of intermixture with them.
>
> (Endacott, 1964, 122)

To ensure a stable distance between the Chinese and European communities, various laws and rules were made to maintain the segregation of the two races. The Peak Reservation Ordinances were passed in 1888 and reaffirmed in 1904 (and was not repealed until 1946). Some hotels such as the Hong Kong Hotel, only allowed Chinese into certain rooms and they were not allowed to stay overnight (Carroll, 120). There was also the Light and Pass Ordinance — a law formalized in 1857 (Sinn, 10) which clearly reflects the European distrust of the Chinese community, and was not abolished until 1895.

There were, of course, the more liberal-minded groups of colonialists who frowned upon such absolute segregation. Sir John Pope Hennessy, Governor from 1877 to 1882, whose wife was of a Eurasian background, was shocked at the rift between the two races. His liberal policy of inviting the Chinese to Government House so shocked the European community that many stopped accepting invitations to Government House (Courtauld, 31).

John Carroll argues that racial discrimination in Hong Kong actually increased in the first part of the twentieth century as local groups become richer and attained more socio-economic power (118). Racial barriers seemed to become more rigid. This phenomenon, Carroll says, can be found in Dutch and British colonies, where spatial segregation becomes more stringent with the rise of a strong native merchant class (118–119).

Professor Lancelot Forster in the late 1920s described the relationship between the two races as being entirely for mutual material gain. 'There is contact but no fusion, no community of thought or feeling ...' (quoted in Sweeting, 342).

Sir Cecil Clementi, Governor from 1925 to 1930, expressed his alarm at the mutual aloofness of the two races:

> Although in daily contact with each other, the two communities nevertheless move in different worlds, neither having any real comprehension of the mode of life or ways of thought of the other.
>
> (Spurr, 154)

Until the Second World War, many institutions continued to abide by segregation rules. Clifford Matthews, a Hong Kong-born Eurasian, and an avid cricket player, remembers playing at the Hong Kong Cricket Club, but added that it was not possible for him to be admitted as a member because of his racial identity (Oral History Project, Track 5).[1] These segregation practices persisted even in the midst of the Japanese invasion. As a wounded Volunteer, he recalls how he was turned away from the Matilda Hospital when he described himself as Eurasian on the admission form.

During dangerous times of hostilities, the segregationist desire in some remained acutely strong. Gwen Dew remembers hiding inside the Repulse

Bay Hotel with other European ladies. Amid the Japanese sniping and bombardment, a British lady (who had recently came from the Peak Hotel) suddenly looked around her and in a penetrating voice said, 'What are all these Chinese doing in here? What right have they to be here?' (Dew, 83).

But despite such rigid segregation practices, Hong Kong never had any laws against miscegenation. Interracial marriages were very rare and often involved much sacrifice. Any European employee who violated the colonial etiquette by interracial romance was jeopardizing not only his career but was also risking ostracism by the European community. Kenneth Andrew, who came to Hong Kong in 1912 to join the Royal Hong Kong Police, recalls that the first document he had to sign was a promise not to marry a Chinese female (Langford, 1998). Governor Henry May (1912–1919) boasted that under his administration no European police officers or prison officers were married to Chinese or Eurasians (Great Britain Public Record Office, CO 129/392, 14/12/12, 58). Employees in the Public Works Department who married Chinese or Eurasians were not allowed, by regulation, to live in government quarters, nor were prison warders (Carroll, 121). Michael Wright, an architect in the 1930s with the Public Works Department, also had to sign a document to say in no uncertain terms that should he marry a Chinese or take one as a concubine then he would be liable to be dismissed (Gillingham, 11). Sir V. M. Grayburn, the Chief Manager of the Hongkong and Shanghai Bank, wrote in his letters in 1937 how he looked 'with disfavour on most marriages to non-British women', and so far as the wives of British executive staff were concerned, 'Foreign, native, half-caste are definitely taboo' (King, 1988, 286).

This constant anxiety towards interracial romance and its effect on colonial propriety was not unlike that found in Kipling's India in the late nineteenth century. His narrator in the story 'Kidnapped' says, 'Marriage in India does not concern the individual but the Government he serves' (1987, 135). The only Englishman in Kipling who actually marries an Indian woman is McIntosh in 'To be Filed in Reference'. McIntosh, however, has to forfeit his status and even identity as a member of the governing race.

Traditional Chinese attitudes towards mixed marriage were equally forbidding, if not worse, even though on the surface Chinese attitudes might appear more tolerant. Vivienne Poy, daughter and biographer of Richard Charles Lee (son of the famous Hysan Lee) says that in 1917 at the age of 12, Richard and Harold Lee were sent to England to study. Before the two brothers left, they were told that if they married non-Chinese while abroad, they would be automatically disinherited (Poy, 6).

In order to understand such an aversion towards mixed unions, it is important to look at the traditional racial thinking in China, and how in the early twentieth century, Chinese racial consciousness became intensified with the rise of racial nationalism.

As Chow Kai-wing has pointed out, prejudice against outsiders in China had always been universal. Records of Chinese contempt of foreigners abound in traditional Chinese historical accounts. However, Chow argues that the most negative and prejudiced remarks about foreigners were impressionistic, fragmentary, ethnocentric contempt. Chow claims these were not based upon any racial hierarchy (1994) such as those found in the eighteenth and nineteenth century European race discourse discussed in Chapter 1.

Beginning in the late nineteenth century, Chinese race theory was more rigorously adopted into the Chinese political context as an assertion of Chinese racial pride in face of foreign aggression. Zhang Binglin (1896–1936), a reformist, promoted a revolutionary Chinese nationalism based on the notion of race in his attempt to expose the racist policy of the Manchus.

Dikötter quotes a Chinese nationalist, writing in 1903, who explains that the notion of *quo* 'country' was no longer merely a geographical expression, but had a distinctly racial connotation (109). Yan Fu, who translated T. H. Huxley's *Evolution and Ethics* in 1898, declared that 'the sentiment of patriotism is rooted in racial nature' (Dikötter, 110).

In fact, racial nationalism was one of Sun Yat-sen's 'Three Principles of the People' (*Sanminzhuyi*). Sun's principle of racial nationalism, as Dikötter explains, is based upon the principle of 'racial solidarity' (123). L. Sharman describes how 'Sun Yat-sen made his appeal to an emerging national consciousness, strongest in its racial form of prejudice against foreigners' (quoted in Dikötter, 124). The theme of racial humiliation was intensely articulated in nationalist writings during this period. Students' writings consistently reflected the humiliating treatment and derogation to which the Chinese were subjected by Europeans and Japanese (Dikötter, 124). To counter this sense of humiliating inferiority, Sun claimed that only nationalism could forestall racial destruction (Dikötter, 124). It was in this mood of racial nationalism in the early twentieth century that attitudes towards mixed marriages and Eurasians became acutely negative.

Han Suyin, in her first autobiography *The Crippled Tree* (1965) recalls her conversations with her Chinese uncle, who described to her the emotional upheaval, the intense bitter sorrow and havoc within the gentry-official Chou family when their son Chou Yen-tung (Han Suyin's father) wrote home in 1913 to request permission to marry Marguerite Denis, a middle-class girl from Brussels (Han, 207).

Han also recalls her own experience in Chengtu in 1940. Her husband Pao, a highly race-conscious military officer, aide-de-camp to Generalissimo Chiang, would not let the warlord Hu Tsungnan to meet his wife Suyin. Han writes:

> Pao was afraid that Hu Tsungnan might not approve of me; might look at my face and deduce some 'foreign' blood; and Hu Tsungnan's xenophobia was notorious. This might spoil the good impression Pao had made; he wrote to Hu that I was 'so shy' that I refused to see anyone; I lived in the bosom of my family from which I could not be extricated …
>
> (130)

The negative Chinese perception of an interracial person can be more or less tested through the terms used to describe such person. Eurasians were (and occasionally still are) often referred to in derogatory Chinese terms like *tsap chung* (half-caste), *da luen chung, tsap ba lang* (mixed/messed up breed). Other Chinese terms like *boon tong fan* and *wun hyut yih* are less derogatory but still suggest a kind of genealogical abnormality.

Amid all this feeling against interracial unions and their offspring, there were a few isolated voices that held very positive views on racial hybridity.

Tang Caichang (1867–1900), a well-known Chinese reformer, advocated the amalgamation of the white and yellow races, for it was only through 'racial communication' that China would flourish again. He put forward ten arguments in support of intermarriage. In his seventh argument, he says, 'In Hong Kong, Singapore and the Pacific islands, intermarriage between Chinese and foreigners had produced offspring of unparalleled intelligence and strength' (Dikötter, 87).

The Hong Kong barrister and Chinese diplomat Wu Tingfang (1842–1922) also speaks in favour of mixed unions: 'There is no doubt that mixed marriages of the white with the yellow races will be productive of good to both sides' (Dikötter, 87).

But these isolated voices in favour of interracial mixture, like their European counterparts discussed in the last chapter, were inevitably drowned by popular prejudice against interracial people. The Hong Kong Chinese community, in its close proximity to the vast Chinese nation, was very much under the influence of its cultural and political climate. Interracial unions between Europeans and Chinese in Hong Kong were, therefore, not only warily avoided by the European community but very much frowned upon by the Chinese community. Yet amid all the unspoken condemnation and the quiet aversions, interracial alliances were in fact quite common in Hong Kong.

For reasons of career and climate, the majority of foreign traders, sailors, soldiers, missionaries who came to the colony were usually young bachelors. The '"fishing fleets" of husband-hunting English girls which set out hopefully for British India, did not appear to have come as far as Hong Kong; little wonder, then,' writes Courtauld, 'that a Eurasian community began to emerge' (27).

Affairs between Europeans and Chinese women were conducted in a highly discreet manner. The corseted European wives found svelte young Chinese women a sexual threat to their marriages, says one Hong Kong historian, and they sometimes reacted violently against including Chinese among their family acquaintances (Lethbridge, 1968, 128).

Carl Smith claims that most European men and Chinese women[2] in the early days had their long-sustained affairs without living together. Most of the time, their affairs were conducted under what he refers to as the 'protected women' arrangement.[3] European fathers of early Eurasians of this period were usually merchants who remained in the colony for a limited time. Having made their fortune, they usually returned to England or Europe. Provisions were customarily made by the putative husband for the Chinese women and their offspring in form of an annuity, a trust or gift of real estate (Smith, 1969, 13–17).

In describing these protected women, E. J. Eitel, also recorded in his Minutes of 1 November 1879 that these women were:

> as a rule, rather raised in their own esteem by the connection, of the immorality of which they have no idea; they are also, as a rule, better off than the concubines of Chinese well-to-do merchants; they are generally provided for by the foreigners who kept them, when the connection is severed, and at any rate these women are as a rule thrifty, and always manage to save money which they invest in Bank deposits, also in house property, but principally in buying female infants whom they rear for sale to or concubinage with foreigners, by which they generally gain a competency in about 10 years.
>
> (Sweeting, 235)

This practice of concubinage, whether or not it was really a widespread practice, had seriously affected the perceived moral standing of these kept women and, consequently, on how the early Eurasians were looked upon by both the European and Chinese communities.

The Hong Kong colonial government was not unaware of the emergence of a growing number of Hong Kong Eurasians. As early as the 1850s, Sir John Bowring, Governor from 1854 to 1859, had already observed that 'a large population of children of native mothers by foreigners of all classes is beginning to ripen into a dangerous element out of the dunghill of neglect. They seem wholly uncared for' (Endacott, 1964, 94–95).

The issue of coping with the rising number of Eurasians in Hong Kong was addressed in a letter by the Hon. Sir John Smale, Chief Justice, to the Colonial Secretary on 20 October 1879:

> No-one can walk through some of the bye streets in this Colony without seeing well-dressed Chinese girls in great numbers whose occupations are self-proclaimed, or pass those streets, or go into this Colony, without counting beautiful children by the hundred whose Eurasian origin is self-declared. If the Government would enquire into the present condition of these classes, and still more, into what become of these women and their children of the past, I believe that it will be found in the great majority of cases the women have sunk in misery, and that of the children the girls that have survived have been sold to the profession of their mothers, and that if boys they have been lost sight of or have sunk into the condition of the mean whites of the late slave holding states of America ...
>
> (Sweeting, 235)

In 1880 Eitel responded with a more positive view of the conditions of Hong Kong's Eurasian children in the *Hong Kong Government Gazette*:

> The children of these women are invariably sent to school. In fact, these women understand the value of education and prize it far more than respectable Chinese women do. The boys are invariably sent to the Government Central School where they generally distinguish themselves, and as a *rule* these boys obtain good situations in Hongkong, in the open ports and abroad. The girls crowd into the schools kept by the Missionary Societies. These children are generally provided with a small patrimony by their putative fathers. They dress almost invariably in Chinese costume and adopt Chinese customs, unless they are taken up by ill-advised agents of foreign charity. I am quite positive, as far as my experience and the information I have received from many gentlemen in the best position to judge goes, that they do not in any way resemble the mean whites in the Southern States of America.
>
> (Sweeting, 236)

The fact that some early Eurasian girls got accepted into missionary schools in the nineteenth century does not automatically guarantee their immunity from concubinage. In Eitel's letter to the Colonial Secretary in 1889, he says:

> The Diocesan Female Training School[4] in 1862 found itself compelled in 1865 to close the School on the ground that almost every one of the girls, taught English, became on leaving school, the kept mistress of foreigners.
>
> (CO 129/342; quoted in Sweeting, 248)

This sad fate of many Eurasian females is well represented in historical texts and memoirs.

More than half a century after Eitel's letter, the image of Eurasian females was still associated, borrowing Han Suyin's description of Eurasian women, with the notion of 'moral laxity' (1952, 198).[5] In his camp narrative, Wenzell Brown describes how he met Lucy Reynolds in the Stanley camp:

> Lucy was Hong Kong's leading madame. The fame of her brothel had spread over the world. British civil servants in Delhi speak reminiscently of Lucy's Eurasian girls. In Wapping or Limehouse, in Shanghai or Cairo or Caracas, Lucy Reynold's name brings a twinkle into the eyes of the knowing.
>
> (128)

What Eitel said concerning the success of some Eurasian boys was undoubtedly true. But as an indication of official ambivalence it can be added that it had been a tradition for the government to place Eurasians to man the lighthouses, until lighthouses were automated in the 1980s (Waters, 142). These jobs were well paid, had good benefits and security and, perhaps most importantly, they were away from the city, out of sight, unseen. In these posts, Eurasians became officially marginal area. Positions for the senior civil service had traditionally been reserved for expatriate British officers. According to historian Frank Welsh, 'it was not until 1942 that the Colonial Office dropped its demand that all candidates should be "of pure European descent"' (381).

Eurasians, says Lethbridge, were perceived as a threat to the Europeans principally because of their anomalous and ambivalent social position. 'Eurasians were both European and Chinese, and as such difficult to apprehend as social beings.' Hence, Eurasians as a group could not be 'allocated with ease to their proper niche in the colonial social structure' (Lethbridge, 1978, 176).

⊷⊶⊷○⊶⊷⊶

By the 1920s, the Eurasian community had not only gained in terms of size but in their socio-economic status within the Colony. Yet, their nebulous and ambiguous identity continued to worry some people, particularly when there were legislations that applied only to one of the two principal races.[6] Fixing the Eurasians in either one or the other race would greatly facilitate colonial administration. The Hon. C. G. Alabaster, OBE, member of the Hong Kong Legislative Council and later Attorney-General, in his 1920 article 'Some Observations on Race Mixture in Hong Kong', urged the colonial government to deal with the problem of race mixture in Hong Kong by 'declaring marriage between certain races invalid or a punishable offence, or at least certain decisions as to the degree of blood making a particular person a member of one race or of another' (248).

Racial mixing for Alabaster is less an offence under God or the law than a major inconvenience to the bureaucracy. Alabaster says that prior to 1911, there had been no such need for legislation since 'the Eurasian problem did not exist; or perhaps it would be more accurate to say that before that year classification could be effected easily without too close an inquiry into a person's pedigree'.

Alabaster divides the Hong Kong Eurasians before 1911 into three distinct groups. The first group is the Portuguese. With their strong Roman Catholic ties and Portuguese names, the Portuguese Eurasian 'would never be regarded as Chinese, even if Oriental in feature and with only a fraction of European blood in his veins'. What seems to worry Alabaster is the ambiguous status of the 'Chinese Eurasians' (the Eurasians that oriented towards the Chinese culture) rather than the 'British Eurasians' (the westernized Eurasians). Regarding the Chinese Eurasians, Alabaster says,

> One would have no difficulty in giving a Chinese classification to a half-caste, even though his father were English, who wore Chinese clothes and a queue, who passed under the name of Wong or Chang, who had married according to Chinese customs a 'Kit Fat' (wife) and had three concubines, and who after some years' business training in the compradore department of a foreign firm was trading on his own account under a Chinese 'hong' name, besides being a member of the Chinese Chamber of Commerce.

Whether deliberately or not, the Chinese Eurasian that Alabaster has depicted resembles in almost every way Ho Tung, the Eurasian doyen to be discussed in the next chapter. As for the British Eurasians, Alabaster says, he would have

> an English surname who dressed as a European and lived as such, both in business and in his home life, would not be regarded legally as a Chinese, although his parentage might affect him socially.

> (248)

These racial markers in terms of names, clothing and lifestyle, as set out by Alabaster, were no longer distinguishably reliable anymore after 1911.[7] After the emergence of the Republic, there was a widespread westernization in habits and customs of the better class Chinese, and with them those of the Chinese Eurasian. The first effect was the cutting of the queue and the adopting of European dress (a cultural transformation that Ho Tung also addressed in his article to be discussed in Chapter 3). Given this lack of racial markers, it became quite easy for some Chinese Eurasians to cross the racial divide whenever they thought fit. Alabaster mentions how some Chinese Eurasians became Europeans in order to capture their share of war profits (248). With the liquidation of German firms after the First World War, many new firms owned by Eurasians were quick to capture the trade by discarding their Chinese names for English ones — an ethnic change which gave them a commercial advantage, and an early example of the kind of strategic ethnicity we will encounter later.

Alabaster is not unaware that these Chinese Eurasians were also treated with some suspicion by the Chinese community as there was an 'awakening in the pure Chinese of a spirit of nationality which is resulting gradually in forming in their minds the idea that the Eurasian Chinese should no longer be classed as Chinese, or at any rate as the leaders of the Chinese community and the exponents to the British of Chinese thought and sentiment' (248).

The legislation Alabaster recommended was never enacted, but the proposal reflects a deep-seated uneasiness about the shifting identities of the Eurasians on the part of the European communities, as well as a potential distrust of the Eurasians by the Chinese communities, an ethnic distrust instilled by a rising Chinese racial nationalism. The issue of perception and trust in the triangular relationship between the Eurasians, the Europeans and the Chinese in Hong Kong has much preoccupied the Eurasian consciousness — it is a theme, which keeps resurfacing in the memoirs examined in this book.

Eurasians were liable to a double distrust, for having a different identity in the first place, but also for not really having an identity at all, being neither one thing nor the other, and consequently sneaky and opportunistic. Whatever people like Alabaster felt about the chameleon identities of the Eurasians, the rise of the Eurasians in the colonial power structure became evident. Eurasian leaders such as Ho Fook [half-brother of Ho Tung], Chan Kai Ming [George Bartou Tyson], Robert Kotewall, and Lo Man Kam [Ho Tung's eldest son-in-law], had been appointed to either one or both of the Legislative and Executive Councils.

Norman Miners explains this phenomenon as a result of the fact that governors did not find it easy to locate suitable Chinese to fill the seats customarily reserved for them. The appointed Chinese member had to be fluent in English so as to be able to take a full part in the business of the Council. He had to be a man of standing and influence within the Chinese community. He had to be a British subject and loyal to the British Crown. But Chinese possessing all these qualifications were rare. Given the difficulty in finding acceptable Chinese, Eurasians were sought to fill the places reserved for Chinese. Governor Stubbs, however, acknowledges that the Eurasians were looked down by pure-bred Chinese who habitually referred to them as 'the Bastards' (CO 129/462; quoted in Miners, 1987, 128).

W. K. Chan has also pointed out that the Eurasians gained seats in the Legislative and Executive Councils not because they were racially closer to the Europeans but because of their mastery of the colonial language and their colonial loyalty (116). The Eurasians might be acting as Chinese for the British administration and taking the seats reserved for the Chinese, but Ming Chan, in a 1995 article, insists rather vigorously that Eurasians like Ho Tung and Kotewall were never seen by other Chinese, either in Hong Kong or on the mainland, as Chinese (257–58).

Whatever the Chinese community thought of them, they became, in the eyes of the British administration, ideal members of the colonial elite as envisaged one hundred years before in Macaulay's Minute — the desiderated cultural hybrid naturalized in a body.

The Eurasians were welcomed into the colonial elite because they could perform or mimic the part of the public Englishman. They also represented — or performed — the Chinese for the English. Poignantly, then, in this capacity, they assumed a double identity, whereas in other contexts they seemed to others to be neither one thing nor the other and to have none. But their very capacity to play the part often led to suspicion about their sincerity and loyalty.

Their role in maintaining stability during various colonial crises in the early twentieth century remained crucial to the administration but was not without a concomitant suspicion. In a despatch to the Colonial Office on 16 September 1922 in anticipation of a boycott and general strike, Stubbs writes rather apprehensively:

> That is the beginning of the end. I told you the other day that I believed we should hold Hong Kong for another fifty years. I put it now at twenty at the most ... . They [the Chinese] will tend more and more to associate themselves with China rather than with England (the tendency exists already) ... . We can rely on nobody except the half-castes and even they will throw in their lot with the Chinese if they think they will be on the winning side.
>
> (Sweeting, 1986, 8)

The Eurasian community in pre-war Hong Kong is in many ways similar to the Creole communities in the Americas as described by Benedict Anderson. They constituted simultaneously a colonial community and a privileged class. With their local rootedness, they were essential to the stability of an empire. In describing the Creole communities, Anderson sees a certain parallelism between the position of the Creole magnates and of feudal barons, crucial to the sovereign's power, but also a menace to it (59). In Chapter 3, we see in Ho Tung's article, how he is able to dispel that potential menace by striking a satisfying balance between his colonial loyalties and his local Chinese national and cultural rootedness.

3

Pioneer Hong Kong Eurasian: Ho Tung

He decided to claim Chinese nationality — possibly because he knew that the Chinese would not be so discourteous as to disown him openly … I used to feel sorry that he should have thrown in his lot with the Chinese.

(Gittins, 1969, 11)

Father was tall and handsome. Though he wore European clothes when he was young, he later always dressed in Chinese clothes … he wore long silk trousers tied at the ankles and black Chinese shoes and sometimes, ordinary European shoes.

(Yeo, 11)

Few leading Hong Kong figures have inspired so many written words as Sir Robert Ho Tung. Vignettes and stories of the Eurasian magnate can be found in almost any book on the origin and history of Hong Kong, Hong Kong travel books, biographical encyclopedias, Who's Who, popular magazines and other similar publications. His ambiguous ethnic background, legendary wealth and his dynastic power captured the imagination of popular writers like James Clavell and Robert Elegant.[1] His personal chronicle over time has become a part of the Hong Kong story. Ho Tung himself often symbolizes not only the successful compradore but also the compradore culture itself. The reason for my including a short section on Ho Tung is that not only was he related to all three authors, but also his own life story and generous contributions to Hong Kong had caused very interesting speculations on his ethnic identity from the Chinese as well as European community.

'Compradore' invariably refers to a Chinese or Eurasian individual who acted as a go-between or middleman between European or American companies and their Chinese business contacts and employees (Sweeting, 1990, 196n4). The word 'compradore' stems from the Portuguese *comprar*, meaning 'to purchase': a compradore is a purchaser. The Chinese equivalent term *maiban* originally referred to the official broker who purchased supplies for the Chinese government in the Ming dynasty. 'Compradore' was also used to describe the staff of the *cohong* of Canton in the eighteenth and nineteenth centuries. The term 'compradore' was later used to identify the middleman between Western (or later Japanese) merchants and Chinese markets (Hui, 37).

Ho Tung was born in 1862, two years after Kowloon was ceded to Britain under the first Convention of Peking. His mother was a Chinese female whose family name was Sze. His father was believed to be a British of Dutch descent by the name of Bosman.[2] Florence Yeo, his youngest daughter, describes him 'as almost as old as the Colony of Hong Kong … and was known as the "Grand Old Man of Hong Kong"' (Yeo, 11).

Ho Tung graduated from The Central School (later to be known as Queen's College), the first Government-sponsored English school. In nineteenth century Hong Kong, there was no equivalent to the Anglicist educational policy, which prevailed in India after Macaulay's famous Minutes on Indian Education. In Victorian Hong Kong, educational policy was based on a mixture of both Oriental and Anglicized ethos. In the early days of Queen's College, while English was taught, classical Chinese was also rigorously pursued. Ho Tung's teacher was Frederick Stewart[3] who had been criticized by members of the government for not emphasizing teaching English more (Bickley, 155). Hence, Ho Tung, notwithstanding his great mastery of the English language, also showed traces of his Chinese scholarship. Growing up in his Chinese mother's household, he was very much imbued with Chinese culture and customs.

Ho Tung joined Jardine Matheson & Co. as a clerk in 1880 where he was quickly promoted to Chief Compradore. By 1900, after working in different departments and subsidiaries of Jardines, he resigned from his compradore position and started his own business empire. He made his debut as a public benefactor in Hong Kong by establishing the first school for children of European parentage (now King George V School) (*Biographical Dictionary of Republican China*, 75).

Ho Tung's more well known political causes in the early twentieth century included his donation of ambulances and airplanes to the British government, as well as contributions to the Prince of Wales War Fund, during the First World War. As a result, he was knighted by King George V in 1915, becoming Sir Robert Ho Tung (*Biographical Dictionary*, 75). In the 1920s, he sponsored a round-table conference inviting the warlords in China to settle their differences face to face (Cheng, 136). In the late 1920s, he also contributed the building for the Sun Yat-sen Mausoleum in Nanking. During the Second World War, he presented a warplane to the Chinese government, and a couple of fighters to the RAF to fight the Japanese (Morris, 1988, 179). He was resting in Macau during the entire duration of the Japanese Occupation in Hong Kong. At the end of the war, Ho Tung returned to Hong Kong with Admiral Sir Cecil Harcourt, the military governor (*Biographical Dictionary*, 76).

Ho Tung's image in his later life remained that of a Chinese patriarch in silk robe and venerable white mandarin beard — an image that barely camouflaged his prominent European features. He had twenty-two decorations. When Oswald Birley painted his portrait in his old age, Ho Tung wanted to be shown wearing all his twenty-two decorations. Birley declined for aesthetic reasons, but painted the decorations themselves in a separate picture, to be hung nearby in its own frame (Morris, 179).

As a successful Hong Kong compradore, and by 1915 a well-known international figure, he was requested to write something about the story of the Hong Kong Chinese for inclusion in the section on Hong Kong in *Present Day Impressions of the Far East* (1917). This book is an introduction to different cities and treaty ports in the Far East, and served as a kind of travel guide for Europeans. The chapter on Hong Kong states:

> To visit Hongkong after having studied its history and the long record of difficulties and disasters from which it has triumphantly emerged, and to witness the transformation wrought in the barren, treeless, pirate-peopled rock of less than eighty years ago, is indeed to realize something of what the British race is capable in the realm of colonization.
>
> (Feldwick, 527)

Whether or not Ho Tung wrote it himself, the article is in his name and expresses his views as a representative of the local Chinese community in Hong Kong. Written in 1916, it presents a picture of how Hong Kong had changed since its inception as a British colony almost eight decades before. It is instructive to look at this article as it offers an insight into the multi-dimensional worldviews that the Eurasian middleman negotiates as he skillfully positions himself in relation to different ideological spheres. The introduction on the Hong Kong Chinese is fundamentally a celebration and justification of British imperialism in Hong Kong, a theme that resonates with the overall controlling discourse of the book. Interwoven within this writing is also a rather ambiguous discourse on Chinese nationalism, as Ho Tung relates how some Chinese were losing their cultural and national identity by adopting Western habits and practices after the Revolution of 1911. As a voice upholding cultural purity, Ho Tung critically depicts the Chinese blind and ludicrous emulation of the West — consciously or unconsciously giving an orientalized picture of the Eastern imitation of Western practices. A strong sense of Confucianism is also felt as he chastises the Chinese females for losing their Confucian virtues of modesty and reserve. Mercantilism and compradorism are clearly at work as he discusses the wonderfully diverse Chinese labour resources offered in Hong Kong.

Ho Tung's colonial story begins by invoking how Hong Kong natives came under British sovereignty:

> It was not, however, until 1841 that Britons and Chinese were brought into close acquaintance with one another by the cession of the island of Hong Kong to the British Government.

There is no reference to the Opium Wars or any unpleasant military or forceful encounter, almost implying the inception as friendly and mutually voluntary. The narrative of colonial encounter offered here is one of benevolent paternalism. In relating the birth of Hong Kong, he invokes what he calls the Colony's Magna Charta [Carta] proclaimed by the British Plenipotentiary, that the inhabitants of the island would be:

> Secured in the free exercise of their religious rites, ceremonies and social customs, and in the enjoyment of their lawful private property and interest.

(527)

Here, the voice of a loyal colonial subject also reminds the reader of the first difficult years of the British occupation when 'this distant outpost of Empire would have, from climatic considerations, to be given up for some less inhospitable shore' if not for the 'indomitable courage of its pioneers' and the 'hardihood of the virile race of native fishermen'.

The prosperity of this outpost, he points out, was only assured after the discovery of goldfields in California and minerals in Australia, when Hong Kong became the centre of labour recruitment and emigration.[4]

Positioning himself in a privileged space as a leader of the Hong Kong Chinese community, Ho Tung exercises a Foucaultian power of representation, its authority deriving from his insider knowledge of the Chinese labour market — a power which he possesses not only over the object of depiction (the Hong Kong Chinese) but over the foreign rulers and potential investors. It is the discursive power of the intermediary, with location both in the world of Chinese work and the world of international capital.

Ho Tung describes the half million Hong Kong Chinese in 1916 as 'essentially transient' (Feldwick, 527). He divides the population into three sweeping categories. He maps out their places of origin in the vicinity of Hong Kong, which dictate and define their profession — constructing different kinds of provincial identities that reflect the class and labour stratification by the treaty port compradore.

The first group (and probably the highest in the implied ethnic hierarchy) was the traders, merchants and domestics in the employ of foreign residents. These were from 'the populous and wealthy province of Kwantung'. The second was 'birds of passage' from Fukien, stopping on their way to the rubber plantations of the Malay states and Dutch East Indies. Other 'birds of passage' included the natives from Sunning and Sunwui 'who repaired to California, Australia and the Mexican ports' and to other South American republics in the early days. The third group from Swatow and Tungkun was the coolie class, 'a hardy and sturdy lot, [who] and can be seen in hundreds any day handling loaded trucks on the quays and in front of the warehouses at Kowloon'.

Ho Tung also reports with pride the intention of the French Government Commission to recruit Chinese labour 'to make good the deficiency caused by the war and to repair the havoc and damage wrought by the enemy in the cities and towns of France'. With much optimism, Ho Tung says, 'it is not too much to expect that in the course of time … Hongkong may be expected to be the headquarters for the southern recruiting field' (Feldwick, 527). The statement here expresses not only the mercantilist's eye on a major business expansion but also a curious subtle loyalty with the Allied Countries, as he refers to the Central Powers as 'the enemy'.

In his representations of the Hong Kong Chinese colonial encounter, there are basically two trajectories: first, the Chinese, with their 'ingrained ignorance', 'deep-rooted prejudice' and 'primitive and unscientific methods', were being enlightened by Western traditions, particularly in medicine and education; second, the Chinese were much misled, confused and potentially polluted by their encounter with the West and its traditions.

It is worth noting that in referring to 'the Chinese', Ho Tung never uses the pronoun 'we' or 'our', but 'they' and 'their'. It could well be a distance dictated by rhetorical etiquette. But it could also be a conscious strategy to create a distance between him and the Chinese populace, even though, as we have seen, much of his authority as an expert and insider derives from his closeness to them. The Eurasian middleman obviously finds it crucial to speak in a tone that would not jeopardize his positions as both the native-informer and the compradore.

Ho Tung speaks of the remarkable material and intellectual progress of the Hong Kong Chinese owing to the educational efforts of the missionaries and the government. He praises the Church Missionary Society as well as the grants-in-aid system of the government, through which 'a perfect revolution has been wrought in the moral and physical life of the Chinese by the well-directed efforts for more than half a century' (528). The adoption of the system of Western medicine was 'a mark of progress' from the 'more primitive and unscientific methods' of the Chinese. The growth of the printing press in Hong Kong must be credited to the government which 'concedes much latitude in regard to freedom of the press, [so that] Chinese newspapers in Hong Kong have thriven in remarkable degrees' (529).

Thus far, the story suggests that everything good about the Hong Kong Chinese and this community is the result of the beneficent influence of the West. But, while Ho Tung acknowledges how the reception of Western methods had brought about wonderful progress to the Hong Kong Chinese, this has not been accomplished without some costs to the 'native mind' where Western influence had 'left its impress' (528). A cultural anxiety about being hybridized by the foreign Other is plainly manifested.

> However beneficial the assimilation of Western thoughts and manners may be, there may be the danger of the girls losing that decorous reserve which is such an admirable Chinese characteristic in the views of the members of the older school of thought … .

Not only were Chinese females losing their traditional reserve but Chinese generally were hastily and foolishly abandoning their Chinese attire for unsuitable western clothing.

> When the old regime was cast off for the new, it was thought the proper thing to discard all that appertained to national custom. Thus, for instance, the national costume — economical, comfortable and eminently suitable from a hygienic point of view — was hurriedly discarded for foreign clothing. Even in the matter of footwear the Chinese, generally speaking, rushed to adopt the Western style. This exuberance of spirit has somewhat subsided, although the hybrid fashion of the Chinese coat with foreign skirt now worn by Chinese Ladies on ceremonial occasions still offends aesthetic taste. On no ground can the absolute denationalization of Chinese customs be defended.
>
> (528)

It is curious that Ho Tung, himself both an ethnic hybrid and a professional facilitator of the East-West liaison, should profess such disapproval for the outward signs of 'hybrid failure', particularly, in the costume of Chinese women. And it is the Chinese *women* that he seems most concerned about. This perhaps points to the belief that women have always been seen as the carriers of traditions and protectors of culture.

In matters of religion too, he asserts the Chinese had a very ill-conceived notion of Western religious practice. Association with churches being 'sought as a means towards social or material advantages or for personal aggrandizement, the hypocrisy of the adoption of an alien religion cannot be too strongly condemned' (529). Chinese culture and national customs, in their exposure to Western influence, had yielded ludicrously undesirable hybrid effects. Interestingly, Ho Tung in 1916 seems to see that to compromise Chinese customs was in a way a breach of national loyalty and therefore, a form of denationalization.

Ho Tung sees it as the duty of Chinese leaders to set an example for the populace in their reception of Western practices.

> It is left to the leaders of Chinese society in Hong Kong to set up some standard of correct observances that would not offend any code of morals or good taste. Admittedly, such a task is not easy of accomplishment. Better far to make an early attempt than to delay until objectionable practices have received the sanction of usage.
>
> (528)

As a leader of the Chinese community and the 'doyen of the Eurasian community' (Gittins, 1969, 11), Ho Tung is speaking in this article as a Chinese. He represents Chinese essentialism and embraces Chinese cultural purism. Ideally, for Ho Tung, a Hong Kong Chinese should be familiar with Western thoughts and practices but he should also faithfully abide by Chinese customs and traditions. It is good that the two cultures should meet, but they should never amalgamate.

A political motivation can perhaps be read behind this Chinese cultural-nationalistic discourse. As this article is written for a British and European audience, it is only by being more Chinese on the cultural level, that he can be more British on the political level. His Chineseness and his representativeness of the moral and cultural ethos of the Hong Kong Chinese community were a kind of asset in dealing with his imperial masters. His involved engagement in a Chinese cultural discourse asserts an independence that not only dispels any suspicion of his being a passive and fawning colonial subject, but also lends him a kind of political foothold in his role as an authentic insider and agent representing the Hong Kong Chinese. Besides, this Chinese cultural loyalty can certainly help to balance his gyrating celebration of British Imperialism from sounding too obsequious. Furthermore, warnings against the 'denationalization' of colonial subjects were a familiar feature of conservative colonial discourse in the nineteenth and twentieth centuries. In other words, his 'resistance' rhetoric is of a kind entirely sanctioned by the colonial power. In his own way, Ho Tung is satisfactorily performing what he was supposed to: both facilitating the traffic of western goods and ideas into China, and being the acceptable voice of Chinese 'difference' for the West.

As the article turns to politics and mercantilism, Ho Tung's 'cultural resistant' tone gives way to a complicitous and collaborationist rhetoric. There is an overwhelming filial sense of gratitude and reverence. Speaking of the political status of the Chinese, he says:

> In this matter, as in all others, they have no reason to complain the Government does not extend to them a fair measure of equality of treatment with other races in the island, for two unofficial members, nominated by the Government, enjoy the distinction of representing the Chinese there on the Legislative Council.
>
> (529)

In speaking of commercial progress, he says:

> The Chinese are excluded from no department of commercial activity in Hong Kong ... . They rank to-day amongst the successful companies operating in friendly rivalry with similar British companies. Another notable fact is the inclusion of Chinese names in the directorate of British companies ... The companies that have thought fit to relax the rigid policy of exclusivism are amongst the largest capitalized and most influential of those registered in Hong Kong.
>
> (530)

Sir Robert has painted a near Utopian picture of race relations in commercial co-operation in 1916 Hong Kong. The Chinese presence at the senior level in foreign firms seemed in 1916 to still have a long way to go.[5] His representation of Hong Kong as a prosperous, stable British colony with established Chinese traders and unlimited labour resources can, of course, also be read as an effort to promote Hong Kong's competitiveness over other growing treaty ports in China. But in the portrayal of a fortunate community, in which the two races combine to create wealth without sacrificing their cultural independence, we can also see the outline of the great intermediary's own self-assessment, an idealized self-portrait in which the city itself is represented in the image of its most successful son.

In closing, Ho Tung once more assures the English reader of the benevolence of British colonization.

> So great is their [the Chinese] faith in the permanent prosperity of the colony, and the safety of domicile under the folds of the British flag, that the Chinese are said to own more than three-fifths of the landed property in Hong Kong ... .
>
> (530)

The eloquent voices in the article, in his multiple capacities — as native, trusted citizen of the Colonial government, representative of the Chinese populace of Hong Kong, Chinese patriot and protector of Chinese customs — have demonstrated the important need to maintain that precarious balance of involvement and detachment, of not appearing too European at certain times and of not sounding too Chinese at other times, but always insisting on a safe distance from all sides. Thus Ho Tung has delicately positioned himself somewhere at the intersecting discourses of Chinese essentialism and traditionalism, colonial collaborationism and mercantilism.

It was in this atmosphere of cautious multi-faceted worldviews that the compradore culture flourished — a culture that formed an integral part of the pre-war Eurasian ethnic ethos.

4

Memoir as a Self-asserting and Self-censoring Tool

Memoirs are always, to a certain degree a revenge on history.

(Gusdorf, 36)

[A] sort of curriculum vitae retracing the steps of an official career that, for importance, was hardly more than mediocre.

(Gusdorf, 37)

The age is characterized by a need to testify. Everywhere in the world women and men are rising up to tell their story out of the now commonly held belief that one's life signifies.

(Gornick, 5)

Before discussing in detail each of the selected Eurasian memoirs, I wish to consider some generic issues concerning the memoirs and how they stand within the traditions and history of life-writing.

The memoir, as a mode of writing through which the memoirist recalls and records her own life story is perhaps one of the most popular forms of autobiographical writing. The autobiographical motivations behind writing memoirs vary. Some write to preserve, commemorate, celebrate or immortalize one's life's experience and achievements. Still others write to confess, explain, to talk back, or to break a silence. But there are also others who write to reinforce a silence, to speak in order to cover up gaps and omissions.

The memoir has never enjoyed a high generic status. It has been viewed as a mode of writing practiced by amateur writers, or as James Olney says, by people who would neither imagine nor admit that they were 'writers' (1980, 4). As Olney has once described it, memoir is often regarded as the 'least literary' kind of writing in literature. It is the amateur's genre. Some have been of interest mostly to local historians who see them as part of the semi-historical social records and have paid little attention to them as writing. Memoirs are often distinguished from traditional autobiographies, such as those by St. Augustine and Jean-Jacques Rousseau, whose works are treated with that special reverence given to great literary texts. Memoirs have often been received with reservation 'as a kind of stepchild of history and literature, with neither of those disciplines granting it full recognition as a respectable subject for study in itself' (Olney, 1988, xiii).

Under the rubric of autobiography, an umbrella term for self-life-writing, we can distinguish basically three overlapping forms of autobiographical writings: First, the autobiography, second, the memoir and third, the autobiographical novel. For our purpose here, I shall look only at the first two, since the third kind, with its disguise of autobiography as the novel, really has quite a different generic status. The boundary between the first two categories, that is, the traditional autobiography and the memoir, is not always clear, and in many cases the two terms are often used interchangeably.

Most scholars in the past tended to emphasize and distinguish the difference between autobiography and memoir. Traditional autobiography, such as those by St. Augustine, Margery Kempe, Bunyan and Rousseau, belongs to a more elevated form of self-writing that focus on the intense introspection of an inner life within an interior domain. Its direction delves inward on a kind of teleological itinerary into the self to find an irreducible unified core, stripping away mask after mask of false selves for the true and pure self at the center (Smith, 1993, 18). It is, therefore, a history of a soul attempting through self-scrutiny to explain itself. With this intense concentration on the life of the soul, the author's outward life and events become somewhat blurred. Temporal references to sociopolitical occurrences have relatively little significance and are often relegated to the background. The traditional autobiography usually offers a continuous, coherent narrative.

The memoir, unlike the autobiography, usually has less sophisticated structural designs and thematic deliberations. The memoir is often less connected, more fragmented, and often lacks continuity in the narrative process. It is often a collection of reminiscences and personal observations and impressions of certain public events — a feature that is strongly evident in the Eurasian memoirs discussed later.

Bottrall distinguishes the memoir from the traditional autobiography by describing the memoir as being conceived in an extrovert temper (8). The memoir, instead of searching for some authentic inner self which explains why the writer is the kind of person he or she has turned out to be, often relates how the writer arrived at the point where he or she is standing at the time of writing. The memoir is more interested in giving a record of its times than in discovering the essence of a spirit or personality. The motivation of the memoir is often memorial, or mnemonic, rather than one of self-portraiture and self-discovery.

Beginning in the 1990s, most scholars have begun to pay less attention to the demarcation between traditional autobiographies and memoirs. Memoirs, together with other modes of life writing are now recognized as having an exemplary and crucial position in public culture (Zuss, 56). Zuss describes them as a culturally recognized primary genre faithful to lived experience. They are "public records of the personal, exposures of the internal, they function as a rhetoric of experience's own voice, an unsullied source of knowledge" (218–19).

Among the numerous celebrated features of memoirs and similar modes of life writing, what I found most relevant to the discussion of Hong Kong Eurasian memoirs is its role as intersecting points between individual experience and social history. These memoirs not only offer historical experiences but reinterpretation of these historical experiences. They allow interventions and interrogations into the unquestioned racial, ethnic and hegemonic cultural discourses that pervaded everyday life.

I would like to draw attention to two self-defining features in the selected memoirs, which quite separate them from memoirs of other contexts. The first of these is the autobiographical subjects' acute consciousness as historical beings.

An often-heightened sense of awareness as a historical being suffuses the memoirs. It is true that most memoirs with their focus on external events and people usually provide a 'window on history from which the narrative is presumably observed' (Eakin, 1992, 139). But in the case of these memoirs, history is not treated in such a detached and distant manner, history is not something to be observed through a window, history is not something ancillary or background to the narrative. These Eurasian subjects are *in* and *of* history in almost every aspect of their existence. They are inextricably and inexorably entwined with the historical process, whether intellectually in the abstract sense, externally and physically in the temporal sense (their actual experience as Hong Kong residents who went through and lived under the Japanese Occupation), or biologically in the genetic sense (as products of the intertwining Anglo-Chinese histories in Hong Kong and descendants from unions between nineteenth century European traders and Chinese women). The memoirist is no longer perceived as mere witness to history. At certain moments in these memoirs, we feel that the Eurasian subject becomes 'the site where history is experienced and transacted' (Eakin, 142) simultaneously on different levels. Eurasian memoirists are recasting history in their own mirrors.

Another self-defining feature of these memoirs is their quest for an identity and selfhood in the extrovert temper. Instead of the inward quest for the self and intense retrospection on one's identity found in traditional literary autobiographies, the subject's quest for identity is conducted through external events and their vigorous engagement with the two opposing cultures and the two (sometimes antagonistic) communities. The memoir addresses the question of 'what happened?' more than the question of 'who am I?' The Eurasian memoirists are in many ways extroverted women, looking back on a career of social prominence and involvement in public life. However, in reading these memoirs, we will find that the second question keeps intruding on the first, so that the narrative of the past keeps running into the autobiographical question of identity in the form of ethnicity. Although none of these Eurasian subjects are particularly oriented towards introspection, the narrative of their past — their memoirs — is punctuated by moments of autobiographical crisis, in the form of recurrent questions of 'Who was I? A Eurasian. What did that mean?' These questions yield very different answers in different Eurasian memoirs, and at different moments in each.

Memoirs, for these writers, become a wonderful vehicle for identity affirmation where the memoirist asserts her own perception of her Eurasian identity. But at certain moments when the self-perceived identity is challenged, the memoir also becomes a self-silencing tool for deliberate muteness — a narrative refusal, deferral and equivocation towards Eurasianness.

Part II

Readings

5

Joyce Symons

Pre-War Hong Kong: 'The Likes of Us'

*'We must carry ourselves with colossal assurance and say: "Look at us, the Eurasians!
Just look. How beautiful we are, more beautiful than either race alone. More clever,
more hardy. The meeting of both cultures, the fusion of all that can become a world
civilization. Look at us, and envy us, you poor one-world people, riveted to your
limitations. We are the future of the world. Look at us."'*

(Han, [1952] 1992, 230)

*Only I had the courage (or the foolishness) to scream against the general contempt
for Eurasians, 'But we are the future.' I stuck to my 'foolishness' ...*

(Han, 1980, 314)

*They knew no homeland, dearer on distant view...
In these lone hills, unsung, unhonoured, unknown
They sowed in blood that we in joy may reap*

(Law, 1998)

*L*ooking at the Stars: Memoirs of Catherine Joyce Symons* was published in
1996, a year before the handover, during a time when every bookstore
in town was suddenly inundated with an abundance of books on Hong
Kong, books re-thinking Hong Kong's colonial past, speculating on its
Chinese future and questioning the notion of a Hong Kong identity. *Looking
at the Stars* is very much an individual version of the common quest for
identity at this uncertain period in Hong Kong.

Joyce Symons was born in Shanghai in 1918. She came to Hong Kong when she was six years old. After being principal of Diocesan Girls' School for more than three decades, she retired in 1985 — a few months after British Prime Minister Margaret Thatcher signed the Sino-British Joint Declaration in Beijing — to the quiet neighbourhood of Walton-on-Thames in England. Away from her hectic public career in Hong Kong, Symons embarked on what many public personages had done in their retirement — the autobiographical project. Retirement had not been easy for the extrovert Symons. When asked what it was like to retire, Symons says, 'It's like dying. Painful and empty, but your heart tells you it is not the end' (1996, 90).

Keenly conscious of the plethora of books on Hong Kong in the months leading up to the changeover of sovereignty, she says, 'I have felt it unnecessary to add much to these works. But a number of people have been interested by my experiences and asked me to tell them stories of my life. So it is for them that I write now' (1996, 1).

Her modestly self-effacing attribution of her autobiographical impetus to the request of her friends seems no more than a polite gesture. In reading through her personal narrative, we feel an impetus much more intense than a memoir written at the request of others. It seems to originate from a heightened sense of isolation as a Eurasian woman, a stubbornness to continue against all odds, a desire to render her life-writing as a form of signature, a final imprint on the world which had alternately appreciated and rejected her. Writing becomes for her very much, as Amy Ling says of autobiography, an act of self-assertion, self-revelation and self-preservation (Ling, 135).

Adjusting her retirement from a bustling public career in the colony of Hong Kong to a lonely existence in an English suburb, her autobiographical project became a kind of reconnection through memory with that vibrant and pulsating past. It bridges the gap between who she once was (principal, JP, Unmelco, OBE, CBE, Honorary Doctorate) and who she is at the time of writing (retiree in a quiet English town). Writing her life helps the autobiographer to gain a more unified and organized sense of self in this stocktaking exercise.

The literary merit of memoirs written by public figures is often doubted by scholars like Gusdorf, who says, 'as soon as they have the leisure of retirement or exile … write in order to celebrate their deeds … for posterity that otherwise is in danger of forgetting them …' (Gusdorf, 36).

It is true that this element of self-celebration or what Gusdorf calls 'posthumous propaganda' is commonly found in autobiographical works of famous public figures. But the presence of this self-celebratory tendency does not necessarily render these autobiographical efforts in self-narrative and self-construction unworthy of the readers' attention. In Symons, though there may be at times a certain propensity to celebrate her personal achievements, there is also a strong confessional impulse where the autobiographer quite uninhibitedly reveals the private self behind the public figure. There is an effort to balance the successful external figure with the lonely, isolated private figure, which tended to be too trustful, potentially short-tempered, occasionally brusque, and at times quite oblivious to sentiments around her.

It is common practice for amateur authors to include in the memoir some kind of foreword, preface or introduction, written by a well-known figure, to direct the readers to some distinctive features of the life the reader is about to read. In the memoirs of Jean Gittins and Irene Cheng, we have forewords to their memoirs written by a Governor, by a university Vice-chancellor, by an English professor and by a senior Legislative Council member. Yet in *Looking at the* Stars, there is no such foreword or introduction by a well-known third party to introduce the author to the reader. The introduction to her memoir is written by Joyce Symons herself.

What marks Symons out from other memoirs published during the handover period is her candid foregrounding of her sense of her Eurasian identity — an issue which not many would be willing to deal with in such a forthright manner, and an issue which, of course, is closely bound up with the birth of Hong Kong as a British colony. Symons reflects upon her own ethnicity and the different responses it evoked quite openly without the kind of reservations, anxieties and blustering that one sometimes finds in other Eurasian memoirs. Yet, she also admits that at the age of 78, she is still painfully aware of the difficulties of being a Eurasian.

Her story begins with, 'In my veins runs the blood of several ancestors from England, Scotland, Austria, Spain and America who first visited China and Hong Kong' (1996, 1). Writing in some quiet corner south west of London in England in the late 1980s and early 1990s, Symons is acutely aware of the dispersal, assimilation and disappearance of the Hong Kong Eurasian community to which she had belonged. She is self-consciously writing as perhaps one of the last surviving members of that pre-war Eurasian community — a closely-knit community that enjoyed a kind of exclusively privileged bourgeois East-West niche in pre-war Hong Kong. But also flooding back with these memories are events and scenes of the internal dissension and invidious divisions of the community as their sense of ethnic loyalty clashed, specifically between the 'Chinese' Eurasians and the 'British' Eurasians. Occasional doubts and lingering bitterness find their way into her writings, contradicting her every attempt to represent the cohesion and collectiveness of her community.

Most memoirists like to see themselves as detached chroniclers of people and events in their lifetime, (as in the case of Irene Cheng to be discussed later). Some memoirists foreground the separation of the subject of discourse distinctly into a narrating self and an experiencing self. But in Symons, the distinction is not very clear, and we feel frustration and anger in the voice of the elderly narrator constantly filtering into the reconstructed narratee at every turn as she reacts to her own process of telling her story. In reading Symons, perhaps it is appropriate to invoke what Roy Pascal says of autobiography, that it 'involves an interplay or collusion between the past and the present, that indeed its significance is more truly understood as the revelation of the present situation of the autobiographer than as the uncovering of his [sic] past' (11).

The 'Pre-war' section of this chapter will look into the different aspects of the construction and representation of Joyce Symons's Eurasian identity through her childhood memory, and examine how the autobiographer defines her sense of Eurasianness and how it was reinforced and nurtured in the pre-war colonial culture, and eventually how her Eurasian ethnicity was destabilized by the experience of war. The 'Post-war' section of this chapter will look closely at how Symons adjusted or refused to adjust her own sense of Eurasianness in a fast changing colony under the process of gradual decolonization, localization and vernacularization.

⊷⊶⊙⊷⊶

The need to articulate and define her mixed ethnicity is undeniably one of her major autobiographical imperatives. There is an unflinching tendency to foreground her hybridity not only as a simple racial mixture, but also as a clearly prescribed ethnicity separate from the Chinese and the Europeans — a cultural, historical and social synthesis from two antitheses.

'All my life I have felt slightly uneasy, for to be Eurasian — certainly when I grew up — has been like suffering from an emotional form of Aids. I was not totally accepted at best by either culture, nor totally despised at worst' (Symons, 1996a, vi). The emotional freight of this unsettling statement is acutely expressed through the image of Aids. Yet alongside this constant awareness of stigma, there also exists a strong sense of Eurasian pride — a pride not based on the biological and cultural superiority of Eurasians as suggested in Han Suyin. Symons's ethnic pride seems to derive more from a sense of adversity, exclusion and ambiguity. In speaking of the fate of the Eurasian community she grew up in, Symons, towards the end of her memoir, says 'Eurasians, in a sense did not exist — certainly they were not ignored, for often they held their own in work or play; but they were not accepted except grudgingly' (1996a, 95).

Symons insists on a carefully prescribed hybrid site — the insistence of a third and liminal space — a 'thirdness' between those two opposing cultural/ethnic powers (British and Chinese). Ideally, this should be a space that should serve as a bridge between the two races but sometimes, it is also a space that finds itself contributing more to the separation of the two races.

An unmistakable craving for a stable, fixed and essential sense of Eurasianness is evidenced. Yet in this craving, there often lurks a subterranean sense of unsettledness, of always having to defend and to protect her own conception of Eurasianness. As her narrative progresses, something akin to the Bakhtinian mode of hybridity seems to emerge, a hybridity that 'has been politicized and made contestatory: hybridity as division and separation' (Young, 21).

⊱──◆─○─◆──⊰

Symons includes in her introduction (not without some amusement) the sometimes-confusing reaction that her ethnic image could elicit. She once described herself at a social gathering as being 'a human cocktail' to a curious audience. A waitress said to her in English, 'You half half?' and Symons replied in Cantonese, 'Not quite' (1996a, vi).

The metaphor of being "a human cocktail" expresses a concept of such eclectic race mixture down many generations that it simply defies any acceptance of race categories and race differences. For Symons, her Eurasian heritage cannot be based on any simplistic common mathematical description (if it is at all mathematically divisible in her case). Her Eurasianness is not just a simple matter of biology. It is the arrival of early European visitors to this part of China and their alliance with the 'Chinese or Eurasian women down the generations' (1996, 2) that she and her community had come into existence. History becomes a kind of defining feature of her Eurasianness. In a way, Eurasians can be seen as living legacies of European mercantile history in China and Hong Kong.

The preference for a historical rather than a biological paradigm to articulate her Eurasian heritage could partly be due to the fact that Symons is very much conscious of the heterogeneous mix of the Hong Kong Eurasian community. Precisely because of its racial heterogeneity, Symons's perception of her Eurasian identity rests heavily upon what Benedict Anderson describes as 'historical destinies' (Anderson, 149). Eurasians were all bound together by the common imagined notion that they were all descendants of an early alliance between European traders and their Chinese 'wives' (Symons, 1996a, 2) throughout Hong Kong and other treaty ports.

To Symons, the Eurasians are a community created by colonialism and mercantilism which, venturing into the East, had spun the intertwining destinies and overlapping histories of two very different races and cultures.

⊳━◆━○━◆━⊲

Peter Hall, the Hong Kong Eurasian author of *The Web* (1992), and a distant relative of Symons, uses this historical paradigm in defining the Eurasians. The Hong Kong Eurasian families and their mutual relationships, he says, are like interlocking roots and branches of the banyan tree (xvi). Hall's process of tracing the first Hall who came to Hong Kong from England in the mid-1850s had inadvertently brought to light the many illicit relationships as well as the illegitimacy of many well-known Hong Kong Eurasians. His research project had at one point caused much bitterness within some sectors of the Eurasian community.

Undaunted by the taboo of illegitimacy, Symons says at the beginning of her first chapter: 'Almost all early ancestors of Eurasians were illegitimate, until the young generations got married to Chinese or other Eurasians and followed a Chinese way of life' (1996a, 1). In fact, she has inserted in her text two genealogical charts of her paternal and maternal ancestors, through the courtesy of Peter Hall. Rather than embarrassment, Symons shares with Hall the detective's ecstasy and historian's thrill in unearthing the long forgotten past in her family history. In Nicola King's discussion of autobiographies, the searching for genealogy, the tracing of family trees, become crucial ways of establishing a history and finding a point of origin, which is central to the reconstruction of the author's identity (7–8). But in Symons's case, the point of origin always seems to be receding before the author's grasp and resisting any verifiability.

The narrator begins her story by accepting that impossibility of locating the point of origin of her Eurasianness — when the first Anderson arrived in Hong Kong. She says if she looks back at her family history, she can only go to her Eurasian grandfather, Henry Graham Anderson, with any real accuracy. Tracing any further back in time is not possible. Her great grandfather was a Scot from Glasgow who worked for a big British shipping company. There was in fact a Graham Anderson who served as a ship's officer on a Jardine Matheson ship. But the Anderson family had no proof or evidence of the connection (Symons, 1996a, 1).

It seems impossible to ever fully know who exactly their European ancestors were. Their identities would remain blurred and subject to question. The only confirmation of their existence remains no more than the genetic legacies manifested through the European features of the Anderson family. Yet Symons seems ready to accept the blurriness of the existence of her ancestors as one of the conditions of being a China Coast Eurasian of their generation.

⊷─◦─⊶

Symons sees the Eurasian community as a distinct ethnic group stranded between two opposing cultures. Precisely because of this position in the middle, she believes that Eurasian children are in a way provided with a condition to excel. Like many other Eurasian children, young Joyce was often bewildered and confused by trying to cope with vastly dissimilar languages, and contradictory codes of conduct or even table manners. There was never any discussion or explanation on these contradictory bi-cultural practices. Having to constantly juggle with these two cultures in their everyday life, Eurasian children, Symons says, often choose the easiest way of doing something, so honing a sharp sense of opportunism. Such adaptability, Symons suggests, applied to school life, often led to academic success, athletic distinction, and being awarded responsible positions at school. She remembers how expatriate teachers usually expected Eurasian children to do well and naturally enough, this apparent favouritism often made them detested by the Chinese children. 'Being in the middle was not easy' (1996a, 3).

Eurasian achievements therefore are in a way attributable to the kind of alienation, separatism, resilience and ambiguity that young Eurasians experienced in the process of enculturation between the two cultures. Here, we see Park's theory of the Marginal Man or Person enacted in real life. Robert Park, the American sociologist, had formulated his theory of the Marginal Man. He sees the Eurasian in Asia and the Mulatto in the United States as examples of the marginal man. The person of mixed blood 'is one who lives in two worlds, in both of which he is more or less a stranger' (Park, 1928, 893). Symons's description of the Eurasian child resembles in many ways the Marginal, 'one whom fate has condemned to live in two societies and in two, not merely different but antagonistic, cultures' (Park, 1961, xiiii). Park argues that living between two opposing cultures has fostered in the Marginal Person a 'keener intelligence' (1950, 376) and 'restlessness' (1928, 893). Looking back at her own Eurasian experience, Symons describes the embattled emotional middle-space as the 'no-man's land' of Eurasian isolationism (1996a, 3). Her construction of an Eurasian identity is clearly based more on the sense of being in the 'middle', of being trapped in between, rather than 'marginal' or 'peripheral'.

The Hong Kong Eurasian culture as delineated by Symons is basically a culture that ultimately inclines towards the West, despite its adoption of some Chinese practices. According to Symons, the typical Eurasian life-style such as food, and certainly female dress, were mainly Chinese, but some expatriate ideas and habits were admired, and gradually assimilated when a family could afford to move up the socio-economic scale. She believes that this pattern of grafting a Western culture onto the indigenous ethnic culture was evident for many decades in Hong Kong and in the other treaty ports of Shanghai, Tientsin, Amoy, Swatow, and Hankow (1996a, 3).

Symons's description of changes in the Eurasian ethnic identity as the individual or the family moves up the economic scale offers a clear example of how ethnicity, rather than being a kind of fixed, stable and concrete category, should be seen as a process, a continually evolving category, where social, economical and political forces determine the content and importance of racial categories (Omi, 61).

Based on Symons's theory of the Eurasian ethnic shift, we can now see how pre-war Hong Kong Eurasians were afforded a kind of 'mobility' to cross the colonized/colonizer, native/expatriates, Chinese/Europeans, yellow/white lines through economic advancement. Examples of such 'crossings' of ethnic boundaries can be found in Symons's representation of her own parents during the 1920s.

Charles Anderson, Joyce Symons's father, was a classic example of the Eurasian figure that crossed the ethnic boundary during times of crisis. The narrator recalls how her father was a very outgoing thoroughly Westernized Eurasian in lifestyle and outlook. He was good in sports like cricket, golf and tennis (Symons 1996a, 3). A graduate of Queen's College in Hong Kong, he married Lucy Perry. Charles found work as a stockbroker in Shanghai where Joyce was later born. She was called Katherine Eleanor, but later renamed Catherine Joyce. 'The reason for my change in name was because Father was a very keen golfer, and renamed me after Joyce Wethered, who won the British Open' (1996a, 2). The image of the Anderson home she invokes during their life in Shanghai was one that had all the luxury and privileges of European life in China. Their house at No. 9 Tifeng Road had a spacious garden and tennis court. The Andersons kept a carriage and several servants, under the command of a 'Head "Boy", who could be relied on to always wear long white cotton Chinese gown over black gaiters' (1996a, 2).

Around 1924, this European exclusiveness began to slip away as Charles Anderson got into financial difficulty. The young Eurasian family moved south to Hong Kong to a small flat at 5 College View. The move was a drastic socioeconomic change. The narrator recalls how, 'I always felt as a child that Hong Kong was a village and Shanghai was a city' (1996b, Track 1). But as things turned out, the change was not only socioeconomic but also brought with it a change in ethnicity. As they came down the economic scale, the narrator recalls how her father Charles edged towards his Chinese side.

Charles Anderson felt alienated from the Europeans in Hong Kong. He began to dislike and disapprove of the expatriate foreigners. The author recalls how her father started to accentuate his Chinese heritage. His attitudes actually affected his appearance and Charles Anderson looked increasingly Chinese, as he grew older, spending most of his days at the Chinese Club. Like Kipling's Lispeth who reverted back to the indigenous culture when she had cause to resent the English, Charles Anderson's case is also one of reversion as he found himself descending down the sociocultural hierarchy in Hong Kong.

During this period of economic dislocation, Symons recalls how her mother Lucy Perry 'was drawn to the West' (1996a, 4). While Charles Anderson was out at the Chinese Club, Lucy Perry became a 'constant worshipper at St. Peter's Church in Western Hong Kong, where the congregation was largely composed of Eurasians' (1996a, 4). Miss Pitts, an English missionary there, taught Lucy English.

As can be seen, Lucy Perry was marginalized on different levels by her class, gender and most importantly language. Lucy's mother, Annie Overbeck (daughter of the Austrian Vice-Consul and his Spanish-Chinese 'wife' [1996a, 1]) died young. Lucy had lived in Macau under a dominating grandaunt who insisted on raising her within the confines of Chinese traditions. A tutor was hired to give her Chinese lessons at home. Unlike her cousins who went to Diocesan Girls' School, Lucy, who came to Hong Kong later, went to the Church Missionary Society School in Hollywood Road. This arrangement kept her on the fringe of the Westernized Eurasians. In the absence of a firm mastery of the colonial language, Lucy Perry was not only excluded from contact with the expatriate society which the larger Eurasian community aspired towards, but she was also marginalized from within the Eurasian community where the mastery of the colonial language played a crucial role in determining one's social status. Her contact with missionaries then can be read less as a colonizing experience but more as a liberating force from her marginal status. The economic dislocation had therefore caused one reversion and one conversion in the Anderson family.

Since their move to Hong Kong, and Charles Anderson's metamorphosis into a Chinese, Symons recalls life in the family, within the conventions of Chinese traditions and practices, as 'rather dull'. Birthdays or Christmas were never celebrated. Chinese New Year remained the most important

Plate 1   Family portrait of the
Andersons taken in 1922, from
Looking at the Stars, courtesy of
Dr Joyce Symons.

time of the year. Children were given new clothes, including shoes, and were taken to call on rounds of relatives and friends. They were instructed to bow to the elders and 'nod to a descending hierarchy of aunts' (1996a, 5).

But young Joyce's cultural confinement was to end soon with her entry into Diocesan Girls' School (DGS), originally called the Diocesan Home and Orphanage, established in the mid-nineteenth century. According to a Hong Kong Guide 1893, 'The Diocesan Home and Orphanage is ... principally for the care and education of Eurasians. It belongs to the Church of England and is managed by a committee, of which the Right Rev. Bishop Burdon, Bishop of Victoria, is chairman' (Sweeting, 1990, 244).

In 1926, at the age of seven, Joyce entered the English-speaking world of DGS. 'At the time I knew not one word of English, nor any alphabet, or numbers'. The young subaltern, who until then had not met a Caucasian before, was completely overwhelmed at meeting 'a tall, austere-looking women with "yellow" hair'. A stranger to the language, young Joyce nodded helplessly at every English word spoken to her. Sitting nervously at the back of an enormous classroom, the author remembers, 'No-one greeted me or spoke to me, and I spoke to no-one' (1996a, 9).

Joyce's entry into DGS marks the gradual affirmation of her Eurasian identity and departure from her early Chinese upbringing through the medium of the British colonial elite education system. She soon found herself able to code-switch comfortably and naturally from Chinese to English with the same ease she found in her Uncle Joe and Aunty Kitty in Shanghai (1996a, 11).

Outside of school, Joyce's life revolved closely within the Eurasian network that consisted of the Chans, the Hos, the Choas and granduncle E. H. Ray. Settling at their new home in Kai Tak Bund in 1926 was a great relief after the cramped flat at 5 College View near Bonham Road with their paternal extended family. The Kai Tak house was one of many in a small terrace of 17 houses, which was to be her home for 16 years. The Andersons felt like pioneers in the yet to be developed area of Kai Tak. 'No-one else in the little community where we had previously lived had ventured out into the hinterland of Kowloon'. But soon, several other Eurasian families joined them in their new settlement. Eurasians had always been scattered around Hong Kong and lived in the midst of Chinese clusters. The actual experience of living within a Eurasian settlement contributed much to her growing pride as a member of the Eurasian community.[1]

The house at Kai Tak Bund was a gift from E. H. Ray, Joyce's wealthy granduncle on her mother's side, who lived at MacDonnell Road. Ray was a Eurasian curmudgeon and was very close to the Anderson family. He bought the Andersons a house and sent one of the Anderson boys to read law in England. Ray was their link into the world of expatriate lifestyle with 'his shiny knives and forks, his European food and, most glamorous of all, his grand presents round a well-decorated Christmas tree' (1996a, 8).

⊳—⊷—○—⊶—⊲

By mid-1930s, the quiet city of Hong Kong suddenly found itself crowded with refugees from Shanghai. Shanghai was seized with panic by the Japanese invasion and foreign nationals fled the city. Fleeing relatives and friends were now called 'refugees'. Hong Kong was suddenly flooded with different Shanghai non-Chinese racial groups, and there was an almost carnival-like atmosphere about the city.

Joyce was born in Shanghai and her tie with her Shanghai Eurasian relatives had always been close. Many Andersons came from Shanghai and some stayed at their house. These newly arrived Shanghainese Eurasians, the 'Shanghai people', were clearly unhappy with the inter-ethnic relations in Hong Kong: '[The] Shanghai people found Hong Kong customs irritating — they considered that we were cowed by the expatriates, and that we treated "the Chinese" far too well' (1966, 21). Symons found such attitudes, particularly the latter one, quite annoying.

The triangular relationship between the Eurasians, Chinese and Europeans in Shanghai are well represented in sociological and literary writings. Herbert Lamson in his 1936 article says that the Eurasian in Shanghai tends 'to look down upon the native side of his ancestry' and resists 'assimilation to native ways and loyalties' (643). He describes how the Eurasians with their hybrid-racial visibility often imitate 'the alien [foreigners] in belittling the native' and become 'a class of native-despising hybrids' (642–43). This 'Chinese-despising temper' of the Eurasians could invoke greater resentment towards the Eurasians than towards the foreigners, 'since the native expects that if the Eurasian has part-Chinese blood he ought to be less imperialistic and less haughty toward Chinese than the traditionally native-dominating alien' (643). Lamson concludes that Eurasians in Shanghai, rather than facilitating cultural contacts between the Chinese and Europeans, in fact perpetuate their separation. Yet given the diversity of the Eurasian community in Shanghai, there were, of course, Eurasians within the community who tended to lean the other way towards his Chinese side. Novelist Diana Chang (a second generation Eurasian herself) describes in her novel, *The Frontiers of Love*, how Feng, a Shanghai Eurasian youth finds these self-satisfying attitudes disdainful.

Chang also illustrates quite vividly the Eurasians' psychological ambivalence towards the power their Eurasian presence invoked over the Chinese and the resulting superiority they felt. Sylvia, one of the Eurasian protagonists says,

> There were too many Chinese; yes, she felt that to be true; and it was so easy to claim distinction, to be ennobled as though one had somehow achieved it through conscious effort just by speaking English and looking, not even Aryan, but just non-Chinese.
>
> (Chang, 86)

Yet, this sense of ethnic power or superiority was felt only when they were among the Chinese. This 'distinction', as described in Chang's novel, was looked at very differently by the expatriates. Emily Hahn recalls how her friend in Shanghai, Grace Brady, felt ashamed of her large number of Eurasian nephews and nieces in the way that Southerners in America do about mulattoes. This sense of shame, Hahn believes, reflects the general expatriates' attitudes towards Eurasians in the China Coast.

> I had the customary American attitude towards the people we call
> 'Eurasians' ... . I had toward them none of the definite reaction we
> are all given by environment toward the Negro race. Probably we
> Americans, even before China became our ally in this war, thought
> it romantic to have a touch of oriental blood. Certainly it added to
> the glamour of a movie actress or a dancer if she could claim a Chinese
> or East Indian ancestor, not *too* recent ...
>
> (1944, 29)

Eurasianness in the China Coast remained a form of exotic glamour in the distance, particularly within certain glitzy social milieu. Any *close* blood connection, however, would invoke an instant sense of embarrassment and unease.

▷─◆▷─◇─◁◆─◁

Coming to Hong Kong, some of the Shanghai Eurasian relatives of Joyce felt indignant about the social apartheid in pre-war Hong Kong, particularly when they found themselves pushed to the other side of the colonial divide. Charles Anderson himself, as narrated in the beginning, had felt the same kind of indignation now experienced by the Shanghai Eurasians. Joyce's own family's move back to Hong Kong in the 1920s had been a difficult one, particularly in locating their socio-ethnic position in the colonial hierarchy. 'In Shanghai, people were Chinese, or non-Chinese — foreigners — who included British, American, Irish, German, Filipino, or even Eurasians. But in Hong Kong throughout the colonial period, people were either expatriates or Chinese[,] no one mentioned Eurasians' (Symons 1996a, 2).

Despite their lack of public recognition in Hong Kong as an ethnic group, the Eurasian community was able to muster some sense of cohesion through the establishment of The Welfare League in the late 1920s — perhaps the most important social institution that not only articulates a strong communal awareness but represents a form of collective Hong Kong Eurasian identity (The Welfare League is still in existence today). Joyce herself later sat on its committee in the late 1940s. It was from Eric Ho, a nephew of Sir Robert, that Symons learned that her father Charles Anderson was secretary to The Welfare League in the late 1920s. During a meeting on 23 December 1929, Anderson appealed to his fellow Eurasians:

Gentlemen, it has been said of us that we can have no unity, and since even the semi-civilized tribes of Africa have it, this, though palpably absurd, is a challenge to be faced and an insult to be wiped out. Our detractors little know that if we have not coalesced sooner it is simply because the urge to do so has not been pressing. They do not realize that, after all, there is no gulf between a Chan and a Smith amongst us and that underlying the superficial differences in names and outlook, the spirit of kinship and brotherhood burns brightly. We Eurasians, being born into this world, belong to it. We claim no privileges but we demand our rights for which we must contest to the last ditch. With the blood of Old China mixed with that of Europe in us, we show the world that this fusion, to put it no higher, is not detrimental to good citizenship. If 'Peace on Earth and Goodwill towards Men' is not to be mere gibberish, then the Eurasians within the seven seas are some of the people sent into this world to assist in the accomplishment of this idea. In this part of China, we are a force to be reckoned with, a force to be respected and a force to be better appreciated when it is shown that we can look after, not only ourselves, but also the destitute of our kith and kin.

(Eric Ho, 9)

In this piece of elegantly crafted racial rhetoric, part of which Symons quoted in her memoir, Anderson is attempting to re-articulate a collective identity by offering to the Eurasians a fresh view of themselves and of their world, one that is revamped from the common perception or misconception. In his efforts to counter the negative stereotypes of Eurasians, he is using a rhetoric that is highly informed by a kind of biologism of race, and places Eurasians in a very special racialized position. He is using their mixed heritage, 'a fusion between old China and Europe' as a unifying force to form a kind of Eurasian solidarity. The differences in physical attributes and names (some Eurasians have more European features, some Eurasians use only their Chinese family name) are 'superficial differences' and should not be used as dividing forces to break up their sense of a common ethnic bond. Eurasians, because of their mixed heritage, are sent into this world endowed with a mission to act as ambassadors of peace. In a sense, they are represented as a kind of chosen people to bring harmony to the different races genetically manifested within them.

In 1935 after graduating from DGS, Joyce entered Hong Kong

University (HKU). In many ways like DGS, the student body of the 1930s HKU was fairly mixed ethnically. She stayed at the St. Stephen's Hostel run by missionaries for women undergraduates. The English girls took their meals with the wardens. But Joyce preferred to take her meals with the Chinese girls. As far as culinary preferences are concerned, Joyce seemed quite consistent — her ethnic orientation seemed more readily inclined towards the Chinese side.

It was at this time that she met her future husband Robert Symons (Bob), a Eurasian medical student. The narrator fondly recalls the European features of Robert Symons, who had 'a fair complexion and light wavy hair, he had a rather pronounced nose and greyish-green

Plate 2   Joyce Anderson as a "budding teacher" in the late 1930s, from *Looking at the Stars*, courtesy of Dr Joyce Symons.

eyes, with a splash of red in his left eye' (1996a, 20). As she has traced her own genealogy, the narrator also traces the Eurasian background of Robert Symons, whose grandfather was an Englishman from Devon and an engineer working on boats along the Yangtze River. On Robert Symons's mother's side, her father was a Jewish businessman with the name of Salinger (1996a, 79).

⊱━◆➤━○━◆◂━◆⊰

In September 1939, Joyce, having graduated from the Hong Kong University, was starting out as a young teacher at DGS. One morning, she heard Britain's Prime Minister Neville Chamberlain announcing on the radio the declaration of war on Germany, followed by the playing of the National Anthem. The war might still seem far and remote for most Hong Kong people, but Joyce was already feeling concerned about what was to escalate into a world war that very few could escape. The global effect of the Second World War was slowly reaching Hong Kong. Every British colony was involved one way or another in colonial defence under the British Empire. The Compulsory Service Ordinance of 1939 was passed and Hong Kong was Britain's first colony to follow her lead in introducing conscription. Under this Ordinance,

> All British Subjects of European origin coming under the Registration Ordinance were made liable to some form of compulsory service, and if fit, to be enrolled in a Defence Reserve.
>
> (Endacott, 43–44)

Since most Eurasians were British Subjects, they were required to join the Hong Kong Volunteer Defence Corps (HKVDC) (Fisher, 114).

By June 1940, with the fall of France, the possibility of an attack on British possessions by Japan became less remote. After the fall of Canton in October 1938, the Japanese had already reached as far south as the Shum Chun River. The possibility of open Japanese invasion of the British colony now became more real than ever.

On 28 June 1940, an urgent order for evacuation of all British women and children was received from the War Cabinet in London. A special meeting of the Executive Council held the following morning approved the order for compulsory evacuation. The Governor, Sir Geoffrey Northcote, made a broadcast that evening which was followed by formal announcements in the press (Wordie, 1997, 7).

But what did 'all British women and children' mean? Did Eurasian women and children who were British subjects fall under this category? Many Eurasians were at a loss as to their eligibility. Some Eurasians who had family members in the Volunteers thought that they were surely eligible. Others like the Gittinses were not so sure. Still others like the Mathews never even thought the order applied to the Eurasians at all (Wordie, 1997, 41).

Joyce, however, was not quite ready to accept that Eurasians were not eligible for evacuation. The Andersons possessed valid British passports, they were a Volunteer family, and because of their belonging to the non-Chinese part of the community, they had shared in the war work. Joyce could not see why they should be excluded.

The two Anderson sisters, Joyce and Marjorie, went to the registration tent for evacuees, which was set up on the Cricket Club grounds next to the Supreme Court. In the Oral History Project transcription of an interview, Symons recalls that there were:

> Lines with British, British-India, British-Portuguese and British-Chinese. But she [we] could not go into any categories, so I said to my sister 'We go out for a drink and come back towards the end.' So I asked one officer 'What time do you close?' He replied '12:30'. So we got back at 12:10. They [we] walked up to the United Kingdom's line and told them I was not pure-British, but my ancestors were part Chinese and five other nationalities, but I wanted to get away.

> (1996b, Track 1)

Unable to fit themselves into any of the categories, Joyce tried the line for United Kingdom (presumably for just British in a general way). Their applications were rejected on the spot. Joyce was told by the authorities that they really had no idea what to do with 'the likes of you' (1996a, 23). The phrase 'the likes of you', referring to Eurasians like Joyce, quite clearly questions the legitimacy of her Eurasian identity being categorized as British. The phrase suggests not only a denial of this intermediate identity but also a strong suspicion of its utterly uncategorizable status.

Here, we feel the narrator re-living that intense moment of indignation and as if justifying her own anger after five decades, she tells the reader:

> However, 'the likes of us' were ordered to share in the war effort, with our young men conscripted into the volunteers and trained for battle, and everyone with a non-Chinese name having to take on some kind of war work.

> (1996a, 23)

Joyce's father had joined the Rice Control Office. Her mother Lucy had became an ANS (Auxiliary Nursing Service). Her brother, a young magistrate, belonged to the Defence Volunteers. Every one of the Andersons was in some way sharing the war effort. She herself had been a patriot and loyal to her British heritage and that was the result — excluded and rejected by the British authorities. The authorities had refused to recognize their eligibility for evacuation and by implication, the 'authenticity' of their being European and British. The official's reaction had very much de-stabilized

Joyce's own confidence in her Eurasian identity and her European heritage. Being métissage, her citizenship and nationality were instantly subject to query. The response of not knowing 'what to do with the likes of you' unequivocally expresses the colonial bafflement about 'métissage' — and the group of non-descript racial types and 'pseudocompatriots' (Stoler, 201) that unsettled the neat order of colonial hierarchy.

As the narrator recalls the humiliating event, one memory leads to another. The disparaging phrase 'the likes of you' leads Symons to reflect on the other kind of 'the likes of you', the apostate Eurasians who had escaped their patriotic duties by changing their ethnicity through the simple process of 'adopting Chinese names' (1996a, 23).

Symons's bitterness towards these turncoat Eurasians extends also to the Chinese. The narrator cannot reconcile herself to the fact that the Chinese were not included in the war effort. She says in the 1996 interview:

> It is [*sic*] not British fighting Japan, it was a common enemy, how can they [the Chinese] need not do any war work. The government didn't have the guts to ask the Chinese to do anything.
>
> (1996b, Track 2)

The colonial government at that time had their own concerns. Endacott, the Hong Kong government's official historian of the war, justifies the government's reluctance to appeal to the Chinese community in war work.

> The Chinese remained Chinese at heart and few were absorbed into the western community ... Basically law-abiding, they gave little trouble to the authorities, they asked for no share in political control or for any form of State aid, and by the same token they did not expect the State to make any demands on them ... There was but slight feeling of belonging to Hong Kong, scant loyalty to the State, and little spirit of willing sacrifice for the community. To them, Hong Kong defence was a matter for the British. Hong Kong was, therefore, an artificial society and the vast majority were there temporarily, seeking economic advantage or escape from Japanese attack, and only Eurasians, Portuguese and some local Chinese, Indians and others of long standing became westernized and regarded Hong Kong as a home worth fighting for. The refugees were an unknown quantity and the British authorities were understandably hesitant about appealing for co-operation from the resident Chinese community.
>
> (1978, 27)

As a result of the colonial government's distrust of the Chinese community, the responsibility of contributing to the defence of the Colony fell upon the shoulders of the small Eurasian community (and other small minorities like the Portuguese and the Indians). The Eurasian community which had hitherto acted as a bridge between the British government and the Chinese community, now found themselves in danger of becoming a sacrificial victim as a result of the mutual distrust and indifference between the British and the Chinese. Symons's memory of this Eurasian victimhood shows no sign of abating as she retells her story.

In the early summer of 1941, Charles Anderson sent his two daughters Joyce and Marjorie as 'refugees' to his brother, James Graham Anderson in Shanghai. Symons recalls how the British and other foreign communities steered clear of the Germans. But one afternoon when Joyce and her Eurasian cousins were passing by a German school, a group of young Nazis surrounded the girls and shouted, 'You dirty British, you're finished, Herr Hitler will enter London soon' (1996a, 23).

Joyce and her Eurasian relatives were much shaken. Their British heritage, which all along had invoked a kind of colonial prestige, now became a target of abuse by Germans and later by the Japanese. This incident marks her first realization of the possible costs of being 'British'. After the summer, the two Anderson sisters, returned to Hong Kong.

⊱—◆⟩—○—⟨◆—⊰

The Hong Kong Centenary year drew to a close in December 1941. Partly because of the apprehensiveness towards the possibility of war, the Centennial celebration, compared to the Golden Jubilee celebration 50 years ago in 1891, was much more subdued. The Japanese had already evacuated their own civilians by July 1941. The young Eurasian teacher found herself teaching smaller classes in DGS. As the expatriate girls and some of the teachers had been evacuated to Australia (1996a, 23), the school had shrunk considerably. Joyce, and the many Eurasians who were rejected by the Evacuation Authorities, probably shared the same helpless indignation at being abandoned and stranded in the colony. Woo Mo-han, a Hong Kong Chinese, recalls in her memoir how as a child she could not understand 'why we cannot be evacuated like the British and the Japanese, instead of being stuck here to wait for the war to come' (4).

At around 8 a.m. Monday, 8 December 1941, five hours after the Japanese had started their strike at Pearl Harbour, Kai Tak aerodrome was attacked by 30 Japanese planes (1996a, 23). Dr Li Shu-fan, in his memoir remembers how he saw 'coils of black smoke overhanging Kai Tak airdrome … It seems strange now that no one around me was at all excited. The incident was generally assumed to be connected with air maneuvers of some sort — at least, this was the answer I received to all my inquiries. With the exception of the armed forces and the police, hardly anyone realized that the Japanese invasion had begun' (Li, 80).

The Anderson family, living on 23 Kai Tak Bund, was directly within the target of this first bombing. Symons recalls how the drone of aeroplanes and the air raid siren directly above the area confirmed what she had dreaded for so long — the real war had begun.

The war narrative in Symons's memoir can be read as operating on three different levels, interweaving into each other at different points. On the first level, there is the historical narrative, the larger scene of the war between Britain and Japan, between the 60, 000 well-trained Japanese troops and the tragically ill-equipped Hong Kong force of British, Indians, Canadians and volunteer civilians. On the second level, there is the narrative of Donald (Symons's brother) as an officer at the front line. In this section of the narrative, Symons is fulfilling what she saw as her moral duty to record the story of Donald's sacrifice to the war. Not being an eyewitness to the battlefront, Symons relies on her memory of the pieces of information that filtered back from Donald and other soldiers, Donald's letters, and occasionally relying on historical research on the Hong Kong Volunteers. The third level is the autobiographical. The narrator recalls her own experience as a civilian in the non-combatant sphere of the war. With the exception of the chaos and fleeing in the initial days of the fighting, the rest of this civilian narrative after the surrender consists mainly of anxious waiting, listening and more waiting. Helpless passivity became a major action.

On the historical level, there is a strong sense of fatefulness as the narrator describes how the Hong Kong force was ridiculously outnumbered. Symons wistfully recalls how the two peace missions offered by the Japanese on 13 and 17 December were refused by the British (1996a, 25). Donald died on the 19 December — a death that perhaps might have been averted if one of these peace offers had been accepted.

On the narrative of Donald, Symons has reconstructed Donald's experience as the youngest of the four officers in No. 3 Company. The No. 3 Company composed principally of Eurasians (while No. 5 and 6 were mainly Portuguese). Only the two older officers survived. Telling the story of her brother's fighting at the front line is in a way giving voice to the many 'unsung, unhonoured, unknown' Eurasian youths who never lived to tell their stories of the battlefront (Law, 1945). Donald had fought 'unflinchingly', responding to General Maltby's Order of the Day to 'become a great example of high-hearted courage to all the rest of the British Empire who are fighting to preserve truth, justice, and liberty for the world' (Symons, 1996a, 25). But Donald had also become part of what Jan Morris describes as the 'grand tragedy' where 'so much rhetoric was expended, and so many lives were thrown away to demonstrate so desolate a point' (247). In Donald's last letter dated 17 December, written two days before his death, we feel the sense of quiet premonition in the consciousness of the lone soldier. At the time of his writing the letter, Donald was based in Wong Nei Chong Valley (Wong Nai Chung Valley).

> We are still where we were on Sunday, with little prospect of going anywhere else. So far we have no shelling or dive bombing but I feel certain our time will soon come ... Do you find yourself looking back to the 'good old days?' I do so, quite often. I wonder what has happened to [our house at] No. 23 and the servants ...
>
> (Symons, 1996a, 25)

The 'good old days' were irrevocably gone for the Andersons and with them the Eurasian community's privileged existence. Donald and his company had been transferred from the Peak where they had been trained for months to be stationed to the Wong Nei Chong Valley. The Peak was to be manned by the Canadians. Wong Nei Chong was one of the bloodiest battle sites of the 18 days of fighting. The fighting at Wong Nei Chong Gap, manned by the Eurasian volunteers under Lieutenant Bevan Field, had been recorded by Robert Gandt:

> The Eurasians were enthusiastic soldiers. Subtly discriminated against in the cloistered business community of Hongkong, they'd found a source of pride in the Volunteers. They had their own company — No. 3 — and they often distinguished themselves by beating even the regulars of the Middlesex Battalion in machinegun competitions.
>
> (119)

The Eurasians were the last surviving unit in Wong Nei Chong Gap. Cut off and unsupported, the pillboxes at the Gap were manned by remaining Eurasian Volunteers still trying to deter the advance of the Japanese by their machine guns. Donald's No. 3 Co. suffered 85 casualties in a mobilized strength of 115 (Symons, 1996a, 25). According to Gandt, 'when the Eurasian company's pillboxes had finally been captured after a 16-hour resistance, Colonel Shoji felt compelled to send a message of apology to his division commander'. Colonel Shoji had won his victory, but at a fearful cost. In the fighting for Wong Nei Chong Gap, the Third Battalion on the Japanese side had lost over 800 troops, including the battalion commander (Gandt, 122).

The actual mobilization of Eurasian volunteers was later criticized. It was alleged both by Eurasians (especially wives of Eurasian soldiers) and the Japanese that the British authorities deliberately stationed Eurasian soldiers in the front-line positions to save white soldiers (Fisher, 115). This notion of sending Eurasians to the front to save white soldiers might have been a part of Japanese propaganda. But Emily Hahn recalls how the two young Gittins widows (sisters-in-law of Jean Ho Tung Gittins), who had stayed with her during the war, had believed that this was the reason for the high casualty rate for Eurasian boys (1946, 167). Despite Symons's resentment of the Evacuation Authorities, she does not seem to harbour any such bitterness towards the military authorities. She quotes the British Field Office (Lieutenant Bevan):

> I was particularly impressed by the fine spirit and steadiness shown by the Volunteers under my command. They were all Eurasians, most with a British father and a Chinese or Eurasian mother, a type which in Hong Kong had not been credited generally with the character these men showed.
>
> (Bruce, 250)

The third level of the war narrative in Symons's memoir functions within the scope of the autobiographical, based on Symons's first-hand experience. The narrator traces how the Andersons abandoned their house to their four servants and worked their way through the swirling crowds of panicky people that flooded the streets, some to locate their friends and relatives, some to escape, some to just find a safe hiding place from this sudden Japanese invasion. 'In the space of a few hours Hong Kong had been transformed into a place of terror — of unknown dangers and threats' (1996a, 24), leaving unmistakable signs of fear on the faces of people trying desperately to flee — but to where? — was the question that crept into the consciousness of so many people like the Andersons.

That was indeed a pressing question for any Eurasian at that time. The local Chinese might have their village of origin somewhere in China, but most Eurasians had no village of origin to which they could return. Strictly speaking, Hong Kong was their place of origin. As Wordie pointed out, most Eurasians neither read nor write Chinese and could hardly be expected to survive well if forced into the Chinese interior (1997, 21).

Like hundreds of other Hong Kong people who were trapped in Kowloon, the Andersons waited anxiously for a way to cross the harbour. They managed eventually to board a sampan of a friend moored on the waterfront. As their sampan made its way through the harbour, Joyce witnessed with emotion, through the gap of the tarpaulin on the sampan, the last British destroyer leaving the harbour. It was not until 5 p.m. that day that Joyce finally reached their granduncle's house on MacDonnell Road only to realize it had been commandeered by the military. As the days of fighting continued, Joyce and her family moved from house to house, from flat to flat in different parts of the badly-shelled Mid-Levels, crowding into the already crowded homes of relatives and friends.

After the surrender, like all the rest of Hong Kong, the Andersons waited in fear and uncertainty. A heavy foreboding descended on the city. The Crown Colony, as Hahn has described, was now being claimed as an actual possession of Japan, not a part of 'liberated China' (1944, 320).

The Andersons had heard from others that Eurasians had the option of being considered civilian prisoners of war, but it would be preferable if they avoided internment (Symons, 1996a, 24).

In Japanese-occupied Hong Kong, many Eurasians were much confounded by the Japanese perception of their ethnic identity. The Gittins sisters (Phyllis and Irene), as recalled by Hahn, said the Food Control Board would not give them rice ration cards. Chinese could have these cards but

Eurasians could not; they also could not get flour because they were not Europeans (Hahn, 1946, 169). Unable to fit into the racial categories of Chinese or European, the Eurasians were left in limbo.

The Andersons were now pinning their hopes on Phyllis, the eldest Anderson girl, who had married Henrique Nolasco. This Eurasian-Portuguese union now provided for them the possibility to a new land of freedom — Macau.

The head of the family, Charles Anderson, went to the first floor of the Hongkong & Shanghai Bank (which had been commandeered by the Japanese government) to a section called 'Third Nationals' to apply for an exit visa to Macau (1996a, 7). Third national identification passes were usually given to Vichy French, Portuguese, Russians, Norwegians and some Eurasians. These passes did not necessarily signify special privileges, and pass-holders of this category were sometimes stopped in the streets to have their passes examined. The Andersons' applications for evacuation had been rejected by the British colonial authorities, yet their applications for exit permits were granted without much aggravation — under their new identity of 'Third Nationals' — prescribed to them by their new Japanese ruler.

During the days of Japanese occupation, Eurasians in Japanese-occupied territories were often called upon to identify with their Asiatic heritage. Many historians had pointed out that the Japanese at that time were very much interested in Eurasians who could understand and speak Chinese dialects and the English language as potential recruits to their Intelligence Service and, perhaps, as a living embodiment of their propaganda of racial unity in Asia (E. W. Clemons, 218, 220). Failure to conform could very well be interpreted as evidence of unwillingness to co-operate in racial unity under the motto of Pan-Asianism.

In Hong Kong, many prominent Eurasians were under great pressure to declare their political loyalty to Japan, which meant the necessity to identify themselves as 'Chinese'. These Eurasian elites who had always served as bridge figures between the British rulers and the Chinese populace now found themselves reluctantly serving as bridge figures between a much-hated Asiatic ruler and a considerably shrunken and much harrowed Chinese population. This was the tragic face of the intermediacy, which Symons's father had celebrated in his speech. Marginality and hybridity could mean a position between more than one upper and nether millstone.

As Ed Gosano, a Hong Kong medical doctor who worked briefly at the Argyle Street POW camp, describes in his memoir, the occupied Hong Kong at that time was very much like 'a patient nearly drained of the lifeblood' (Gosano, 24). M. K. Lo, brother-in-law of Jean Gittins, was kept in solitary confinement until he agreed to join the new government (Gittins, 1982, 38). Many other Eurasians were under similar pressure now to serve their new ruler.

The Andersons were one of those more fortunate Eurasian families who were not forced to make an identity or political shift. As Third Nationals, they were able to officially leave the Japan-occupied Hong Kong for Macau.

Dislocation, hunger and poverty were part of everyday reality for many refugees in wartime Macau. But for those who could afford it, the small Portuguese enclave was a haven to escape the uncertainties and worries of war. Macau, according to Stanley Ho, the grandnephew of Ho Tung, 'was paradise during the war'. The Japanese honoured the neutrality of Macau and did not interfere with the administration (McGivering, 108). Sir Roger Lobo, a Legislative Council (Legco) member, remembers wartime Macau as a place of fun and spirit. 'We played tennis, we went dancing, learnt the jitterbug' (McGivering, 74). A. de Oliveira Sales, another Hong Kong Legco member, recalls that the Portuguese city which had a population of only about 70,000 before the war, found itself coping with a population of half a million during the war (McGivering, 66).

The wartime British Consulate in Macau was under Consul J. T. Reeves. Gosano, who also escaped to Macau during the war, says of Reeves: 'Had it not been for him being in Macau during the war, the Portuguese and other refugees including British affiliates, [sic] from HK [Hong Kong] would have a different story to tell of the horrors of war on civilians. John Reeves redeemed much of the bad image we second-class citizens had of Colonial domination' (34). Reeves, upon learning that Donald Anderson had been killed in the war, offered Derek (Joyce's younger brother who was barely

16) a job as an archivist at the Consulate (Symons, 1996a, 27). As British subjects, the Andersons were also able to draw a subsistence allowance from the British Consulate. With the connection of their Portuguese in-laws, the Andersons resumed a life of comfort and privilege. They occupied a spacious flat with two servants.

As evident in many war narratives by Hong Kong residents who sought refuge in Macau (including those by Ed Gosano, Stanley Ho, Roger Lobo, A. de O. Sales) Macau was a pulsating wartime city for affluent refugees. Yet Symons's Macau narrative offers a stark contrast to these other vivacious Macau narratives. There is an overwhelming sense of isolation and melancholy that pervades her narrative domestically, socially and politically.

In Macau, Joyce stayed at home as an English tutor and homemaker. Away from Hong Kong, she kept to herself, living on the few sporadic letters she received from the interned Bob via the Swiss Red Cross. Derek was working with the British Consulate and was out of the house most of the time. Phyllis was in French Kwangchow Wan as an undercover British agent. (She was awarded the King's Medal after the war [1996, 29]).

On looking back, the narrator confesses how she felt 'deeply ashamed' of her quiet life. Donald was killed in action. Her sister Marjorie was interned in the Shanghai Lungwha Camp. Bob, her fiancé, was locked up in Shanghai Yangchow internment camp. Both Phyllis and Derek were involved in dangerous underground work for the British anti-Japanese resistance. Everyone of her generation except herself was in one way or another involved in a form of patriotic existence (whether in the form of working for the British anti-Japanese resistance or interned for being British). Symons's memory of her life in Macau is tinged with a strong sense of exclusion — of being left out from the participation in the British resistance movement. There is this nagging sense of being excluded from history, that history was going forward without the narrated subject — a phenomenon that has been described by Eakin as the Jamesian 'stigma' (1992, 139). In discussing the autobiography of Henry James, Eakin says James, speaking from the sidelines of the American Civil War, felt the wounded possessed an 'indefinable shining stigma', 'the strange property or privilege … looking through us or straight over us at something they partake of together but that we mayn't pretend to know' (quoted in Eakin, 1992, 139).

More and more Hong Kong Eurasians joined the mass migration to

Macau. A small network of Hong Kong Eurasians in Macau emerged. Yet, Joyce had found herself unable to become part of the network of the Hong Kong Eurasian refugees. Despite their close relationship with the Choas, they were not invited to the Choa wedding in Macau. The narrator says, 'we were ostracized for being British' (1996a, 27). Many of the refugee Eurasians had abandoned their identity as British subjects. Many were probably enhancing their Chinese heritage and, in some cases, moving towards the Japanese side. The Andersons, who continued to be faithful to their British connections, became quite isolated and alienated by their own community. The narrator's tone here is infused with a kind of ambivalence. On one hand, she was thankful for being away from the Japanese and yet, on the other hand, the ostracism was acutely painful. The sense of exclusion was two-fold, from being British, and also from not being able to participate in the British resistance.

Joyce's only connection to the outside world was listening to the BBC Overseas Service on a short-wave radio, which Phyllis brought home. (The Macau newspapers were in Portuguese and Chinese. There was only one English language newspaper called the *Macao Tribune*, published weekly by journalists from Hong Kong [McGivering, 66]). The narrator recalls, 'Even now the sound of Big Ben's chimes gives me a thrill, but in the limbo of those war years it was pure magic' (1996a, 28). The magical chimes of Big Ben representing the British Empire become a soothing source of constancy, of surety, amid the isolation that the Eurasian refugee felt in the Portuguese enclave.

To keep her mind active, Symons started to learn Chinese: '... 40 or 50 words a day, and [I] was able to read a newspaper after six months. With this new skill, each day I translated Wendell Wilkins's (US Vice-President) account of his visits to Russia for Derek to take to the Consul' (28). It was perhaps a wartime re-connection with her early Chinese upbringing.

The dawning of the bright and hot VJ Day in early September gave rise to mixed elation and worry. Symons says:

> There had been many rumours about the fate of Hong Kong. The Nationalist Chinese would claim it — General Ho Sai Lai (a son of Sir Robert Ho Tung) would ride a white charger to receive the Japanese surrender or, another story, Chinese troops would move in and a Chinese flag would flutter from The Peak. All untrue, thank

God. The British naval forces soon sailed in, to install Admiral Harcourt as Military Governor pending the return of a Foreign Office appointee.

(29)

For a Eurasian like Joyce, whose political sentiments and cultural sensibilities had never been close to China, a future under a Chinese government was utterly inconceivable. The fear that Hong Kong would be handed over to a new Kuomingtang master could be extremely disconcerting even though General Ho, a member of the Hong Kong Eurasian community and a relative, would be among those in power. Robbie Ho Sai-lai might be a Eurasian, but in public, his ethnic and political identity had been unquestionably Chinese.

Joyce did not really have time to ponder or speculate about her own future or the future of Hong Kong. A telegram from the Hong Kong Administration requested her presence at DGS. She was summoned back to Hong Kong from Macau so that Miss Gibbins, the pre-war DGS principal, who had come out of internment, could take her repatriation leave to England. The Macau refugee 'came home on an Australian corvette of the Royal Navy' (1998, 164) but the city that greeted her was a depleted and depopulated ghost town.

> The harbour was deserted … It was about 5 p.m. and the dream-like rickshaw ride along a deserted Nathan Road seemed interminable. There were very few pedestrians, no traffic, and just a rickshaw or two. Shops and offices were bolted, no-one peered from windows and the whole scene was almost eerie. I felt like an intruder and was glad to turn off onto Jordan Road.
>
> (1996a, 29)

This image of the ghostly south Kowloon becomes a dramatic contrast to the south Kowloon she left on the day of the Japanese invasion with its panicky crowds and swirling chaos. Would the Colony be the same again? At the gate of the school, Miss Gibbins was waiting with a couple of naval officers. The principal ran towards Joyce. The narrator recalls '… I thought to myself — it will be fine' (29). Joyce had returned to that Eurasian sanctuary she knew so intimately — confidence and hope came flooding back.

Alone in Hong Kong and well settled at DGS, Joyce received a telegraph from her sister Marjorie in Shanghai saying she was returning to Hong Kong on a Jardine ship. The narrator recalls watching Marjorie, a wan little figure carrying a small suitcase walking down the gangplank. Coming out of internment in Shanghai, Marjorie had sneaked on to the ship as a sort of stowaway, paying a small fortune to share the purser's cabin with a few other women. Having been an official private secretary with the United States Command in Shanghai, Marjorie would have had no difficulty securing a job in Hong Kong. But her 'determination to leave the East was rock solid — she had had enough. The problem was how to get a passage to England; a free passage, to which she was surely entitled as a former civilian prisoner-of-war'. But again, being Eurasian, the matter might not be so straightforward, as their previous experience with the British Evacuation Authorities was still vividly edged in their memory.

> We went together to that bastion of officialdom, the Colonial Secretariat, which was ruled by Admiral Harcourt of the newly-formed Military Administration of Hong Kong. After an interminable wait, we were ushered into the office of a very senior civil servant who listened coldly to Marjorie's story, pronouncing at the end: 'Miss Anderson, this is your home. I'll see that you are taken off any ship at any intermediate port if you try to get away.' ... The sneer on that official's face and his manner stuck in my mind for years.
>
> (31)

This high-handedness of the official was another assault on their Eurasianness since the last one at the Cricket Club ground five years ago. The senior official from the Colonial Secretariat was performing his duty by adhering to the conservative biopolitics of the Empire. Eurasians had often been perceived as a kind of unwanted by-product of the colonial encounter, some form of 'eternal contaminations' of white prestige in the East (Anderson, 149). In consequence of which, Eurasians could only be seen as Europeans who could never be considered full-fledged citizens of England.

The Andersons might have been a Volunteer family and contributed to various war works. But to the officer, they nonetheless were part of the indigenous population of the colony. They should be barred from taking advantage of the free passage to a place that was not their 'home'. No matter how European they seemed (in physical attributes, language, etc.) the official was still probably very uncomfortable about some, borrowing Stolers's (203) term, 'invisible protean essences' that lurked behind their European façade.[2]

The dejected Anderson sisters walked down Battery Path. On reaching Des Voeux Road, they passed the missing lions (a landmark removed by the Japanese from their place outside the Hongkong & Shanghai Bank) and Joyce spotted a billboard with the words 'Repatriation of Civil Personnel — 3rd Floor' — there was still hope. At this place, the Andersons experienced a new British colonial liberalism embodied in a very friendly young army captain. Joyce recalls:

> Without preliminaries I demanded: 'Have you ever been east of Suez before?'
>
> 'No, I haven't' he replied.
>
> 'Then,' I announced dramatically, 'you won't know about the likes of us!'
>
> He heard me out, then smiled and turned to Marjorie: 'Miss Anderson, we will fly you home by RAF. When can you leave?'
>
> (1996a, 31)

There is distinctly a strong sense of dramatic (and narrational) satisfaction in the way Joyce quotes to him the very words used to exclude the Andersons from treatment as British citizen four years earlier. This time things were different for the likes of them. Within an hour or so, the 'home' of the Andersons had dramatically changed from Hong Kong to England. The young army captain represents the liberal colonial discourse of inclusion, humanitarianism and equality that very much informed the post-war policy of the British Empire at that time. Marjorie was a British subject who had been interned as a civilian prisoner of war; her mixed-descent should not in any way affect her being identified as a full-fledged citizen entitled to a free passage 'home'.

The afternoon of interviews by representatives from the Colonial Secretariat and the Repatriation Office demonstrate how the Eurasians — a colonial racial group which because of their ambiguous status within the colonial structure — could become an embodiment of the tension between the colonial inclusionary impulses and the colonial exclusionary practices. The former insisted on exclusion and deemed it paramount to safeguard the boundaries from the onslaught of 'dubious' citizens while the latter advocated inclusion and equality among British subjects throughout the Empire. In a sense, the Hong Kong Eurasian hybrids under the newly resumed colonial authorities of late 1945 can be read as a metonym for the conflicting 'biopolitics' (Stoler, 199) of the pre-war and post-war Empire.

The end of the Second World War marks the end of a privileged and gracious era for the Hong Kong Eurasians. The experience of war had changed Hong Kong and its perception of this small privileged sector of the community. The humiliation done to the European community during the Japanese Occupation had not only blemished white colonial prestige in Hong Kong but had also tarnished the exclusiveness of other intermediate groups like the Eurasians, whose very status in the colonial hierarchy was closely connected with the prestige of the European community in Hong Kong.

The 'imagined' Eurasian community of Symons, which rested upon common 'historical destinies', testifies to a crucial early living mode of hybridity in Hong Kong before the war. The period after August 1945 marks the birth of a new Hong Kong — a phoenix transformed — 'a resurgo' as symbolized in the rising phoenix under the oval portrait of King George VI in the Victory issue of a Hong Kong postage stamp.[3] But what was resurrected was also subtly changed. For Joyce Anderson, life in post-war Hong Kong was to bring her recognition and fame as a civic leader, but somehow she seemed unable to shake off a feeling of uneasiness, a form of historical melancholy as a Eurasian in the midst of a rapidly decolonized Crown Colony.

▻─┼─◂▸─○─◂◂─┼─◃

Post-War Hong Kong: Eurasian Isolationism

> *[T]he 'no-man's land' of Eurasian isolationism is still a hazard for those born into two cultures as they try to blend the different threads together. Today, at the age of 78, I am still painfully aware of them.*
>
> (Symons, 1996a, 3)

This section will look closely at Joyce's ascent in the colonial hierarchy, from a displaced Eurasian teacher to the first woman appointed to the Hong Kong Executive Council. In many ways, her narrative can be read as a glorification of a public life — a public career that witnessed some of the major political changes in post-war Hong Kong: the communist infiltration in the 1950s, the 1960s riots, the quasi-decolonization within the colonial context during the 1970s — changes that marked the uneasy equilibrium between the ambivalent British administration, the discontented Chinese masses in Hong Kong and the vast Chinese communist regime next door.

Apart from its detailed narrative of Joyce Anderson's experience in the war years, *Looking at the Stars* also recounts most of the major sociopolitical events of post-war Hong Kong within its finely printed 97 pages. The implied reader in *Looking at the Stars* is therefore someone who has to be quite familiar with the major sociopolitical developments in Hong Kong as well as the changing sentiments of its population towards the colonial rule during these decades. Partly because of its limited narrative space, or partly as a matter of narrative style, not much narrative space is devoted in mapping out the sociopolitical background. Events are paraded out continuously without much didactic interruption. I have thus included in my readings the sociopolitical and historical matrix necessary for the reader to appreciate the difficult circumstances surrounding a Eurasian woman like Joyce Symons.

In speaking of self-representation, perhaps what separates *Looking at the Stars* from other memoirs of public careers such as Li Shu-fan's *Hong Kong Surgeon* (1964) (a memoir in which, borrowing Gusdorf's description, the 'penetrating insight and skill' of the subject were never wrong [Gusdorf, 36]) is that Symons's narrative has a tendency to alternate between self-glorification and self-satire. Symons could be unabashedly self-congratulatory in her recollection of her colonial loyalty and recognition, particularly in her meeting with Admiral Harcourt, her celebration of the 1953 coronation, her appointments to the Urban, Legislative and Executive Councils, her affiliation with top civil servants and taipans of the large British trading houses. Symons's life and her ascent within the colonial hierarchy serve as a rare example of the rise of the subaltern to the ruling elite. The autobiographical subject is often represented as a heroic figure defying all odds. Yet at other times, the subject is unapologetically created as a fool with utter lack of awareness to the changing colonial sentiments around her. Very often Symons would swing in the other direction to a self-directed satire, particularly in her memory of her appointment as supervisor to the communist workers' schools, her ignorance of the Chinese national day, and her position as a political pawn. But underneath all these memories, both self-congratulatory and self-satirical, there is occasionally a betrayal of a deep sense of uneasiness towards the Colony in transformation. While on the surface, Symons's memoir could be read as a *Bildungsroman*, as we follow the story of how the young Joyce reached maturity. But also operating alongside the progression of the *Bildungsroman*, is a narrative of her ascent in the colonial structure. We see how Symons developed from being a young silent Eurasian subaltern (a new student at DGS who spoke not one word of English), to a member of the Eurasian elite as she began her public career in the Urban Council, and finally to becoming a British in the eyes of many people as she was appointed to the Executive Council.

Ethnic identity continued to play an important role in her life as a community figure. Her British patriotism nurtured during the war had fostered in her a deep colonial loyalty. While closely bound to the shrinking Eurasian community in her private life, she identified herself more and more with her British connections in her public life. Yet the pre-war sense of Eurasian solidarity was now to be replaced by a feeling of Eurasian isolationalism. Her Eurasianness and what it represented in the post-war colonial context had at times rendered her a source of resentment among the leftist schools and Chinese members of the public from the lower economic strata. During the anti-colonial and anti-British riots, her Eurasian face became the physical embodiment of imperialism and colonialism resented by harassed taxi drivers and angry leftist mobs. Her elevation to positions at the Urban and Legislative Councils provided a channel for her to express her pro-government stance and colonial loyalty. At the Urban Council, Symons was much disturbed at the way liberal and radical British members and other Chinese members were criticizing and attacking the government. Her alienation from the Chinese community, and the more liberal British members left her very much isolated as a loner in the political arena.

Her Eurasian isolationism as a civic leader also coincided with the tragedies in her personal life. Her narrative becomes almost confessional as the narrator describes the collapse of her private world, which contrasted dramatically with the successes of her public life. This discordance between her private and public existence foregrounds the tragically ironical autobiographical ethos of her personal narrative.

The Empire's inability to defend the Crown Colony of Hong Kong as well as other colonies in Asia from the horror of Japanese aggression had cast a shadow on Britain's unquestioned prestige in Asia.

Whitehall had insisted on maintaining British rule in Hong Kong after the war, but it seemed ambivalent towards reviving its pre-war position in China. More conservative elements in London believed in the importance of maintaining its former influence, but others had questioned the wisdom of such policy. In the midst of much unspoken ambivalence, the process of disbandment of the British Empire had subtly begun.

As Jan Morris says, Hong Kong was profoundly and permanently changed by the experience of war. The pageantry of government was soon restored, but this was never again to feel quite like a British colony. Its balance had irretrievably shifted. The last vestiges of segregation between the ruler and the ruled were renounced (Morris, 261). The relation between the two races had been altered by the Japanese occupation. The Peak Reservation Ordinance was repealed in 1946. In 1947, the Central British School (later renamed King George V) first admitted non-Europeans (Sweeting, 1993, 83). Notwithstanding the fact that it still flew the Union Jack, and was headed by a British governor, post-war Hong Kong had become a kind of colonial mutation. Old European residents returning after the war were ruffled by the casual and carefree relations between the races, and as Jan Morris describes:

> The social life of the expatriates was never quite the same again —
> the tea-parties never quite so ineffable at the Repulse Bay Hotel, the
> Club never quite so inexpressibly club-like, the bathing beaches, once
> so comfortingly reminiscent of Bournemouth, now swarming with
> Asians. Very soon Chinese had broken into every sphere of life, social
> and economic, and were challenging the British for the financial
> dominance of Hong Kong.
>
> (1989, 262)

Sir Alexander Grantham (Governor 1947–1957), a pre-war Cadet Officer in the 1930s, returned to Hong Kong as Governor in 1947. He remarks on the changes he saw:

> A marked decline in social snobbishness was one of the first things I
> noticed after my return. The 'taipan' and the senior government

official was no longer regarded, nor did they so regard themselves, as demi-gods ... I observed, too, a greater mixing of the races ...

(104)

After Miss Gibbins, the principal of DGS, was repatriated back to England to recuperate from her internment in the fall of 1945, Joyce was left in sole charge of the DGS. The memory of re-starting the school is cherished all the more by its association with the Royal Air Force, Royal Navy and the Royal Marine Commando. The RAF not only guarded the school from the Chinese looters, but also helped in rebuilding and running the school. The Commando Officer had supplied Joyce with six Japanese POWs to work on the dilapidated tennis courts. Admiral Harcourt himself also came to visit the school signifying a rare colonial privilege.

Lacking even the most basic and fundamental resources, Symons recalls her almost heroic efforts in re-opening that old institution of DGS in the fall of 1945. She welcomes her new identity as acting head of DGS with a mixture of elation and apprehension:

> A new headmistress would have to be found. I was to be acting headmistress to open the school; to run it without adequate staff and without books and money, and to deal with students who were rushing back to us. This I did, but only with the wonderful help from the officers of the Navy, Army and Air Force. It was a dream and a nightmare rolled into one (1998, 164).

With no salaries, Joyce applied for volunteer rations for the teachers. With Miss Gibbins's card, she got some European food (1996a, 30). As for herself, she was given Chinese food, which, of course, marks another externally perceived ethnic change. In the 1942 ration at May Road, she was given the European diet of flour and bread (25). The Japanese had evidently seen the Andersons as Europeans then. This post-war official perception of her ethnicity, under the circumstances, is quite satisfying as 'we had variety and quantity' in the food ration (31).

The seemingly impossible task of re-opening and re-starting the old school was eventually completed after the frantic but rewarding first few months. Joyce left for Shanghai in early 1946. She and Robert Symons had been separated since the summer of 1941 but war had not changed things for them. The couple was married in Shanghai in the spring of 1946. Symons's memory of her wedding evidences the Eurasian prestige in the British Concession. The young bride was given away by the Commissioner of the Chinese Maritime Customs Service, Mr Hopstock 'the man at the

Plate 3   Wedding portrait of Joyce and Bob Symons
in 1946, from *Looking at the Stars*,
courtesy of Dr Joyce Symons.

very top — it was almost like meeting royalty' (1996a, 34). A reception was given at the Commissioner's house. As an assertion of her British patriotic connection, the young couple also had a civil wedding at the British Consulate three days later after the wedding at the Cathedral. The newly wedded Eurasian couple, who had never been away from the East, set sail for England on a repatriation ship.

Their repatriation ship was to carry British and French nationals from Shanghai and Hong Kong. Symons recalls how on one occasion she saw blond German POWs cleaning out latrines on board, 'I felt oddly uncomfortable but I heard one woman exclaim raucously: "I don't have to go but I will, to make the German swine clean up after me!"' (35). Joyce, whose world up to 1946 had been oriented towards European prestige in both Hong Kong and Shanghai, felt extremely strange at seeing a European being ordered around and performing menial chores. Like most of the Chinese in pre-war Hong Kong who had long been accustomed to feeling the physical presence of 'whiteness' as a kind of exclusiveness and privilege, Joyce was not used to seeing the disruption of the colonial racial distribution of labour.

The arrival at England marks Joyce's physical entry to that imperial political and cultural centre of the British Empire — which also marks her departure from the periphery of the colonial outpost. It was an emotional arrival for the Hong Kong Eurasian. 'As we drew alongside the pier a military band played *Rule Britannia* and tears poured down my face — at last I was in England' (35). The Eurasian teacher had finally reached that unknown land of origin where many of her ancestors had came from. But their reception by her British relatives was hardly what she had expected.

The couple stayed with Charles Anderson's brother, Henry Anderson, a medical practitioner and his wife Ethel in South Wales, of whom they knew very little except probably their name. Their eight-month experience in the mining village ended quite traumatically. For the first time, Joyce Symons found herself being resented as Chinese by her British relative. Her uncle's wife Aunt Ethel, a British lady with an apparently unstable personality, seemed to have some unexplained prejudice against the Eurasian couple whom she saw as Chinese. Aunt Ethel attempted to hurt her several times. One time she threw a bucket of water at her for no reason. Another time she had jokingly threatened to put arsenic in her sugar. In one of her bouts of midsummer madness, the police were called. With her peals of strange laughter she had drawn a crowd of fascinated spectators.

> There she sat on the sill, dressed in the red silk kimono I had given her, shouting to the gathering crowd below: 'They are all against me, those bloody Chinese'.
>
> (1996, 36)

The violence involved in the incident had much shaken the newly arrived Joyce. The fact that her aunt saw her as a 'bloody Chinese', also had had a very disturbing effect on her. Back in the East, whether it be Shanghai, Macau or Hong Kong, Joyce had been used to being seen as British, European or Eurasian, but never before as Chinese. Now in England, she was suddenly being perceived and despised as Chinese — an externally perceived identity, which resonated not at all with her own internally perceived identity. It was an unwelcome denial of who she believed she was. Much shaken by the incident, the couple left for London immediately.

In London, the young couple enrolled for postgraduate courses. Robert enrolled in the School of Tropical Medicine in London University and Joyce for her post-graduate Teachers' Diploma.

By mid-1947, their diplomas were completed. They were ready to return 'home' in Hong Kong. The couple waited for passage home on ships sponsored by the government to take people to work in Hong Kong, 'our finances made it essential for us to utilize this small emigration scheme' (1996, 40). Here, we see the Eurasian couple become a kind of colonial emigrants in transit. The Symonses came to England on a repatriation ship (even though they could hardly be described as repatriates returning home). They returned to Hong Kong on a government-sponsored ship, which was supposed to bring people to work in the colony, but they were in effect returning home — Hong Kong. This is another instance of what might be termed the Eurasian contra flow.

In December 1947, the couple embarked on the *Empire Brent* sailing from Glasgow to Hong Kong. The narrator recalls as they were drawing close to home:

> Bob and I knew for certain we were back in the East when we were laid low by indigestion. It was quite overwhelming to be home in Hong Kong although home we had none — nor did Mother. The Japanese, using British POW labour, had demolished our house at Kai Tak Bund ...
>
> (40–41)

Joyce returned with a nagging sense of displacement. The city of Hong Kong in early 1948 had regained some of its former buoyancy with the influx of both political and economic refugees from metropolises like Shanghai. Housing was a major problem. The young Eurasian couple could no longer afford the kind of genteel terraced houses they had enjoyed before the war. They had returned home, but not quite readily to the privileged class.

In 1949, while working as a private tutor, Joyce was also helping out the Hong Kong Anglican Bishop, Rev. R. O. Hall, as 'unpaid Supervisor' to some Anglican primary schools. In this early post-war era, the number of vernacular primary schools increased rapidly. Among these expanding vernacular schools, there was a new group of schools run by unionists for the children of workers. Trade unionists requested assistance from the Anglican Church to help organize schools for the children of low-paid workers. Many of these workers' schools soon become hotbeds for Communist propaganda (Sweeting, 92, 197).

The successes of the People's Liberation Army in the Chinese civil war had fostered the infiltration of communist ideas in some vernacular schools. By the end of 1948, the new Governor, Sir Alexander Grantham, was already employing Cold War rhetoric in his speech at the opening ceremony of a middle school. He warned the audience of the insidious dangers of politics in schools:

> There are those, and to my mind they are the most evil, who wish to use schools as a means of propaganda and poison the minds of their young pupils with their particular political dogma or creed of the most undesirable kind. This we know is what happened in the schools of Fascist States and is now happening in Communist-dominated countries. This deforming and twisting of the youthful mind is most wicked and the Hong Kong Government will tolerate no political propaganda in schools.
>
> (Sweeting, 1992,199)

The government had intended to close down some leftist workers' schools run by trade unionists. Bishop Hall intervened on their behalf. With a tinge of self-sarcasm, the narrator recalls, 'A compromise was reached whereby each school would accept a seconded Government headmaster and all would serve under a new supervisor — one Joyce Symons' (1996a, 44). It did not take long for Joyce herself to realize the oddness of the appointment.

One Saturday, 1 October 1949, Joyce found it strange that all her private students had cancelled their lessons with her. She decided to put her free hours to better use by visiting the schools newly assigned to her supervision.

> At one school, active hatred was visible on almost every face. The headmaster had locked himself into his office. After a lot of pleading, he reluctantly let me in.
>
> 'What on earth is the matter?' I asked.
>
> 'They want to throw me over the verandah, and you too!' he replied.

'Why?' I gasped.
'Because they demanded a half-day holiday because of Peking
and I said they could not have the holiday because of your visit!' I
foolishly said, 'But what's Peking got to do with it?' He looked
disgusted at me and muttered almost inaudibly: 'Because this is a
Communist school!'

(44)

Mao Tse Tung declared the founding of the People's Republic of China on
1 October 1949 in Tiananmen Square — an event whose significance to
the leftist schools had quite completely eluded Joyce. This incident, on one
level, can be read as the narrator's self-congratulatory impulse in her
construction of herself as a kind of heroic loyalist — with her oversight on
the importance of that day in October, she had unknowingly defied the
communist national day. But on another level, this can also be read as the
narrator's self-deprecatory impulse to represent herself as a fool — with the
propensity to doing the right thing (discourage the growth of communism)
at the wrong time (on their national day).

   To understand Joyce's awkward position in the incident, it is important
to understand the political atmosphere surrounding this co-operation
between the Anglicans and the workers' school and their respective points
of view. The Anglicans had looked at the cooperation as a form of charitable
work for the society. The workers' school, on the other hand, had probably
seen the co-operation as a form of indirect government monitoring. This
new supervisor was seen as a government agent sent to monitor their
activities. The workers' school saw Joyce's insistence on inspecting the school
on this particular day as a manifestation of her lack of respect and indifference
to their Chinese patriotic sentiments. Moreover, the appointment of Joyce
as the supervisor of the workers' school was probably perceived as an
imperialistic political manoeuvre. With her high European visibility, she
stood for everything that the workers resented — British imperialism,
compradorism and the local elite co-opted by the government. When she
entered into the realm of the communist workers' schools, she became the
perfect embodiment of everything that was resented in the Chinese
communist world-view.

   In 1953, Joyce was invited by Bishop Hall to the position of headmistress
of DGS proper. Joyce pondered over it, and accepted the offer not without

some 'inherent caution'. In the 'shifting sands of post-war Hong Kong', she was keenly aware of her duty to the past, present and future of DGS. In many ways, Joyce was conscious of how different she was from her predecessors. Not only would she be the first married woman, but she was also the first Eurasian to head the school, where expatriate women had traditionally occupied the position of principal.

The year 1953 marked the coronation of Queen Elizabeth II. As an 'unashamed royalist', Joyce was able to give full expression to her colonial loyalty. There were full-fledged celebrations of royal pageantry in DGS. Activities were organized to celebrate the Commonwealth and the Royal family. There were displays of heraldic shields, decorations in the national colours and pictures of the Queen. It was an occasion where the new principal was able to give her enthusiasm free reign, and probably as her way to express gratitude for the England who had took her in during the immediate postwar years.

The new principal was not unaware of the underlying indifference and antagonism in the new generation of refugees that came to Hong Kong since 1949. 'Many girls had been refugees from Communist China and I felt they should begin to absorb the underlying tenets of British administration in this their new home' (1996a, 49).

This difference in sentiments between the post-war Chinese and the pre-war Chinese towards the British monarchy is dramatically illustrated in the memoir of Woo Wo-han. Woo is a Hong Kong Chinese born in 1930, who describes her recollection of the 1937 and 1953 coronations in Hong Kong. In pre-war days, Hong Kong Chinese 'were simpler in outlook and quite united in their single-minded allegiance to the British monarch. They revered King George VI in much the same way as they might an Eastern Emperor, loving him with the affection of children towards a foster-parent'. She recalls:

> As a child of six, I had sat on an uncle's shoulders and joined the happy crowds in the street to watch the procession passing along Queens [sic] Road, the main street on Hong Kong Island. I vaguely remembered the many Chinese bands, which continually played the British National Anthem. There was a dazzling pageant of Chinese beauties on open trucks and a parade of historical scenes emphasizing the Colony's Anglo-Chinese heritage. There were clowns, comedians

and acrobats, performing as they moved along. The procession continued all morning. When the enormous picture of the handsome King, framed by fresh flowers and carried on a stand by twelve men, appeared, people cheered, shouted and sang *God Save the King* in Cantonese.

(Woo, 75)

The same festive spirit pervaded the colony in 1953 but underlying the carnival atmosphere, the sentiments of the post-war Chinese towards the British monarchy was markedly different, as Woo recalls:

> But now at the beginning of his daughter's reign, Hong Kong and its people had greatly changed. In place of widespread enthusiasm, I seemed to sense both indifference and antagonism among the people. The refugees from the mainland were Chinese in exile and didn't share our sense of belonging. They were indifferent to the ruler. Furthermore, communist ideas had slowly infiltrated the Colony since 1949. Colonialism was denounced as a great evil, a direct result of imperialism. The working class began to show anti-British leanings. Only people like myself, born, bred and educated in the Colony, and fortunate enough to belong to the privileged class, still maintained our respect and admiration of the throne.

(76)

Joyce's contributions to the coronation year celebrations were acknowledged by Hong Kong's most respected Eurasian leader — 'Even Sir Robert Ho Tung wrote to the school to wish us well in Coronation Year' (1996a, 49).

At the time when Joyce was trying to instill some respect and allegiance to the British monarchy, a strong sense of Chinese racial and national consciousness was growing within some sectors of the vernacular schools. A Chinese national identity was articulated which relied very much on Dr Sun's concept of racial nationalism (Dikötter, 124). This, of course, calls for an allegiance (however imaginary) and an article of faith to Nationalists and Communists alike, which simultaneously pushes aside all those who were of a minority or mixed ethnicity.

Many Chinese in the early post-war years possessed a formidable leaning towards ideas of Chinese racial and cultural superiority. Joyce's cousin Diana (daughter of her father's sister) was a teacher at one of the vernacular schools in Shek Kip Mei. One evening Diana came to Joyce's home and appealed to her not to disclose or reveal their relationship because, as the narrator recalls, 'she was Chinese but I was British. In the circumstances, our connection, if it were known, would not do her any good' (1996a, 51).

Diana's request to keep their kinship a secret and her ready denial of her Eurasian heritage had quite confounded Joyce. Diana Ho was the daughter of Aunt Kate and Uncle Ho Wing. She, like Joyce, was a Eurasian on both her father and mother's sides. In fact, in exercising this ethnic tactic, Diana was practicing an act of strategic identity that a great number of the Hong Kong Eurasians of her generation had to perform at some point or other — yet a choice which Symons had looked upon with disapproval — whether in times of peace or war. For Symons, it is precisely this act of shifting identities, between the public and private spheres, that had perpetuated the gulf between a Smith and a Chan within the Eurasian community.

⊷•✦•○•◆•⊶

The 1960s was a difficult decade for Hong Kong and also a period when Joyce began her public career as a civic leader. There was a drastic economic downturn in the mid-1960s with the fall of the real estate and stock markets. There were scandals on the liquidity of several of the old established local banks, which resulted in massive bank runs. Unemployment was high and the housing re-settlement programme could hardly cope with the population explosion. Ian Scott describes the social malaise of Hong Kong as being a state of anomie which

> ... is characterized by such feelings as the perception that community leaders are indifferent to one's needs, the perception that little can be accomplished in a society which is seen as basically unpredictable and lacking order ...
>
> (83)

Joyce was appointed by the Governor in 1966 to the Transport Advisory Committee[4] (TAC) where she served for three years. Most members of the TAC were members of the Executive Council, Urban Council and senior civil servants (Symons, 1996a, 60). It was at this time when Symons first joined the TAC that the Star Ferry decided to raise its second class fare from 5 cents to 10 cents, sparking a series of social discontentment.

On 4 April 1966, a lone demonstrator went on hunger strike outside the Star Ferry terminal against the new fare. He was in support of Mrs Elsie Elliot[5] who had organized a signature campaign against the fare increase. According to Scott, that soon drew a crowd of young demonstrators in a jovial mood. This mood was replaced quickly by violence and antagonism towards the police. Baton charges were used, followed by shots and tear-gas shells. Rioters began throwing stones, setting vehicles alight, dropping cement and rubbish from buildings (Scott, 86). This incident marked the beginning of the waves of riots that shook Hong Kong for the next 20 months.

The sporadic social violence and turmoil that followed in the spring of 1967 were indirectly stimulated by the feverish anti-bourgeoisie movements of the young Red Guards across the border. Evidences of the upheaval in China arrived in form of 'floating corpses' down the Pearl River into Hong Kong waters. Bombs or 'pineapples' were planted at different corners of Hong Kong. Cars were burnt. Schools were interrupted.

The 1967 violence continued to escalate to the level of specifically anti-colonial and anti-British resentment. According to Scott, these riots were not just fuelled by the Cultural Revolution across the border but could also be attributable to the strong colonial profile of the government, which was quite incompatible with the fact that other British colonies had already gained their independence by this time. Scott describes how the anti-colonial demands of the demonstrators, supported by the Chinese communists, were consistently rejected by the British and Hong Kong governments. At least some sections of the community perceived the government to be discriminatory, high-handed if not oppressive, and an all too visible manifestation of foreign domination (Scott, 81).

With her highly visible European physicality, Joyce was not unaware of how she might be perceived by angry mobs. Woo Mo-han recalls in her memoir the militantly anti-British racist sentiments in the 1967 riots. The protestors jeered at the European police inspectors who were trying to reason with them. They shouted loudly at the English policemen: 'Down with the white-skinned pigs' and to the Chinese policemen: 'Shame on you yellow-skinned dogs, for obeying the orders of the white-skinned pigs' (Woo, 202). Large posters bearing tirades against imperialism, colonialism and capitalism were pasted all over the exterior walls of government offices and buildings (205). Chinese policemen were called on to ignore the orders of their European superiors. The protestors chanted slogans like 'Long Live Chairman Mao', 'White-skinned pigs go back to England' and 'Stop suppressing and exploiting Chinese patriots' (205). As the days passed in rioting and strikes, it became commonplace for troublemakers to brutally attack foreigners in the street. British police inspectors were the first targets, then foreign newsmen and other civilians (207).

As can be seen from the description by Woo, the possession of a foreign face could ignite much volatile resentment in those days of riots. Symons recalls,

> Life became difficult. At 6 a.m. every day, I checked on the state of public transport. Either the Star Ferry or the Yaumati Ferry would be running, but not both. On Hong Kong Island, trams and buses ran only on alternate days. …
>
> My driver took me down to the ferry pier at seven, and once on the Kowloon side I always offered a lift in my taxi to staff or DGS girls. Sometimes, the drivers refused to drive me or expatriate teachers. I always asked the driver in Chinese if he was willing to drive us. If we were then stopped by a hostile crowd, I would plead that he was driving us willingly. All the drivers were morose and rude.
>
> (1996a, 61)

DGS was directly across the street from the South Kowloon Magistracy, the symbol of foreign domination and imperialism. On one of the more violent days, the school found itself literally trapped in the midst of thousands of angry rioters. At this point in the text, the tone of the narrator seems to betray a revived anxiety as she relives the long forgotten tantalizing angst of that day. The sense of confidence and control felt by the Eurasian headmistress, whose mind the narrator inhabited a moment ago, seems to have slipped away momentarily:

> The school was surrounded by disturbance. From my office, I could see that Gascoigne Road was packed with policemen in full riot gear. When I went upstairs, I found that crowds carrying banners were pouring through the side streets between Nathan Road and Chi Wo

Street abutting our boundary wall. Behind the old Alhambra Theatre, there was a third mob — this time without banners. I rang Yaumati Police Station, only to be told that the situation was very tense indeed. About 200 policemen would have to deal with thousands of Communists in the side streets and round the South Kowloon Magistracy while the seven thousand strong rabble near the Alhambra remained an unknown factor. I explained to the Senior Superintendent that a public examination was being held in our Hall …

(61)

As the agitation got worse, the tear gas used by the police to clear the crowds drifted into the school. The principal tried to calm the candidates by promising to ask the Examination Authority for extra time as the students wiped away their tears (62). Combining heroism and invigilation duties, the principal ignored the threat of the approaching rioters and continued the exam. Soon after, the whole school had to be evacuated in the absence of any permission from the Director of Education.

Within the walls of the school, the principal was in complete control of the situation defying the hostilities outside. Once outside of its walls, the headmistress with her European features realized that she was completely vulnerable to the moods of the Chinese mobs. From an undaunted figure of power, Joyce was now an exposed victim. How was she going to leave? No taxi would be willing to take her.

Just as we reached the main gate, hordes of Communists rushed past. Mr Chan turned round with a radiant smile: 'Headmistress, it's going to be alright. I see the panic in their eyes.' No taxi would stop for me so Mr Chan walked away to try to hail a cab. Luckily, his driver agreed to let me in. We had a nightmarish one-mile journey to the ferry through the dense crowds.

(62)

Embattled in her own community, Joyce was literally under siege by a hostile crowd. The heightened terror of someone with a European face riding in a taxi in the midst of a feverish anti-British crowd can only be imagined. The sight of a European, at times like these, has the potential of igniting new fury and aggravating further the riotous mood.

Symons's mother and her sister Phyllis's family, on the other hand, were in Sha Tin away from the city. They had no trouble from their neighbours or the surrounding villagers. However, Symons notes that 'dead rats were thrown into the garden by young boys keen to make their mark as patriots' (62).

The Eurasians were seen as living symbols of British colonialism as well as a convenient scapegoat for the ubiquitous Chinese patriots to vent their frustrations against the government. Many expatriates at senior levels tried to stay away from the riots:

> Governor Trench himself was away on summer leave and was too ill to return and other expatriate civil servants were said to be taking extra leave to be out of it. Those, such as Jack Cater, who remained earned their spurs that summer by staying to ride out the fight.
>
> (Courtauld, 79)

Yet, despite the demands of the leftists and Mao supporters for the overthrow of the British colonial administration, the Peking leadership had no real wish to 'export' the Cultural Revolution, as the Chinese premier Zhou Enlai put it (Courtauld, 79). The Chinese authority had no desire to take over the Colony in 1967. As Morris says, 'their proxy intervention had been no more than a demonstration' (1988, 274). In fact, many agree that even at the height of the feverish riots and demonstrations on the streets and outside Government House, the general public of Hong Kong, for once, was quite sympathetic and supportive to the plight of the law enforcement branch of the administration. The crisis ended. The colony survived.

The confidence lost in the stability and future of Hong Kong seems never to have been fully restored after the end of the 1967 riots. Symons herself stayed through the riots though she was not unaware of the beginning of a diasporic movement of old time Hong Kongers:

> Some very rich people started to buy property overseas and send their children away for tertiary and even secondary education. I consider that this was the beginning of emigration from Hong Kong. There were many subtle changes in our lives. Some of Robert's Shanghai patients began to move to the United States. At school, more and more girls made plans to study at Canadian and American colleges after the School Certificate Examination taken in Form V.
>
> (1996a, 62)

This general middle class tendency to emigrate from Hong Kong also marks the beginning of the gradual dispersal of the Eurasian community. The Eurasian community was shrinking. Yet in 1969, Joyce's public career began to take a new turn. She was appointed by the Governor to the Urban Council.

The Urban Council in the 1960s was a statutory body responsible for the management of health, resettlement and the low-cost housing scheme. For any Hong Kong citizen, becoming a member of the Urban Council could be the first step to getting a seat in the Legislative and Executive Councils. In the 1960s, the Urban Council had 20 unofficial members, half of them nominated and the rest elected.[6]

The narrator recalls the exhilaration over her appointment. 'When the news broke, the press corps were tremendously excited, for the Government Information Services had issued my curriculum vitae in full, extending to three columns! Robert seemed very proud and Mother was deliriously happy' (63).

During her three years (1969–1972) at the Urban Council, Joyce 'enjoyed the camaraderie and the limited friendship' (77). Yet, this limited sense of camaraderie was somewhat blemished by opposition from British liberals like Elsie Elliot. Unlike Elliot who had a network of Chinese supporters from the lower socioeconomic stratum, Joyce did not represent anyone, whether Chinese, Eurasians or Europeans. Her position was not always welcome in the Council. In her work at the Urban Council, Joyce found it especially trying to have to tolerate the criticism directed at the government by the elected members and the public. 'I really hated the way some members merely pretended to toe the party line, without any genuine appreciation of the British contribution to Hong Kong' (77). Some of the ward offices too had been difficult for Joyce.[7]

> I did not enjoy this work as the cases were based on too much antagonism[,] everything the Government did was wrong[,] though of course occasionally something was. I could not share the enthusiasm of elected members for this aspect of Urban Council responsibility.

(81)

Joyce was unable to ward off her sense of isolation not only from the elected members but also from her gradual realization of her inability to connect with the Chinese public, particularly those who came to seek help in ward sessions.

> I was a loner, stepping on no toes, but equally refusing to be stepped on. Being on ward duty was interesting enough. I had replaced an elected member, Dr Alison Bell, an energetic Scotswoman who often matched Mrs Elliot's zeal. Dr Bell had mastered Cantonese, so she was able to conduct council surgery without an interpreter. I did the same, but was not popular with some of the strident claimants who wanted more and more of everything from Government. They could not understand why I was not as 'helpful' as Dr Bell. I remember in particular one man, a cripple with a loud voice and a rather malevolent expression, who demanded that I telephone the magistrate before whom he was due to appear on a charge of fraud. When I refused, and before I could explain why, he swore at me using words I had never heard before.
>
> (64)

In many ways, Joyce was very much a stranger in the flux of the changing political setting of the late 1960s in Hong Kong. Perhaps being marginal to those prewar structures caused her to cling to them more faithfully and left her less able to adapt to a post-war Hong Kong, which was becoming a dramatically different place. Obedience, respect and reverence for the government authority could no longer be assumed automatically. Elements of distrust and suspicion towards the administration were common particularly in the lower strata of the society.

⊶⊷⊙⊶⊷

The 1970s marked a great many changes for Hong Kong as a colony. After 1971, the governors of Hong Kong were not former Colonial Service officers, but diplomats conversant in the knowledge of China. As Morris suggests, Hong Kong's affairs were now seen more as a matter of foreign policy than of imperial duty. The Colonial Secretary was also renamed the Chief Secretary in 1976 (Morris, 1988, 213). Hong Kong was being described less and less as a colony and was often being referred to as a 'territory' (Courtauld, 86).

In Symons's life, the 1970s was a decade marked with uncertainties as well as distinction. The DGS boarding school had to be closed. There were no more war orphans or Eurasian girls left fatherless. In 1972, her husband had been diagnosed with cancer. The narrator recalls that period with a painful sense of loneliness and devastation which she likens to a dull constant pain, an aching muscle, 'nothing organic, nothing that would react to a medical diagnosis' (1996a, 66).

Yet, as if fate was playing on her, her ascent in her public career was gaining pace. In June 1972, Symons was awarded an OBE with Sir Kenneth Fung and Sir Albert Rodriguez as sponsors. In that same summer, Governor MacLehose invited her to join the Legislative Council as an Unofficial Member. She was the second woman on the Legislative Council following Dr Ellen Li.

The implications of an appointment to the Legislative Council for a Hong Kong citizen during this time cannot be taken lightly. The Legislative Council (Legco) in the 1970s was very much like Hong Kong itself. It remained, as Morris describes it, an astonishingly well preserved and preternaturally lively fossil of British Imperialism (203). N. J. Miners wrote in 1975:

> If the first British governor of Hong Kong, Sir Henry Pottinger, were to return to the Colony today, practically the only things he would recognize would be the outline of the Peak and the system of government, which has hardly changed in 130 years.
>
> (xv)

The Legislative Council[8] came into being in 1844. As in other colonies across the Empire, it consisted of Officials (senior government servants) and Unofficials, which were all appointed by the Governor. Morris wrote in 1988 that the current constitutional situation of Hong Kong was more or less like the constitutional situation of Gambia or Jamaica half a century before. It was the very last of the classic British Crown Colonies; even dependencies like St. Helena or the Cayman Islands, had by then achieved legislatures with an elected majority (Morris, 1988, 203). Hence, in Hong Kong, being appointed to the Legco signified not the winning of votes in an election but a kind of favour granted personally by the Governor himself (Miners, 1995, 114).

The lustre and exuberance of Symons's public life continued to be dimmed by a gnawing sense of foreboding in her private life. One fine November day, she went on a trip to Macau with her Eurasian relatives, and on spotting a minute Chinese temple, she suggested going in.

> Without thinking, I paid the monk's attendant $2 for a bunch of sticks which I tossed in the air for him to read my fortune. The man inspected the higgledy-piggledy mess from which I picked two or three sticks.
>
> He seemed lost in thought, then murmured quietly: 'You are a foreigner; you won't believe anyway. Here is your money back.'
>
> Astounded, then perturbed, I immediately thought he had spotted a bad omen. I was glad to escape from the dark temple into the brilliant sunshine.
>
> (1996a, 70)

Despite being a fervent Anglican, Joyce seemed unable to resist the Chinese custom of fortune-telling. This incident itself is somewhat paradigmatic. Joyce made the classic recoil between the cultures, from the darkness of Chinese fatalism to the sunshine of European enlightenment. Her Eurasian dimension comes poignantly into play first, in her unconscious affiliation with Chinese culture (she entered the temple 'without thinking'), then the fact that as part Chinese, the bearer of traditional Chinese culture initially entertained her. However, she was later rejected by him, disqualifying her by her belonging apparently to an out-group ('a foreigner'). This was followed by her readiness nonetheless to interpret the 'real' meaning of his rejection (he had spotted a bad omen which he was unwilling to disclose). The reaction of the joss-stick interpreter had left her with characteristically mixed feelings — perturbed by what she instinctively felt but half-understood. Glad to escape, but unable, years later, to forget. This piece of memory in Symons's memoir could hardly be a more comprehensive little allegory of the Eurasian condition.

Emily Hahn describes in her months of living with the Gittinses how the two Eurasian women tended to resort to fortune-telling in times of crisis. Hahn describes the Gittins sisters as 'completely English types'. In their months of living together never had she run into anything different 'until we got onto the subject of fortune-tellers. Then it seemed as if the girls moved a long way off, into another sort of landscape' (1946, 186).

Joyce was in a way very much like the Gittinses, despite her thoroughly European outlook and Christian sensibilities, she seemed utterly unable to cast off the ominous feeling from the joss. The fact that the monk had refused to reveal the unexplicated oracle on grounds of her foreignness, only exacerbated her apprehension more.

>—+>·—O—·<+—<

After a tortuous and woeful battle with cancer, Robert died in the summer 1974 while seeking medical treatment in Perth. His funeral in Hong Kong was held at St. John's Cathedral. Before the funeral,

> Someone from the Government House had rung to say that the Governor, Sir Murray MacLehose, would attend the service. He would give up his pew on the right of the chancel to me and my family, taking the left pew which before the war had been known as 'the General's pew'. Also, he wished me to leave before him.
>
> (1996a, 75)

The grief-stricken widow was completely overwhelmed by this colonial honour. In Hong Kong, since the nineteenth century, the location of one's house was an infallible guide to one's social status, and the position of a pew in the Cathedral was another indication of rank and self-esteem (Morris, 1988, 104).

The large Estoril Court apartment seemed too large without Robert Symons. 'Our twin beds looked strange, now that one was empty… for now I was alone — really alone'. Joyce moved out of her Garden Road home and moved into DGS, where she installed a headmistress flat on the top floor of the school — 'a public figure in the city and in school, desperately alone and forlorn'.

It was during this period of her emotional numbness that Joyce began to be more conscious of the support she gained from expatriate colleagues. In private unofficial meetings, the narrator recalls, 'when I made a stand, support came mainly from expatriates' (1996a, 77). At the same time, however, she began to be keenly aware of the invisible barrier between herself and her Chinese colleagues. Her rejection by the Chinese fortune-teller seemed to anticipate her alienation from the Chinese community. As her father Charles Anderson once felt alienated by the expatriate society and sought refuge in the Chinese community, Joyce Symons now felt alienated among her Chinese colleagues and sought refuge in her expatriate friends:

> The very first function I attended a month after Bob's service was to be a typical test of my fortitude, as well as an affirmation of friendship. There was no doubt that I had to attend the Chief Secretary's dinner party, but I dreaded arriving at Sir Denys Roberts' home on the Peak. As soon as Denys saw me, he crossed the huge drawing-room to greet me warmly. It was noticeable that as we had our pre-dinner drinks, several expatriate friends came up to me, though the Chinese councillors kept their distance. I put it down to 'face'.
>
> (77)

As the distance between Joyce and her Chinese colleagues widened, she also began to doubt her own position between the Chinese public and the administration. When she first started her public duties, she had been motivated by the fact that being a Eurasian would allow her to contribute more objectively to the positions of the Chinese people and the British Administration. But the ground had shifted and the Eurasian could no longer stay in that fast shrinking middle space. There is an unmistakable tinge of defeatism when the narrator recalls a ward session:

> Once when I was on ward duty, a Member of Parliament was visiting the Umelco[9] office. He was surprised when I spoke to the applicant in Cantonese, and briefed him in English — others were also taken aback. I immediately felt that only Chinese members should deal with members of the public.
>
> (82)

Apparently, the MP, not knowing Joyce was Eurasian, had taken her for a European. Joyce's sudden switch to Cantonese had crossed the linguistic and colonial divide within the ward session. She had bypassed the official interpreter. The sense of unease on the part of the Chinese public can also be imagined since it became difficult for them to fit this Eurasian lady into any readily comprehensible colonial category.[10] Was she part of the Cantonese-speaking public? Or was she part of the governing British officials? Had she faithfully and accurately interpreted the grievances of the Chinese claimants/public? Did she sympathize with them? Where did her loyalty lie? The narrator's usual sense of undaunted sprightliness seems to have been dampened by her memory of the different reactions she had invoked in the session. Symons's intrepidity was replaced by a poignant sense of resignation, of defeat — resigning to the fact that as a Eurasian she could never fit into the Chinese-speaking leadership to serve the Chinese public.

The year 1976 marked Joyce Symons's further ascent in the colonial hierarchy. She was appointed to the Executive Council[11] by the Governor. Being appointed to the Executive Council was the highest point in the colonial hierarchy that a private citizen could ever hope to attain. The position of the Executive Council in the government of Hong Kong corresponds to that of the cabinet in Britain (Miners, 1995, 75).

Times have changed the roles of many Eurasian civic leaders. Unlike her earlier Eurasian predecessors who served as bridge figures and middlemen between the government and the Chinese masses, there was no longer any such traditional roles for Joyce Symons to perform. In fact, it is likely that many people no longer considered this first women Executive Council member a Eurasian, as Norman Miners in his discussion on the pattern of appointment of the Unofficials in the Exco in the 1970s, seems to confirm:

> In 1976, two Chinese Unofficials resigned and were replaced by one Chinese and one British member. The latter is Joyce Symons, the first lady ever to be appointed to the Executive Council.
>
> (1977, 68)

Joyce Symons served the Executive Council from 1976 to 1978. Following the colonial tradition, she was awarded a CBE in that same year. In March 1985, at the age of 67, she retired from DGS, three months after British Prime Minister Margaret Thatcher signed the Sino-British Joint Declaration in Beijing. Having attended the endless rounds of farewell parties, she boarded the British Airways aeroplane and landed in England at 6 a.m. one day in April 1985.

Her reception at Heathrow was a dramatic contrast to the overwhelmingly emotional farewell she had at Kai Tak airport. The Eurasian retiree's national/racial identity was to undergo one more trial. Back in Hong Kong, she was Eurasian and sometimes British. Now in England, her ethnic and national identity once again reverted to an ambiguous status.

> It took some time to collect my luggage after a long wait at passport control, for my Hong Kong passport seemed an anathema to the passport control officer who managed to project intense suspicion and anger, even at that early hour. Not even the sight of my birth certificate, issued by Somerset House, could appease the fellow.
>
> (1996a, 91)

The 1985 encounter with a suspicious Passport Control Officer in Heathrow was not unfamiliar. It was merely repeating what had happened to her in 1940 and 1945 where Joyce had experienced the same difficulty in establishing her British racial and national identity to the Evacuation Officer and the Repatriation Officer. The difference is that this time her status was complicated by the series of parliamentary acts, including the 1962 Commonwealth Immigration Act and the 1971 British Immigration Act, which deprived Hong Kong British subjects of any resort to the principle of *civis Brittanicus sum*. The same old familiar suspicion and wariness were directed at this Eurasian Hong Kong-British subject.

In fact, the national identity of many Hong Kong-British Subjects was predestined for an ironical twist of fate. After all the fight by Hong Kong-British Subjects to have a right of abode in England, the final act of British cynicism came 18 months after July 1997 — the new Labour government announced that all citizens of the remaining colonies were to be given full British passports. Hong Kong was no longer a colony and its people would not qualify (Vines, 123).

As Joyce Symons's story draws to a close, there is a strong sense of wistfulness, a sense of irretrievable loss, particularly towards the once privilege-laden Eurasian community to which she belonged. Tides of Eurasian migration out of Hong Kong after 1945, after 1949, after 1967 and finally after the 1984 Sino-British Joint Declaration, have dispersed the Eurasian community to different corners of the world. The narrator ponders:

> The Community I belong to is scattered worldwide. Eurasians were not as fortunate as the smallish Jewish community in Hong Kong — they had their prominence in the professions and business — the first Hong Kong peer was that delightful and dedicated man, Lord Kadoorie. The Jews also had their faith, their synagogue and their close ties.
>
> (1996a, 95)

The Eurasian community too had leaders comparable with Lord Kadoorie, such as Sir Robert Ho Tung and Sir M. K. Lo, all of whom were much respected by the Hong Kong public. But they belonged to a different era in the past. There seemed nothing to hold the Eurasian community together. There was no great adhesive and identity-forming force such as the Hong Kong Jews had in their religion. As the narrator meanders along in her memory of other Hong Kong polyglot minorities, she comes upon the Portuguese:

> The local Portuguese had a wonderful sense of camaraderie. Their patois (a sort of Portuguese with Indian and Chinese innovations), their religion — almost all were practising and staunch Roman Catholics. A few became professionals — a good majority were clerks and in particular bank clerks, contributing in that way through their honesty and hard work to the business success of Hong Kong.
>
> (1996a, 95)

'Eurasians', says the narrator 'in a sense did not exist'. There is a painful lack of cohesion and unity among the community internally and externally. Unlike the Jews and the Portuguese, the Eurasian community in Hong Kong was one to which many of its members did not really know, or declare, or feel that they belonged.

Joyce Symons visited Hong Kong several times after her move to England. One of these occasions was in 1995 to participate in the Fiftieth Anniversary of the Liberation of Hong Kong from the Japanese Occupation, which the narrator describes as her 'final pilgrimage for Donald' (96). The Anniversary events included a lunch picnic at the Cricket Club at the Wong Nai Chung Gap, the site where Donald had sacrificed his life. Colonel Lindsay gave a long description of the fighting. Clifford Matthews, another Eurasian veteran in the same No. 3 Company, spoke of Donald's bravery and unselfish sacrifice 'a gentleman and a hero to the end'. The earlier sense of insuppressible bitterness that has suffused Symons's every retelling of the story of Donald seems to have abated, and been replaced by something akin to acceptance. The unsung story of her brother, that needed to be told, had finally been told, and so as her own story of the colonial destiny of the pre-war Hong Kong Creole community, told by perhaps one of its last surviving members.

Excerpt From *Looking at the Stars*

Plate 4 **Dr Joyce Symons, author
of *Looking at the Stars*, courtesy
of Dr Joyce Symons.**

Early Childhood in Hong Kong

I have a treasured photograph taken in the early 1920s which shows Mother dressed in the height of fashion, alongside me, aged four, and Marjorie, born in 1921, who must have been two. Father was a handsome man in those days, with a broad brow, brown eyes and a sharp nose. Phyllis was a pretty girl with a lovely sculpted-looking nose, in contrast to my button nose — the only one in the family. We look a typical happy family, but underneath the still faces was a different story of a troubled marriage and troubled financial circumstances.

We had moved south to Hong Kong Island, to a flat above Father's family. My elder sister Phyllis did not live with us, but became a boarder at the Diocesan Girls' School on the Kowloon mainland, which was considered too far to travel each day. However, my brother Donald, the next eldest child, born in 1912, was a pupil at the Diocesan Boys' School just up the road from our home on Bonham Road.

Although the rest of family settled in, Father missed the vitality of his Shanghai life-style, which had regularly included political discussions with radical young friends, inspired by Sun Yat Sen. Father often remembered those ardent socialists who were often found at our house, arguing and enthusing many long hours about socialism and the new world order.

Now in Hong Kong, Father became unhappy. He began to dislike and disapprove of the expatriate foreigners and started to accentuate his Chinese heritage. As he grew older he looked increasingly Chinese in his appearance, while Mother, on the other hand, was drawn to the West. I remember that Father was rarely at home but when he was, he have terrified me with the fiery outbursts directed at Mother. Their estrangement must have begun at about this time and it was to the church that Mother found solace. She had soon became a constant worshipper at St Peter's Church in Western Hong Kong, where the congregation was largely composed of Eurasians. Not for them the grander St John's Cathedral — that was the natural habitat of the expatriate Anglicans.

Mother lived for Sundays when she could go to church and see and [sic] English missionary, Miss Pitts, who had befriended her. Miss Pitts taught her English and encouraged her to be herself not just a wife and mother — which must surely have been a dangerous doctrine in those days. Mother was a home-loving woman, but not a particularly good housewife. But she adored her children and always put us first. My parents became increasingly distant with one another, and Father spent most of his time with friends at The Chinese Club. For some time, he lived by gambling there, becoming known as the uncrowned king of the casino, but he brought home barely enough to support his family of four children.

At the time our family had regular contact with a few Eurasian families — one of them being the family of Aunt Kate, my father's elder sister. She became known as Mrs Ho Wing after she married one of the sons of the future Sir Robert Ho Tung, who was one of Hong Kong's wealthiest and most powerful men. Aunt Kate's husband was profitably employed as a compradore, or agent, by the Hong Kong and Shanghai Bank. (The title of compradore seems unique to the Far East, and refers to someone employed as a contract broker by large European firms, including banks. The compradore, either a Chinese or Eurasian person, advised the expatriates on their dealings with the native Chinese, and underwrote the contracts, and, through their business knowledge, were often wealthy themselves.) Aunt Kate was also very clever at making money — running chit funds and acting, as money-lender, and was alert to a good bargain. Later, in the last fortnight of the war against the Japanese, she bought a house in exchange for a rather uninteresting diamond.

Excerpt From *Looking at the Stars*

Many other women besides Aunt Kate ran chit funds which were unofficial "insurance" schemes, into which the members would contribute a monthly sum. When loans were required, the prospective borrowers would bid, vying to offer the highest interest possible. Only the winner would be given the loan, then paying the interest back into the fund. At the end of the agreed period, the interest and capital was shared out between the members. It was a good system, unless the head of the chit fund was dishonest. Women servants were especially vulnerable, and sometimes lost their life savings in this way. Aunt Kate was also busy with all her schemes that she had little time for us, so we preferred her husband, who was much more friendly to us. Their children were never particularly close, except for their son, who died suddenly aged 12 from black water fever. It was my first experience with death and I really did not know what to make of it.

At this time of my life, Marjorie was my closest ally. I loved her quick wit, and was envious of her dark curly hair. However, she had bouts of bad temper which sometimes frightened me. I did not realise until years later how bad her health was. She was cursed with dreadful pains in her leg, which caused her to cry loudly at night — much to the irritation of Father, on the rare occasions that he came home, and the neighbours.

When she was not in pain, Marjorie and I played happily together. Every morning, we went downstairs to visit Father's mother, who lived with her daughters in the flat below, where we would carry out our toilet drill. Poised side by side on our little commodes, we would chat until interrupted regularly by the maid asking if we had finished. Later, when I was a teenager, Granny confided that the morning toilet drills were the high point of her day. She would listen with amusement as Majorie and I chatted in Chinese and entertained ourselves.

In less-wealthy families such as ours, a young servant girl would be allotted the daily chore of cleaning the commode, and each night would carry the vast communal commode outside the house, where it was collected by the night-soil coolie. I remember that the father of one of my school friends had successfully tendered for the job of collecting all the night-soil on Hong Kong Island and became very rich indeed. He discreetly described himself, not incorrectly as a businessman. In those days, one of the ways social status was measured, was from the type of commode. A house with its own toilet was a very rich one indeed. Our family did not acquire such a status symbol until 1937.

Looking back now, life in those days was rather dull. We didn't celebrate birthdays or Christmas — traditionally the high points in any child's life. The big occasion for us was Chinese New Year. Despite our troubled financial situation, it was a time when we were all given new clothes, including shoes, dresses — even straw hats. There was also plenty of food and, best of all, the delightful red envelopes of *laisee* or lucky money, that married adults give out to visiting children.

Every Chinese New Year, looking uncomfortably stiff, dressed in our new clothes, Mother took me and Majorie to call on our friends and relations. First port of call was Granny in her flat downstairs. Even on the first visit, I sensed the importance of the occasion. I wished Granny best wishes and wealth and *Kung Hei Fat Choy* (Happy New Year). I was instructed to bow to Granny, and nod to a descending hierarchy of aunts, while Granny would ask us if we had been good ("of course!"). Granny's maid servant would then trot out, resplendent in her new clothes of *sam-foo* (loose over-shirt and trousers) to serve mother [sic] with a cup of tea and offer her a round condiment tray divided into segments filled with melon seeds, sugared lotus seeds, candied ginger, and other Chinese sweets. As instructed, we took tiny helpings from the ornate tray and waited obediently for the grand climax — the presentation of the *laisee*, followed by the ceremonial thanks. Trying not to look too excited at the prospect of opening up our money packets, we were then excused and could leave to meet the children of the house. There was the inevitable boasting by some children about how much money they had, but Marjorie and I always preferred to wait until we were sitting in the sedan chair going home before counting out our haul as greedily as any highwayman after a hold-up. Yet we never disclosed the amount to others for we really had so little to boast about.

Excerpt From *Looking at the Stars*

I liked to spend my money to pay a hawker, whose monkey performed amusing tricks. He carried two bamboo baskets full of ribbons, Chinese sweets and snacks. My favourite treat was to buy a few huge olives covered in salt, which I would happily suck on for hours. Majorie spent her money on ribbons for her hair. Even if my brothers and sisters could not accompany Mother on the Chinese New Year visits, every child was remembered, and when I was nine, I remember demanding — and obtaining — a share of the *laisee* for my stay-at-home siblings. By the time I was about 12, Mother had stopped the New Year visits altogether.

Things remained financially difficult for the family. We had little ready cash and eventually there was no money for new clothes to wear at Chinese New Year. Yet Mother still managed to find funds for two new dresses a year — one for the summer, and one for the winter. Being a tom-boy I often refused them, and further argued there was no need for such extravagance. Yet sometimes my good intentions did no good. When I did decline, Majorie would often successfully claim the dresses for herself!

Reprinted from Catherine Joyce Symons, *Looking at the Stars*
(Chapter 2, pp. 4–5), with the permission of Catherine Joyce Symons.

6

> ⊱—┤ ◆❯ • ⊙ • ❮◆ ┤—⊰

Jean Gittins

Ethnic Indeterminacy: The Eurasian Girl in a Chinese Family

… My leanings, for some reason unknown to me, were always towards the British, and none of us looked altogether Chinese in appearance, this complicated situation was therefore a continued source of embarrassment to us.

(Gittins, 1969, 11)

Even though there is never a perfect correlation between one's self-identity and one's perceived identity, identity can ebb and flow depending upon the response they receive. Those that receive the most support will gain prominence, while those that are demeaned or ignored will become less conspicuous.

(McCall and Simmons, [1966] 1978, 77)

Out of the three lives examined in this book, Jean Gittins's is probably the most traumatically 'marked' and painfully 'branded' by history. Joyce Symons, as we saw in the last chapter, was a bitter witness and an indignant spectator of the Japanese invasion of Hong Kong. Yet, the war remained very much a historical deluge, which she was protected from through her shelter in Macau. Placing the two narratives side by side, the subject in *Looking at the Stars* remains, to a large extent, a keen observer of the violent forces of history, watching anxiously from a relatively safe distance the unfolding of the brutal historical action.

Gittins, on the other hand, was not only caught in the whirlpool of history but at times, we see that she willfully chose to collide head-on[1] rather than to side step the forces of history. The changing circumstances had instilled in her a daringness to take chances. Immediately after the surrender, she ventured onto numerous dangerous trips to Shamshuipo camps to 'sight' her husband and to Stanley camp bringing supplies and news to the interned University staff. She collaborated in the escape of Professor Gordon King, the Dean of the Medical Department, when the university staff was held in a kind of parole. As daily survival became difficult for a single female, she decided to submit herself to camp internment. She sustained drastic physical, psychological, emotional changes during and after her internment. In many ways, the Eurasian subject that emerged in the narrative epitomizes the physical embodiment of the cataclysmic effects of historical realities. The subject becomes, in many ways, 'a site where history is experienced and transacted' (Eakin, 142).

The first part of this chapter focuses on *Eastern Windows – Western Skies* (1969)[2] by Jean Gittins. *Eastern Windows* is the longest most comprehensive retrospective account of Gittins's autobiographical works, which covers much of her childhood and young adulthood. Gittins's other autobiographical texts, *I Was at Stanley* (1946) and *Stanley: Behind Barbed Wire* (1982), deal with her Stanley camp experience. Her last autobiographical text, *A Stranger No More* (1987), concerns her settlement in Australia.

Most memoirs do not have the kind of radical break or emotional trauma which is found in Gittins's that quite literally disrupts the sense of flow from past to present. In most cases, the voices of the mature narrators in their memoirs may sound quite different from those of the narrated childhood or teenage selves, but usually there is an organic continuity and no strongly felt break that interrupts the sense of the self constructed in the narratives. In Symons's case, her quiet refuge in Macau during the war years hardly constitutes a marked stage which may divide her pattern of existence into a 'before' or 'after'. Nor does Irene Cheng's sudden widowhood in April 1942 constitute any marked change. Fortune may change but the self is continuous. But in Jean Gittins's case, the spiritual and physical deprivation, the nervous anxiety, and the humiliation and isolation she suffered during the camp years distinctly mark the emergence of a self 'before' and a self 'after'.

In *Eastern Windows*, Jean Gittins's life can be separated into three parts:

(borrowing the words of Cynthia Ozick's character Rosa),[3] 1) the 'life before' 2) the 'life during' and 3) the 'life after', with her camp experience being the central and traumatic episode.

The 'life before' as constructed by the narrator is her idyllic privileged existence before her camp internment. From the days as the sprightly fun-loving daughter of a Eurasian magnate who resided on the Peak to those of a young wife in the Kowloon Tong Eurasian network, Jean was very much cocooned within the clannish bourgeois and exclusive luxury of the Hong Kong elite. Every time the narrator looks back to this period, her memory seems to have the capacity of increasing the charm and the elegance associated with it. Her pre-camp existence becomes a kind of transcendent reality that serves as a dream-like world to her later stages. The 'life during' is her three-and-a-half years or thirteen hundred days (1982, 151) internment in Stanley, where she experienced material deprivation, physical isolation, sickness and nervous deterioration. The 'life after' is her repatriation to Australia, recuperation, adjustment and finally assimilation in a foreign country. These three different orders of reality are not past and finished. They have the capacity of occasionally filtering into each other, informing and colouring the perception of each other.

Eastern Windows was written during the 'life after' in the late 1960s, two decades after the traumatic 'life during'. The effects of the 'life during' never seemed to have fully abated, it became a memory that surreptitiously confronted the subject at the least expected moment. With new tragedies entering her life in 1966 (both her second husband Sergei Holhov, a Hong Kong Russian from Hong Kong University, and her long-time Australian boss had died within three months), Jean Gittins was thrown into a kind of emotional abyss and wretched dejection. The narrator recalls moaning to an associate, 'I can't seem to remember anything these days and I feel so terribly depressed I could cheerfully drown myself' (1969, 3). *Eastern Windows* became a mode of healing through language. It is an attempt to confront the internal formless mnemonic chaos, to construct and salvage an *auto* or *autos* in the indeterminacy and instabilities of the *bios* through the art of the *graphe*. The primary function of autobiographical memory reflected in *Eastern Windows*, as Fivush says about autobiographical memory, is that of 'organizing our knowledge about ourselves, a self-defining function' (quoted in Eakin, 1999, 111).

Compared to the narrator in *Looking at the Stars*, the narrator in *Eastern Windows* is very conscious of her role as a storyteller as she tells the story of her younger self to the reader. She very often looks at her younger self/ selves in a rather critical manner. When recalling how as a child, she did not bother to give any attention to her Chinese lessons, she says, 'This inattention I was later to regret' (1969, 54). Other times, the mature narrator would put herself again in the position of the younger self and try to understand why she had acted so. Symons, however, does not seem particularly conscious of the distance between the narrator and the narratee. The boundary between the experiencing self and the self who assumes the task of storytelling is often ambiguous. In Jean Gittins, there is a distinct metanarrative. She is keenly conscious of her relations with the different 'I(s)' or different narratees in the text. There is an almost existential need to constantly locate her own identity as distinct from and still relating to that self of before. The narrator starts her journey into the past by first locating and positioning the identity of the narrating self in time and space:

> The name on my passport reads Jean Gittins Hohlov; at the University of Melbourne it is Jean Gittins; to the younger generation in Hong Kong I am simply Auntie Jean.
> It is November 1967. The time is spring ...
>
> (1969, 1)

The process of locating one's identity expressed in the autobiographical act becomes a kind of existential imperative in *Eastern Windows*.

Ethnicity plays a very important role in the personal narratives of Joyce Symons and Jean Gittins. Symons's fascination with her own Eurasian heritage and her racially diverse genealogy is very much foregrounded in her memoir. Like her father Charles Anderson, Symons cherished the somewhat idealized features and essentialized characteristics of Eurasians in Hong Kong and China. Despite her early romantic notion about her racial hybridity, Gittins was less decided about her own Eurasianness. Unlike Symons, Gittins never introduces, identifies or speculates any of her European ancestors in her story. There is a modest reservation which seems to prevent Gittins in being too forthright on her Eurasian blood ties, even though she admits quite openly of her own leanings towards her British side. But at different stages, she felt a kind of gravitational pull towards her Chinese side, while much of her life was completely imbued with European practices, habits and systems of belief. This pattern is in contrast to Joyce Symons, for whom, instead of there being a pull towards the Chinese side, there was a strong sense of estrangement, alienation and isolation from the Chineseness surrounding her. Symons's Europeanness became a kind of emotional prop for her in times of difficulty, as Gittins's Chineseness served as a kind of emotional prop for her in times of adversity.

It is also important to point out that the construction of ethnic identity in Gittins can be seen more as a process with no possible fixtures or stabilization, even towards the end of the text. Her ethnic identity is very much of the kind Stuart Hall has characterized as 'conditional, lodged in contingency' (1996, 3). It is in many ways a situational model of identity as pointed out by Thomas Cooley where one's identity is 'the shifting deposit of a continuing process of adaptation' (quoted in Eakin, 1992, 83). There is a strong disinclination to crystallize her own ethnic conception in any clearly delineated form or what Stuart Hall describes as the 'proper fit' (3). In Symons, there is more or less a *Bildungsroman* pattern of passage to maturity which echoes the subject's mature perception, a kind of 'ameliorative-integrative' pattern (S. K. Wong, 151), coalescing (or half-creating) a firm and stable Eurasian identity — an identity that is collectively bound to the historical destinies of the Eurasian community in Hong Kong and other treaty ports.

In the preceding chapter, I have also discussed how Symons's construction of her ethnic identity was hinged tightly upon her family's socioeconomic strivings. As her family advanced in the economic scale, expatriate habits, ways of thinking and traditions were being adopted. However, in Jean Gittins's case, the application of Symons's economic-based ethnic identity construction can be problematic.

Gittins was the fifth (or sixth)[4] daughter of Sir Robert Ho Tung, 'the doyen of the Hong Kong Eurasian Community' (1969, 11). Yet, despite being a Eurasian from the higher end of the economic scale, Gittins's childhood, in many ways, had been more Chinese and Confucian than most Eurasians and even most Chinese in Hong Kong. This phenomenon seems quite at odds with Symons's own experience where Eurasians of high economic status would usually identify themselves as much as possible with the ruling European community. This form of identification could then be a discursive practice to distinguish themselves from the less preferred Chinese race lower down the hierarchy. But in Gittins's text, this was not the case at all.

As we saw in the earlier chapter on early Hong Kong Eurasians, Eurasians like Ho Tung, as they strove higher in the socioeconomic scale, felt a need to be more consciously Chinese as a strategy to deal with the British colonialists. It was by appearing consciously Chinese that they could legitimize their position as leaders and exponents of Chinese interests in the colonial context. Growing up in the centre of the Eurasian elite at the beginning of the twentieth century, Gittins found herself breathing in a heavy Confucian-Victorian atmosphere. Certain superficial Western practices were selectively adopted, but the strong traditional Confucian discourse that dominated the household was seldom compromised. Hence, on evidence of Jean Gittins's text, the higher one stood on the economic scale, the more one's Chineseness became affirmed. It was only by descending slightly down the economic scale, as she had done through her marriage with Billy Gittins, that her ethnic identity became more European. The irony and reversal became even more dramatic during the war. As Jean Gittins descended down the socioracial scale to the Stanley camp, her ethnic identity was completely Europeanized to the near annihilation of her Chinese self. Set alongside *Looking at the Stars*, *Eastern Windows* offers a kind of strange reversal pattern between race and class in the colonial and wartime context.

⊱─⊷⊷─○─⊶⊶─⊰

This chapter begins by first looking into the narrator's conception of her own ethnic identity in her formative years as she locates the young Jean within the dominating discourses of Confucianism at home and the colonial segregationism outside the Confucian microcosm of the home. I shall then be considering the dual consciousness in the subject formation of Jean Gittins as she grew up, based partly on Rowbotham's theory[5] — the self as culturally defined, namely the obedient Chinese daughter, and the self as different from the culturally prescribed in her part as a liberal and Westernized Eurasian woman. Rowbotham uses the metaphor of mirrors to describe this double consciousness of woman. This mirror, as Friedman explains, is the reflecting surface of cultural representation into which a woman stares to form an identity (38). Not being able to recognize herself in the reflections of the Chinese cultural representations, Gittins felt at times very much alienated from her Chinese heritage. But at some rare occasions, she also felt herself being drawn to that Chinese side of her and she struggled to fit herself into the mode of Chinese female identity. With this duality, there existed a constant sense of dislocation, of double failure to fit comfortably into the cultural definitions of a Chinese context or to escape into a self-defining Western identity. As shall be demonstrated, Gittins's narrative, which articulates the continuously unstable and wavering process of identity, be it situational, conditional or prescriptive, quite dramatically de-stabilizes and calls into question the very notion of race and ethnic categories.

Jean Gittins was a Eurasian born to Eurasian parents in 1908 in Hong Kong. Like Joyce Symons and many Eurasian girls of her generation, she attended school at Diocesan Girls' School. Both girls, particularly Jean, were dedicated Girl Guides at DGS; and both attended Hong Kong University. However, unlike Joyce Symons, who never had any formal Chinese education, Jean went to a *si-shu* for two years of intensive Chinese classics before university. The families of Joyce Symons and Jean Ho Tung Gittins were related, in fact, by marriage. Endogamic practice amongst Hong Kong Eurasians was quite common where strong alliances were formed between the Eurasian families. It is apparent, however, that despite all the ethnic and cultural similarities in the lives of the two Eurasian women, their constructions of their ethnic identities remain extremely different. As shall be seen, both Gittins's and Symons's notions of their Eurasianness do, in their own different ways, resonate with Park's theory of the Marginal Person. In Symons, we feel the 'restlessness' and 'intensified self-consciousness' of the Marginal. In Gittins, we feel more the sense of the 'wider horizon' and detached viewpoint which the Marginal possesses and in some instances, we also feel in Gittins, as in the Marginal, how 'the conflicting cultures meet and fuse' (Park, 1928, 881).

As a young teenage girl, Gittins had begun to relish the idea of Eurasianness as a beautiful mixture and ideal blending of two races with their accompanying cultural, social and intellectual heritages. Her Utopian vision can be seen as an embodiment of racial harmony that dissolves the boundary between races by its physical and genetical manifestation within a person. In this sense, Eurasianness can be read as a sign of the absence of race, the individual subject as melting pot and as a kind of embodied covenant indicating the promise of a future without division and inequality.

Gittins's vision of an ideal hybridity was inspired by a meeting during a sea voyage in her youth. In 1924, at the age of 16, she travelled to England for an operation on the lump behind the ear. On her return voyage, she met many Europeans on board. She recalls how on the journey eastward,

> more than one of my travelling companions remarked on the happy product they saw in me of a dual upbringing: contrary to Kipling's theory, they said, west had met east, and the twain had become unified. Just before our arrival in Hong Kong an elderly lady, whose good opinion I valued, wrote words to this effect in my autograph album, and I blushed with a pride I rarely felt for my heritage.
>
> (1969, 49)

Gittins's vision of her own Eurasianness unsurprisingly was diametrically opposed not only to her family's conception of Eurasianness, but also to the Chinese and European communities' perception of Eurasianness in Hong Kong.

In her introduction of her parents and their ethnic background at the beginning of her book, the narrator says:

> Like so many of the local residents in Hong Kong, my parents, Sir Robert and Lady Clara Ho Tung, had a mixed Anglo-Chinese heritage. In those days and until the end of World War II, racial discrimination in Hong Kong was such that it was a most unfortunate circumstance to belong to a community which, by rights, should have been classified 'Euro-Asian' but its people were, in fact, accepted by neither European nor Chinese.
>
> (1969, 10)

Like Symons, Gittins is keenly aware of the entrenched racial attitudes where Eurasians like her family were excluded by the two main races,

European and Chinese. 'The tragedy of it all was,' she says, 'that until after the Second World War, when so many of the local community [Eurasians] died for the Allied cause', neither the British or the Chinese were willing to recognize and accept them. The Chinese, she notes, were not so forthright and tended to be more cautious in disclaiming them (1982, 8).

She recalls with sympathy how her father in his times had felt obliged to let his 'white' self be entirely dominated and suffocated by his 'Chinese' self:

> He decided to claim Chinese nationality — possibly because he knew that the Chinese would not be so discourteous as to disown him openly ... This did not concern me greatly in my young days but, after I went to school and found that other families like ourselves had merely accepted the situation of their birth, I used to feel sorry that he should have thrown in his lot with the Chinese. Moreover my leanings, for some reason unknown to me, were always towards the British, and none of us looked altogether Chinese in appearance. This complicated situation was therefore a continual source of embarrassment to me.
>
> (1969, 11)

This short paragraph epitomizes the intense ambivalence that young Jean felt towards her father's racial choice. Why did Ho Tung have to throw in his lot with the Chinese, when they were living in the British community on the Peak? The issue becomes even more complicated when the narrator admits 'none of us looked altogether Chinese in appearance' (1969, 11). The discrepancy between one's physical attributes and claimed ethnic identity became a source of embarrassment. From feeling sorry for her father, young Jean began to feel embarrassed about his insistence on a Chinese identity. Why could not her family be like other Eurasian families who 'accepted the situation of their birth' — meaning that they accepted their ethnic hybridity?

Growing up on the Peak as the only non-European family had been an extremely lonely and isolated experience for young Jean. As the narrator says, 'it was strange that we should have grown up in these surroundings at all for, until after the second world war, no other Chinese family had been granted the privilege, special permission from the Governor-in-Council being required to live in this exclusive residential district' (1969, 12).

In fact, the exemption had originally been denied. Governor Sir Frederick Lugard, regarding Ho Tung as a Chinese, refused to grant him exemption under section 4 and castigated him as 'an illegitimate half-caste whose wives and concubines numbered four' (Wesley-Smith, 99). It must be noted, however, that the fact that Ho Tung was eventually granted permission to live on the Peak was not because of his being Eurasian or having a closer racial connection with the Peak residents, but because of his increasing economic influence and social importance in the colony.

This desire to live on the Peak, a kind of European reservation, did seem quite out of character in light of Ho Tung's public claim to be a Chinese.[6] The desire to be on equal geographical footing clearly implied a desire for equal political footing with the British. The Peak in Hong Kong was very much like Fanon's description of Didier in Martinique. Didier, like the Peak in Hong Kong, is on a hill that dominates the city and, according to Fanon, is inhabited by the 'Martinique Whiteys' (who are perhaps not too pure racially but are often very rich) and the 'France Whiteys', most of them government people and military officers (Fanon, 43). Fanon explains that by having a house in Didier, 'it is quite easy to see the place as the dialectic of being and having' (44). By having and possessing a house on Didier or the Peak, one also becomes a European, which belongs to that place. There, Fanon says, 'you have Hegel's subjective certainty made flesh'. In Ho Tung's case, by externally possessing a material, tangible reality on the Peak, he (though still rigorously insisting on his Chineseness) had by possession, belonged to the Peak and became a member of the Peak residents, thereby embodying that sociopolitical power associated with the other Europeans residing there.

In 1906, the Ho Tungs moved into a cluster of three houses on the Peak: The Chalet, [The] Dunford and The Neuk.[7] Gittins prides herself on being 'the first Chinese baby to be born on the Peak' (1969, 12). In all her texts, this is the only time where Gittins specifically describes herself as 'Chinese' with some satisfaction. Other instances where she describes herself as Chinese, such as when recounting her playground experience on the Peak and her University application, are inevitably recalled with an unmistakable sense of helplessness or sarcasm.

Gittins's 'idyllic childhood on the Peak' (1987, 89) was marred by her early confrontation with racial prejudice while playing with other European children in the neighbourhood. There is still a hint of indignation as she recalls the incident:

> She [Miss Hecht, their governess] would meet other governesses and, sitting at some shaded seat, they would knit and chat whilst we played with other children at hopscotch or some other game. This was the highlight of a normal day, except, on occasion and without any apparent reason, the others might suddenly refuse to play with us because we were Chinese, or they might tell us that we should not be living on the Peak. Racial discrimination had extended even to the children and children can be so cruel. Miss Hecht would be really angry at this.
>
> (1969, 15)

The presence of the Ho Tung children in the Peak's playground did cause some anxiety amongst their European neighbours. In 1917, Governor May wrote to the Secretary of State,

> There are many more children now at the Peak than there were in 1904, and European parents are bitterly opposed to any contact between their children and Chinese children ... Chinese residents at the Peak will have with [them] their wives and concubines and numerous progeny, who must be thrown into daily contact with the European children in the children's playground and the few other shady spots to which the European children are now taken by their nurses and amahs ... It would be little short of a calamity if an alien and, by European standards, a semi-civilized race were allowed to drive the white man from the one area in Hong Kong, in which he can live with his wife and children in a white man's healthy surroundings.
>
> (Wesley-Smith, 100)

Whatever sense of Chineseness her family had cultivated in young Jean seemed to be quickly reduced to a wretched sense of 'otherness' once outside the Ho Tung microcosm. The family's determination to live in the white enclave inevitably brought about such snubs. The literal proximity of white and Eurasian elicited an aggressive distancing strategy by the Europeans.

Jean was brought up in a combination of 'the best traditions of the West as well as of the East' (1969, 13). English governesses were hired from England. Piano was taught by a French teacher. Donkeys were bought from

North China for their riding lessons (1982, 12). The narrator recalls how whenever they went riding, they were the envy of other children on the Peak. At other times, Jean's early childhood was spent in practising calligraphy and studying elementary Chinese classics (1969, 15). Occasionally, the children were taken to the Chinese opera whenever Lady Clara's favourite troupe came to town. And young Jean would sit there totally enthralled by the gongs and cymbals and the terrific noise of the battle scenes (1969, 18).

In learning the English language, there was no compromise. The Ho Tung children must have perfect mastery of the colonial language:

> Among ourselves, Chinese was naturally our mother tongue but we were encouraged, especially at meal times, to converse in English so that we grew up to be entirely bilingual, not only in speech but in our thoughts as well as in our dreams. Sometimes we would use a sentence consisting of a mixture of English and Chinese phrases or, if it expressed our meaning more clearly, even a single word might be a combination of the two languages.
> (1969, 22)

This kind of casual code-switching intra-sententially or intra-lexically might be tolerated. But pidgin English remained the forbidden language. 'Mother had a strong dislike for "pidgin" English' (1969, 22) even though it was at that time widely used in the exchange between Europeans and their Chinese domestic support. As members of the colonial elite, the Ho Tungs seemed quite sensitive towards the use of this language. Pidgin was seen as a form of language used by lower class Chinese. Yule and Bernell (1886) describe it as a 'vile jargon'. Gill (1880) calls it 'a grotesque gibberish' and Bird (1883) calls it 'a revolting baby talk' (Bolton, 2000, 44).[8] The hybrid language, of course, implies not only linguistic and cultural impurities, but also class impurity. For a family of ambiguous ethnic status, correct usage of the colonial language is a class marker they could not afford to compromise. Gittins's description of Lady Clara's aversion towards the language, could very well be a projection of her own aversion towards the language as the narrator later describes how she herself forbade her amah from speaking pidgin or broken English to her own children. Neither Irene Cheng nor Florence Yeo mention how pidgin was forbidden in the Ho Tung household nor talk about Lady Clara's disdain of the language.

Young Jean joined DGS in 1917 when she was around 9 years old. Going to school was no simple affair. As Gittins re-lives her childhood experience, the narrator leads the reader along that arduous journey from Victoria Peak to Jordan Road in Kowloon, which the Ho Tung children took daily — first the donkey ride to the Peak Tram Station, the tram ride, the sedan chair ride from tram to ferry, the Kowloon Ferry ride, and finally, the rickshaw ride via Nathan Road to Jordan Road (1969, 31). The single journey itself was enough to exhaust any 9 year old before school even started. Were there no other alternative schools to DGS? The narrator recalls,

> There were alternatives, as for instance, the Peak School for young children, which was quite close by, being only a fifteen-minute walk away, but as far as we were concerned, this was no real solution because no Chinese children were admitted.
>
> (1969, 26)

Her Chinese heritage once again becomes a kind of obstruction to the perfectly legitimate childhood preference of going to a nearby neighbourhood school. Lady May Ride (nee Witchell) who grew up in Hong Kong and herself went to the Central British School for European children, remarks on the ludicrous situation for the Ho Tung daughters. She writes, 'I believe that Sir Robert Ho-tung had put up money for the school, and yet his daughters were not permitted to attend because they were Chinese [although in fact they were Eurasians]. They had to go to the Diocesan Girls' School' (Ride, in Blyth, 9).

Apart from the Peak School, the narrator also recalls St. Stephen's Girls' College 'on the island, not far from Idlewild', where their cousins went. 'St. Stephen's was recognized as *the* school for daughters of Chinese gentlemen but instruction in English at this school was not, in Mother's opinion, of the standard that she had determined to be essential for her daughters. The same, she thought, applied to the French and Italian convent schools run by sisters of their respective religious denominations' (original emphasis, 1969, 26). To ensure their children's mastery of the colonial language and to enjoy the privilege associated with living on the Peak, the Ho Tung children had no choice but to spend hours each day riding on donkeys, sedan chairs, ferries and rickshaws.

The tram ride remains deeply etched in the autobiographer's memory. The daily tram ride was a site where the cultural and racial hybridity of the Ho Tung girls, with their occasionally ill-fitted European attire, stood out most distinctly among the other European passengers (1969, 28). Even though Lady Clara did employ a tailor in town for the girls, the sartorial standards of Lady Clara did not always agree with the sensitivity of the Peak communnity. Gittins remembers how at one time she had to 'wear a voile dress trimmed with a pink ribbon in the middle of winter'. This brightly coloured frock was also reinforced by a woollen singlet underneath which had an annoying habit of peeping out from under the voile neckline. 'Our general appearance was a source of great amusement to our fellow travelers' (1969, 28).

But the tram ride is also the site where they enjoyed a kind of privilege. As the children were on friendly terms with the European Peak Tram employees, they were often allowed to ride on the front row where it was marked 'These seats are reserved for His Excellency the Governor and his Staff' (1969, 30). This innocent incident might seem only a child's desire to sit on the front row but it also signifies how the mature narrator cherishes the colonial privilege of occupying the space reserved for the Governor.

In 1923, Jean passed with distinction in English and Biblical Knowledge (incongruously for someone from a devout Buddhist family) at the Hong Kong University Junior Examination. But she was utterly confounded to learn that she did not qualify to matriculate because she did not have a pass in Chinese. The admission regulations of the colonial University were still very much racialized. Chinese applicants must have a pass in Chinese for matriculation and non-Chinese were exempt.

Kathleen Grose,[9] a Eurasian at DGS who had passes in the same subjects as Jean Ho Tung, was considered matriculated and was accepted into the University. The explanation of this anomaly was obviously that Kathleen Grose, a Eurasian whose family had chosen to use their European surname at that time, was perceived as a European by the University and hence a pass in Chinese was not required. Jean Ho Tung, with a Chinese surname, was perceived as a Chinese and a pass in Chinese was required. The narrator relates this anomaly in a somewhat wry tone, 'because I was Chinese and, as such, Chinese was a compulsory subject for matriculation whereas, for Kathleen, there was no such pre-requisite.' Miss Sawyer, her DGS teacher, went to the University to plead the case, saying Jean Ho Tung 'was no more Chinese than was Kathleen Grose' (1969,36). This is an early instance of a debate before the authorities about who or what Jean Ho Tung actually was. Here, we see in operation Rowbotham's metaphor of the sociopolitical mirror. Our narrator was totally shocked to see the Chinese image of herself reflected back by the colonial institution. Since this image was Chinese, she needed a Chinese pass to be accepted into the university. This alienating experience of not being able to recognize and connect with the image reflected back causes the effects of the dual consciousness, the splitting of the subject into two, to become more acute.

The hapless sense of being excluded because of one's failure to fit into a prescribed ethnic norm grew stronger. All of these exclusions, by European children in the Peak playground, by the nearby Peak School, or by the University regulations, were all directly or indirectly related to her Chinese name, the most powerful Chinese marker of her identity. Yet within herself, she never did feel particularly Chinese. Her Chinese heritage seemed to serve perpetually as a kind of albatross in her girlhood. Gittins's early leanings to her European side could therefore be explained in McCall and Simmons's theory that 'Even though there is never a perfect correlation between one's self-identity and one's perceived identity, identity can ebb and flow depending upon the response they receive. Those that receive the most support will gain prominence, while those that are demeaned or ignored will become less conspicuous.' (McCall and Simmons, 1978 [1966], 77). Her Chinese identity was time and again being demeaned by her childhood experience in the Peak. It was therefore operating less conspicuously and being relegated to a lower status on her identity hierarchy. Within DGS, her Eurasianness seemed to pose no particular problem in view of the large number of Eurasian students. Eurasianness became an acceptable and recognizable category. But once outside the Eurasian space of DGS, the issue of her identity was much complicated by a continuous shifting of external perception and arbitrary attribution. To her surprise, the University admission authority had assigned to her a Chinese identity, which she had failed to assume. She was Eurasian, but people did not seem to recognize her as a Eurasian. As Symons mentions, in pre-war colonial Hong Kong, there was really no such recognized racial category as Eurasian: 'people were either expatriates or Chinese [,] no-one mentioned Eurasians' (2).

⊳—⊷—◇—⊷—◁

The Ho Tung family traditions, according to Gittins, had always been a combination of the East and West, whether in terms of the children's education, living environment, festivities, celebrations, etc. But 'funerals in our family were usually conducted in the Chinese pattern whereas weddings seemed always to follow the English style' (1969, 22). Weddings signify the future — a promise of partnership, alliance and networking of a community. Modelling after the Western pattern seems especially appropriate for an established compradore family like the Ho Tungs with its flexible East-West connection. Funerals, however, signify the past. Conducting funerals in the Chinese manner can therefore be read as the compradore culture of return and reconnection to its Chinese origin.

The memoir has included at least four major Ho Tung weddings, namely, the wedding of the eldest Ho Tung girl, Victoria Jubilee, and M. K. Lo in 1918, which was attended by H.E. the Governor Sir Henry May and Lady May (33); the wedding of the second Ho Tung son, Robbie, and Hesta Hung in 1928, which was graced by H.E. Sir Thomas Southorn and Lady Southorn (67); and her own wedding in 1929, attended by the Vice Chancellor of Hong Kong University (72). Also somewhat briefly included in the text are the weddings of Mabel Gittins and George Hall in 1929 at St. Andrew's Church (85); of her sister, Grace, and Horace Lo in 1933 at 'The Gripps' in the Hong Kong Hotel; and also of her youngest sister, Florence, and K. C. Yeo in the same year (101). Daisy Ho Tung's Chinese wedding in Shanghai in 1924 where Jean herself was the bridesmaid is omitted (Cheng, 1997, 117). But why all this meticulous narrative attention devoted to elaborate western weddings and the narrative erasure of Daisy's Chinese wedding where Jean herself was the bridesmaid? One explanation (apart from memory lapse) would have to do with the deep ideological association of western Ho Tung weddings. Western-style weddings that were graced by major colonial figures loom much larger and brighter in the narrator's memory than the Chinese wedding in Shanghai. That these colonial figures had endorsed these ceremonies had clearly elevated them from a family celebration to a racial and sociopolitical celebration of the Eurasians' station in the community. Perhaps without being consciously aware of it, the narrator is, by recalling and putting into language these major weddings, and its manifestations of power and affluence, re-affirming the collective ethnic identity and prestige of the Eurasian community, which at ordinary times would be more diffused and nebulous.

In 1924, Jean was suffering from the tumor behind her ear. That year, Ho Tung was in London for the British Empire Exhibition. Her brother Eddie had just graduated from HKU in Commerce and was about to join Sir Robert in London. Her mother, Lady Clara, decided that she should join Eddie to meet their father in London and undergo the operation there. The two sailed on the Japanese steamer *Kashima Maru* in June 1924.

At Dover, the narrator recalls the mortifying experience of her 16-year-old self facing an irate immigration officer without her passport. 'I had never before had occasion to show a passport either in China or for re-entry into Hong Kong and had thoughtlessly packed it away in my trunk which was being sent on by sea' (1969, 45). Growing up in Hong Kong in the 1910s and 1920s, a national boundary was still something quite new to her. It was not until after much explanation by Eddie that the immigration officer was assured that his sister Jean was a bona fide British subject from Hong Kong. This experience, of course, serves as a dramatic contrast to Joyce Symons's encounter with the British immigration officer six decades later at Heathrow. Jean Ho Tung, travelling from Hong Kong, was able to enter the UK without any passport in 1924; yet in 1985, Joyce Symons, with a valid Hong Kong passport and a birth certificate issued by Somerset House, was met with much suspicion. The dramatic difference in the two Eurasian women's experience with British Immigration authorities reflects the very different attitudes of the British State in the 1920s and 1980s. In the 1920s, the British Empire was relatively relaxed in its immigration laws towards British subjects from the colonies under the principle of *jus soli*. The Britain of the 1980s had become much more reserved and restrictive, even paranoid, towards British subjects from colonies and ex-colonies. The highly visible European features of these women might have helped to ease the situation in the 1920s but had no such effect in the 1980s.

Her brother Eddie was allowed to remain in England to study. After her operation, Jean, too, was anxious to stay on to learn journalism. Ho Tung's old friend Sir James Stewart Lockhart[10] had even offered to act in the capacity of a sponsor, and Lady Lockhart had invited Jean to make her home with them. Sir Robert, however, declined (1969, 47). Jean's taste of Western modernity in the hospitality of the governing clan in England was short-lived. Her father's refusal to let her stay in England was a bitter reminder that she was still very much under the control of a stringent

Chinese-Confucian patriarchy. No matter how alienated she felt at being the obedient home-bound Chinese daughter, she had no choice but to resign herself into accepting this culturally prescribed identity. Eddie was the son, and she was the daughter — a category in the Confucian context that already defined or circumscribed certain aspirations that Jean as an adolescent might have.

According to the narrative of her sister Irene, family members such as Lady Margaret (Ho Tung's first wife) and Mary (Ho Tung's daughter by his concubine) (Cheng, 1997, 119) were also at the exhibition. But these figures are never mentioned or alluded to in Gittins's text. The omission reflects the narrator's desire to represent the Ho Tungs as a culturally recognizable family unit for a Western reader — an elite Eurasian family visiting with prominent Taipans like the Keswicks and the Jardines in England. The mention of the presence of the first wife and another child by a concubine on the same trip would have marred this ideally colonial portrait.

Back in Hong Kong in 1925, with the hope of pursuing journalism in England shattered and the wish to attend Hong Kong University crushed, Jean was determined to rectify the situation by going to a traditional Chinese *si-shu*. This determination to submit herself to the rigid discipline of a *si-shu* can be read as a conscious effort of ethnic shift on Jean's part to change herself from a Eurasian to a Chinese. It is interesting to note that the title of this chapter on her experience at the *si-shu* was not entitled 'Sheung Fu Girls' School' (or something to that effect) as in her sister Irene's narrative. The title of the chapter in Jean Gittins's text reads, 'I Study the Classics'. A hint of sarcasm can clearly be felt in the title, expressing her own surprise at her sudden determination to pursue the Chinese language at a *si-shu* where she underwent two years of rigorous intellectual and cultural re-orientation.

Sheung Fu Girls' School was one of the old-style private schools or *si-shu* of the traditional type which refused to die out even as the Hong Kong government introduced the eight-year Anglo-Chinese secondary school system (Luk, 119).[11] The traditional *si-shu* was an intimidating world of Chinese traditionalism and learning for a westernized Eurasian girl.[12] Jean's younger sister Florence Ho Tung Yeo recalls her first impression of Sheung Fu:

> My first recollections of school were very frightening as I was sent
> to a Chinese school. This wasn't a *real* school as such because it was
> tiny and run by some elderly Chinese scholars in a couple of dark
> shabby rooms. I was only four years old and it was traumatic to be
> left in these surroundings. I didn't understand anything that was
> taught, not even in the language, so it seemed, as a classical scholarly
> language was spoken and I only spoke and understood colloquial
> Chinese. I just cried and cried every single day until I cried myself
> sick and was too ill to go to school.
>
> (Yeo, 17)

The *si-shu* experience, even for Jean, who by then was 17 years old, had
not been easy. A rigid routine, long hours of rote-learning and regurgitation
of Chinese literature were required in order to obtain a pass in Chinese —
something needed in order to fit herself into the ethnic category that the
University had assigned to her. With untiring doggedness, Jean transformed
herself into a traditional Chinese *si-shu* student after two years — a new
part of her that at times became totally foreign to her Western educated
self. Then in 1926, as if fate was playing on her, the University modified its
regulation for a compulsory pass in Chinese. Jean was liberated from the *si-
shu*. But her *si-shu* experience had been both alienating and transformative.
The two years had awoken in her a connection, no matter how tenuous, to
her Chinese side.

~·→·─○─·←·~

The Ho Tung sisters, Jean and Grace, enrolled as arts students at Hong
Kong University in 1927. They selected the group known as 'Letters and
Philosophy' and their subjects were English, History, Logic and one other
(1969, 57). Grace's 'one other' was Geography while Jean decided to take
Chinese Literature as the 'one other'. Her choice meant twelve lecture hours
per week for Chinese as against two hours for Geography. This determination
to voluntarily pursue the Chinese classics can be read as evidence of that
occasional gravitational pull towards her Chinese side.

In the University of Hong Kong, the narrator met Billy Gittins, a
Eurasian demonstrator in Mechanical Engineering. The Eurasian romance
was met with much disapproval from the Ho Tung parents.

Her sister and brother-in-law, Vic and M. K., had warned that she should expect much opposition from both her parents, not only because the Gittinses were Christians but because there had been some family grievances between Lady Clara and the Gittinses. Some time back in the early 1910s, the Gittinses were evicted by their landlord to allow Lady Clara's brother to move in. But after the Cheungs moved in, the grandmother of the family died and ever since then the brother had all the bad luck in the world. Lady Clara blamed all this ill fortune on the Gittinses (1969, 63).

Ho Tung did not share any of Lady Clara's superstitious grudges but he had his own objections. The narrator recalls the pointed dialogue with her father:

> 'I can't understand your falling in love with him. He is too dark to be considered handsome and he is eleven years your senior in age.'
>
> 'I think he is quite nice looking. As for age, you are thirteen years older than Mother and you have had a happy marriage.'
>
> 'Another thing. You are so extravagant. How is he, on a University demonstrator's salary going to earn enough to support you?'
>
> I suppose I then said an ungrateful and unpardonable thing, but I was stung:
>
> 'As your daughter, I have lived in accordance with your instruction, but, as a poor man's wife, I am sure I shall spend only within his means.'
>
> (1969, 64)

This confrontation with Ho Tung marks Jean's first attempt to assert herself as a modern Western female with her own mind making her own decisions, rejecting the meek and submissive role of a Chinese daughter culturally prescribed for her.

Ho Tung's reference to Billy's skin colour points to the preference for light skin (a stronger European phenotype). Very likely, Ho Tung was concerned not so much with Billy Gittins's looks, but more with the issues of class and ethnicity. Economically, the Gittinses could hardly match the wealth of the Ho Tungs in Hong Kong. They were Eurasians, but they belonged to a more westernized class of Eurasians who did not claim any Chinese nationality and had no inclination to identify with the Hong Kong

Chinese community. Their intra-ethnic but opposing conceptions of their Eurasian heritage was the major hindrance to the courtship. This is perhaps a good example of the myth that race and ethnicity solidify people from different economic classes. Both the Hos and the Gittinses were members of the same ethnic group. But because of their coming from different economic classes and, more importantly, because of their ideological differences in the conception of their Eurasianness, they did not share any sense of community and closeness.

Jean dismissed all her father's comments about Billy Gittins's complexion, age and earnings. Her own conclusion was that 'had Billy had a Chinese name, Father would have no objection' (1969, 64). Looking back in 1982, she says,

> I should have known that he would have been against any daughter of his marrying into an Eurasian family which did not subscribe to his view and adopt Chinese nationality, because he felt that they would not be accepted into any community.
>
> (1982, 18)

The Gittinses were in many ways like the Andersons (Joyce Symons's family) and had their own closely-knit Eurasian community. They did not claim to be Chinese, nor did they claim themselves as Europeans. They saw themselves simply as Eurasians, a self-perceived ethnic identity not supported by any officially recognized racial category, hence locally often seen as an ambiguous ethnic group.

The Gittinses, like the Andersons, were an old Hong Kong Eurasian family. Peter Hall, son of Mabel Gittins (who was also interned in Stanley), tells the Gittinses' story in *In the Web*. Unlike some Eurasians who had sometimes used their Chinese family names, the Gittinses never had a Chinese family name but continued with the name passed on to them by their European ancestor, who was a tea trader in the treaty port of Foochow (Hall, 126). Like many middle-class Eurasian compradore families, the Gittinses had a history of association with Jardine, Matheson & Co. Henry Gittins himself was a staunch Christian and had been an Elder at St. Andrew's Church in Kowloon (Gittins, 1969, 84) 'where many of the Eurasians met' (Hall, 144).

The Gittins children (five girls and two boys) were all raised in a very

Western tradition. Emily Hahn describes the two Gittins girls as 'completely English types. Though they were half-Chinese they spoke English as naturally as they did Cantonese ... Never once in all our months together did I run into anything in Irene or Phyllis different to myself' (Hahn, 1946, 186).

At the end of Jean's second year at the Hong Kong University, she was still quietly seeing Billy Gittins. It was at this time that her parents' pent-up tolerance reached its limit. An ultimatum was given to her:

> To my astonishment and utter dismay, they gave me the alternative of either discontinuing my association with Billy or giving up my course of study to be married. To do them justice, I am certain now that they did not for one moment think that I would take their ultimatum literally, but I was too young, too inexperienced and too rigid in nature to consider compromise.
>
> (1982,18)

Her determination to marry Billy confounded her parents. Four decades after this decision, Jean Gittins believes that her parents 'had most certainly expected that some compromise, in traditional Chinese style, would by degrees evolve' (1969, 71). But she had not responded to her parents by compromise, an interesting strategy that she sees as essentially Chinese. The narrator recalls herself in 1929, as being 'too young, too positively logical, to understand compromise' (70). The 21-year-old Jean had opted for modernity (independence, straightforward volition) over tradition (submission to family wishes and compromise). However, on another level, she was also ironically opting for tradition (choosing marriage) over modernity (university education). The narrator ponders over that decision made by that willful young subject.

> While they, having forced my hand, could not, or would not, retract from my acceptance of one of their alternatives ... It is only natural that I have at times felt sorry that I did not get my degree ... .
>
> (1969, 71)

During this moment of autobiographical narration, the splitting of the first 'I' of experience and the second 'I' of innocence is dramatically highlighted.

Her youthful intransigence had drastically diverted her course of life. There is a strong sense of loss in the severance from the old world of Confucian filial piety and security. Confucianism was a deeply ingrained discourse in the Ho Tung familial existence. Though the young 'I' in her rebellious moment exults in her freedom from the Confucian system, the older 'I' in the narrator seems to feel a wistful remorse. Here, we feel how the consciousness of the Eurasian subject is being split between East and West, past and present. There is a sense that the Eurasian subject is always, borrowing Rowbotham's description of the female split consciousness, 'in transit' like 'immigrants into alien territory' (31).

Lady Clara consulted her 'Red Book' and 19 March 1929 was discovered to be a 'red letter' day. Being a devout Buddhist, she stood firm against a church wedding.

> ... out of regard for her feelings, we were married at the Registry Office. But Mother was not the only bigot; Billy's own minister refused to read over the marriage service with us because I was not a baptised Christian.
>
> (Gittins, 1969, 71)

Much effort was spent in pacifying the staunch Confucianist on the Ho Tung side and the Christian bigot on the Gittins side. The wedding of Jean and Billy Gittins was held at Idlewild with five hundred guests. Probably because the Gittins's Eurasian connection can hardly be compared to those of the other Ho Tung in-laws such as the Los and the Hungs, the narrator says, the wedding 'was small compared to the other weddings' (72), that is, the weddings of the other Ho Tung children.

Becoming a Gittins seemed to give Jean a newly invigorated sense of Eurasian identity. In this new identity, racial hybridity was no longer 'the source of embarrassment' — something to deny, or to evade, but it was an ethnic marker which wanted to be noticed, as being distinguished from the Chinese community. It was this distinction from the Chinese populace that helped to define the collective Eurasian community. Deviating from the 'Chinese ethnic normal image' was something to be positively acknowledged.

The narrator, in retrieving and constructing this part of her life, ceases to refer to herself as 'Chinese' from this point onwards. Eurasianness served as a kind of class emblem indicative of a Hong Kong Westernized and progressive middle-class. The Kowloon Tong Eurasian network in which Jean Gittins found herself was a contrast with the large patriarchal Ho Tung extended family with its Victorian/Confucian mix. As a young couple, they had adopted much of the expatriate habits of engaging 'a houseboy, an amah and a coolie' (76) for their new household.

Jean enjoyed the independence of having her own house and being away from the Ho Tung patriarchy. But soon, this intra-ethnic and geographical crossing from the isolated Confucian extended family in a European reservation to a closely-knit bourgeois Western-style Eurasian network was a cultural shock to her.

The casual manner and forthrightness among the Gittinses were shocking to her. They would say 'the first thing that occurred to them … [which] tended to the way they addressed their parents'. In the Ho Tung family, young Jean had been taught from childhood 'to remember always Confucius' tenet to think thrice before we spoke' (86).

As a young wife and mistress of the house, she felt very uneasy at the way domestic servants were treated:

> The trusted servants I had known were a part of the family; people whom I had called, albeit out of courtesy, brother or sister while I, in turn, was known to them as 'No. 6 Miss'. Now I had to say 'Boy', or 'Coolie' or 'Amah', as the case may be, nameless individuals to whom I was known as 'Missie'.

The narrator recalls how her sisters-in-law Charlotte and Daisy had called round to her house one day while she and Billy were away and had found the cook boy asleep in the sitting room. They had dismissed him on the spot and had engaged another on her behalf (86).

This description of the Gittinses' world, which previously had signified emancipatory modernity, liberalism and enlightened Westernization, on this occasion becomes a critique of colonial habits and modern labour practices.

The Westernized Eurasian culture had adopted the expatriate attitude of seeing domestic labour on a capital/labour basis. With an unlimited supply of Chinese domestic labour, these anonymous houseboys, amahs and coolies could be dismissed and replaced any time on the spot. This attitude towards domestic labour was of course drastically different from the Confucian patriarchal relationship between servants and masters, which emulated a parent-child relationship and which demanded a loyalty from both sides. Servants were part of the family and remained in it for life. Florence Yeo, the youngest of the Ho Tung girls, says in her memoir that 'Sometimes, our home looked like a retirement home!' (20). Relationship with their domestic servants played a crucial part in the Ho Tung family life. Very often, these Chinese domestic servants were transmitters of Chinese folk knowledge, beliefs and customs.

Jean Gittins became a mother one year later in 1930. An amah called 'Kwan Sze' was engaged to look after the baby. Normally, the narrator says, she would have called her 'No. 4 sister', but because this amah had the habit of grumbling about everything, Billy christened her 'Grouser'. The amah was rather flattered at being given an English name — until she found out what it meant. The baby's amah is one of the few Chinese[13] to be granted some narrative space in the memoir.

> She rather prided herself on her ability to converse in English and wanted to use this in speaking to the children, but to her immense disappointment, I would not allow the children to speak broken or pidgin English. Nothing could stop her, though, when she was out with them; for some reason known only to herself, Grouser always regarded it to be beneath her to converse with them in Chinese in public.
>
> (Gittins, 1969, 94)

Grouser had lived in England for some years with her previous employer. She liked to see herself as culturally advanced compared to the other Cantonese amahs. The narrator seems to show extra tenderness in describing Grouser's ardent desire to be an English speaker. Perhaps Grouser's comic attempt at mimicry in some way enhances the authenticity of Gittins's Eurasianness, in the same way as Eurasian figures may be comically described by some white colonial writers — Kipling for example — a way that enhances the authenticity of the truly white. On another level, the comedy of Grouser's mimicry can be read as a displacement, or decoy, of laughter at Jean Gittins's own squirming discomfort in her own hybridity. Jean's banning of the pidgin English is, of course, an echo of her mother's objection to the language, which, despite all her resentment towards her mother's superstition and religious bigotry, expresses her fundamental bond with her mother in their mutual anxiety about slipping back into the pidgin language and the pidgin world.

▻┈✦〉┄○┄〈✦┈◅

Jean's second child was born in 1935. Both Grace and Florence had been married by this time and had become part of the Kowloon Tong Eurasian network. The young Gittins family spent their summers on the Peak or took the Ho Tung yacht *Fook Po* (1969, 99) to the nearby Junk Bay or Silvermine Bay. But this kind of leisurely microscopic privileged lifestyle was soon to be interrupted by the larger movement of history.

Hong Kong was, by this time in the late 1930s, very much under the shadow of war. Canton fell in October 1938 and the colony was staggering with the daily arrival of refugees. Jean's daughter Elizabeth had joined DGS and John was in kindergarten. With two children in school, the young Eurasian mother was not contented to join the leisurely ladies 'at lunch or afternoon tea parties or at games of bridge or mah jong'. She had attended a course of air-raid precautions. 'It occurred to me that I could still study, and rather than returning to the University to complete my Arts course (which was probably what I should have done), I decided to take a secretarial course' (1982, 19). In early 1940, Jean joined the administrative staff of the university as secretary to the Dean of Medicine, Professor Gordon King.

The Evacuation Order from Whitehall was issued in June 1940. All European evacuees had to register with passports and health documents and be ready to embark for Manila en route to Australia on 1 July. The families of the regular armed forces were evacuated forthwith on 1 July. 'Other British women and children of European descent' were told to report on 2 July for registration (Endacott, 14). Yet the evacuation order caused great confusion and nervousness for those whose eligibility was marginal. Emily Hahn who was living in Hong Kong with a few Eurasian women expresses her sympathy for these women in her memoir:

To begin with, the order wasn't clear. Just what women and children, asked the public, were meant? The reply was ill considered: 'Pure British,' said the government. This implied that thousands of Eurasians and Portuguese who held British passports were not considered worth saving from danger … . The officials who answered their charges got in deeper and deeper. 'You natives,' they said in effect, 'are at home here. In a pinch you can go into Free China. Our women from England are in a different category.' … 'We can't help it,' said the harried authorities. 'We are giving free transportation to these women and children, all the way to Australia. We can't send every woman and child in town … And we would have to take the millions of Chinese too, if we start accepting Eurasians.'

([1944] 1987, 205)

Hahn also describes the resentment among the English women or the 'pures' which others began bitterly to use when referring to the English-born women. 'Why do I have to go if those Eurasian women can stay? Why must I go and leave my husband free to play around with Chinese tarts?'

Wordie too describes in an article how during an ex-prisoners of war lunch in Kowloon, two elderly Eurasian women who had been in Hong Kong during the war years looked at each other and raised their eyebrows when asked about the 1940 evacuation of civilians: 'Oh yes, we weren't among the "pures", so we had to stay behind' (Wordie, 9 August 1998). The bitter sarcasm after half a century is still quite evident.

As we saw in the last chapter, Symons never mentions any sense of anxious wariness of her own racial eligibility as she went to the Evacuation Authorities with her sister. Hahn describes how Eurasians born in Hong Kong have been brought up like English people. "They wear foreign-style clothes, speak English, can't write or read Chinese, and consider that they are as British as anyone. After all, that is what they have been taught all their lives …" (Hahn, [1944] 1987, 205). Symons, like most Eurasians described by Hahn, considered that 'they are as British as anyone'. But this is not so in Jean Gittins's case. She was extremely apprehensive about the eligibility of her own racial background.

Was she 'white enough' for the White Australian Policy? She might be of European descent, but she also had a non-European heritage. She had heard that those evacuees who were not of pure European descent were identified and returned to Hong Kong upon reaching Manila.

The narrator does not mention how these Eurasians were identified. How did the authorities manage to 'weed' the Eurasians out? A British passport did not carry in it the genealogy of one's blood descent. Many Eurasians like the Gittins and the Andersons had very Caucasian-looking physical attributes and were perfectly at home with the English language.

Many of the Eurasians felt insulted and indignant at what happened in Manila. The situation had not gone unnoticed by the Hong Kong government. In reviewing the evacuation process at the Legislative Council Meeting, Sir M. K. Lo, himself a Eurasian and brother-in-law of Jean Gittins, stated on record that:

> I have indirect complaints of disgraceful discrimination meted out to some of the evacuees in Manila … My information is that people were weeded out deliberately by Government officials on the advice of two ladies from Hong Kong and sent to places which were not fit places to accommodate anyone.
>
> (*Hong Kong Hansard* 1940, 115)

Probably sensitive to her own children's successful passing off as Europeans in Australia, Gittins does not mention her own brother-in-law's complaint about racial discrimination at the Legislative Council Meeting. But Symons, who had herself been denied evacuation, recalls what she had heard about the circumstances in an interview with local historian Jason Wordie in 1995:

> The Eurasians were separated at Manila — someone went among them pointing them out 'She's Eurasian and she's Eurasian — her mother's a Eurasian' and so on … They were then all separated and sent back to Hong Kong.
>
> (Wordie, 1997, 47)

The weeding of Eurasians, in the absence of any documentary proof, was very much a form of ad hoc ethnic cleansing on the spot. The pre-war European and Eurasian communities in Hong Kong were very small and speculation on people's Eurasian background was an assiduously popular subject for society gossips and malicious calumny.

Jean and Billy Gittins became very anxious for the safety of their two children, who were 11 and 5. Billy did not want their children to have the same fate as those children of Central European countries suffering malnutrition as a result of starvation during the First World War (Gittins, 1969, 119). It was the images of suffering European children, rather than the thousands of suffering Chinese children at that time, that had such a powerful effect on Billy Gittins, an indication that he identified his children more as European than Chinese.

They had considered the alternative for Jean to take them to Australia herself, but her maiden name on her passport would automatically betray her Chinese ancestry. The couple decided that the best way would be for their children to pass as pure whites under the care of a European lady friend. 'Gittins was an English name and they looked foreign enough' (Gittins, 1982, 20). It was an identity choice that reflected *part*, if not *whole*, of their racial heritage.

In May 1941, Jean put her two children under the care of her friend Sybil Jack who, having returned from leave in UK, was obliged under the government's Evacuation Policy to quickly re-embark for Australia. That day of separation from her children etched deeply in the memory of the author. The five-year old John, recalled the narrator not without some pangs of guilt, was too young, too emotionally upset at the thought of the impending separation to understand. He could not feel reconciled to leaving the security of home and parents and even the exciting prospect of going on a big ship offered but small comfort (1969, 120).

The narrator recalls the day of sailing, 5 May 1941. The two Gittins children were standing on board the old liner *Nellore*. John had great difficulty fighting back his tears. 'As we stood on the wharf waiting for *Nellore* to depart, I could see his little hands clenched on the ship's railing. He said not a word' (1969, 120). Elizabeth, the 11-year-old, unable to comfort her little brother, also gave way to her own grief.

The two Eurasian children managed to pass as 'pures', and arrived safely in Australia. Gittins says, 'Some people thought me completely heartless; others appreciated our difficulties' (1969, 120). Grouser, the children's amah, later 'died of a broken heart'. Gittins adds,

> I don't think she ever recovered from the parting with John when we
> sent him and Elizabeth away. As for myself, she had written me off as
> a most heartless creature as she could not reconcile herself to the
> fact that it was in the children's best interests to be sent away.
>
> (1987, 100)

Notwithstanding the defence and justification in hindsight that the
narrator has given to the reader, the incident in a way could still be read as
Jean's double betrayal of her ethnic loyalty and gender expectation. Sending
her children to Australia, passed off as pure white, was a betrayal of their
Eurasian loyalty. Sending her children away to a strange land for an unknown
period of time was also compromising her role as a mother, an identity
which is culturally perceived as responsible for the caring and nurturing of
her children. But ironically, despite accusations from many directions, the
narrator recalls how Ho Tung, the great Chinese patriot who insisted on
Eurasians taking on Chinese nationality, had shown sympathy for this
strategy of his daughter and approved his grandchildren's situational identity
as pure Europeans.

The world of privilege and exclusiveness was shattered on the morning of 8
December 1941. Jean's sense of apocalyptic apprehension was affirmed and
made real. As a Volunteer, Billy Gittins had been called up the day before.
Jean was planning to billet with the Faids when Professor Gordon King
called her at 6 a.m. on that beautiful morning to report immediately to the
University Relief Hospital. They were preparing to receive patients by noon.
As Jean arrived at the university, Japanese bombs fell on Kai Tak airport.

Hong Kong surrendered to the Japanese on Christmas Day 1941. The
white flag flew over Government House. 'Disillusion and dismay were to
come later. Surrender left us stunned' (Gittins, 1982, 24). An editorial in
The Hong Kong News[14] put it in starkly racial terms:

> ... The vaunted supermen of the white race had melted over like
> butter. In eighteen days of conflict it was all over, a horrible
> muddle of inefficiency and helplessness which has bequeathed
> a miserable aftermath.
>
> (Endacott, 1978, 136)

The Japanese invasion of Hong Kong was perceived by the Japanese in terms of a war between East and West, between Asians and Europeans. The new masters saw themselves as a champion of the Asians against Europeans. The Eurasians, being neither Asians nor Europeans, were to become in many instances an awkward wartime group whose identity (and sometimes loyalty) continued to confound and confuse the Japanese, and sometimes the British and the Chinese.

The Japanese had perceived and publicized the war as a form of vengeance for the East against the West. Attempts were made to humiliate the Europeans in front of the Chinese. But the humiliation of the Europeans often had quite an opposite effect on the local people. Instead of cheers, there was often sympathy and as they found themselves under the collective manacles of the Japanese, a sense of common bondage and victimhood, under the circumstances, crossed the race divide. George Baxter, an American, who was the Manager of the United Press, was among those gathered at the Murray military ground and herded in a westerly direction:

> [T]housands of Chinese lined the curbs to watch the white man being ordered around and driven like cattle by the squat Japs. It was plain that humiliation was part of the Jap scheme to convince the natives that the white man had been conquered. Sometimes, Jap gendarmes would break up the crowds just to let the Chinese know that they, too, were under the Jap thumb.
>
> (194–, 22)

John Stericker, a Briton who worked for Hong Kong British Tobacco Co., was also in the march along the Western Praya:

> I will never forget the look of sympathy and sorrow on the faces of the Chinese who stood and watched us go by. We were not always regarded as their friends, nor were we racially connected with them, but for once, they realized what good friends we had been. Recent events had demonstrated that East could show an attitude to East that the West, in its most imperialistic moments, had never shown.
>
> (1958, 141)

These groups of Europeans spent three weeks in the overcrowded Chinese boarding houses on the Western waterfront. The Japanese, even at this early stage, were not unaware of the Eurasians that were among these groups. Like the British Evacuation Authorities who weeded out the Eurasians at the port of Manila, the Japanese Authorities also started weeding out the Eurasians among the interned Europeans at the waterfront hotels. Wenzell Brown recalls how some Eurasians were evicted:

> Rex was mortally afraid of being ejected from the hotel, for to go out into the streets without money or a place of shelter might mean death from starvation or exposure. Soon an order came for the release of all Eurasians and Japanese officials came through the hotel and gave passes to those Eurasians who had reported as British subjects. Rex hid in the toilets until the officials had gone, and then returned to the room apologetically sucking his moustache and bowing and smiling as he resumed his seat on the bed. Briggs left with the Eurasian group and we were sorry to see him go. He left with us a few tins from his provisions and promised to get in touch with our Chinese friends to let them know where we were ... A room at the end of the hall was vacated, as it had been occupied by a group of Eurasians. Now Clyron and Smart and I seized it.

(1943, 59)

Already in this early stage, given the meager resources within the internment, it is not surprising that Eurasians were often seen throughout the rest of the internment as taking up space and resources not rightfully belonging to them.

Jean Gittins was still with the University staff at that time. The two sections of the non-Chinese community, namely, the Peak residents and the University staff, were spared this 'particular outrage' at the waterfront hotels. The Chief Justice Athol McGregor was made responsible for the Peak residents. And the Vice Chancellor was made responsible for the University staff. The narrator, speaking as a member of the non-Chinese community in the University, recalls, 'We were virtually interned within the compound and were honour bound not to attempt escape ...' (1982, 32).

Jean at this stage was torn between the alternatives open to her as an individual of both European and Chinese descent. If she were to claim herself as a Chinese, she could return to the Ho Tung family and remain free. But with Billy as a POW and her children living in Australia as 'pure whites', she could not bring herself to use her Chinese identity to escape internment.

Several days before the University staff received orders to move into

Stanley Camp, a member of the Chinese medical staff, who had been appointed to take over the hospital, asked Jean to stay behind to assist him. She jumped at the opportunity and agreed to stay, but on condition that he would get her an 'Enemy Alien' pass. This 'Enemy Alien' pass was different from the 'Third National' identification passes issued to Eurasians, Portuguese and Russians. The Enemy Alien pass identified its holder as either British or American. With this pass, Jean could identify herself as British and then be exempt from internment.[15]

Her Enemy Alien pass proved to be a valuable wartime document to accommodate her ambiguous identity. Japanese sentries, upon studying her pass, often imagined her as some British or American of importance who had been permitted to stay out of internment on official business. Being perceived as an important foreigner certainly had its advantage, but there were times when Jean desperately needed to be seen and taken as a Chinese. This happened when the Japanese Authorities announced that only Chinese nationals were allowed to withdraw money (a limit of HK$100) from selected banks. Jean went and tried to persuade the Japanese Controller at the Hongkong and Shanghai Bank that she was indeed the daughter of the Chinese compradore Ho Tung, though the narrator recalls that 'in name and appearance I was a foreigner' (1982, 34). The racial test was passed. Ho Tung was accepted as Chinese and Jean, his daughter, was also accepted as Chinese.

There was a certain sense of freedom that Jean enjoyed with this Enemy Alien pass. She took several arduous trips to Shamshuipo camp but could only sight Billy across the barbed wire at a distance. Each trip had been a 'harrowing experience' for her as she saw her husband in captivity.

With the freedom that came with the pass, Jean also made frequent visits to the university staff in the Stanley camp bringing whatever food and basic necessities she could get from outside. During the first month of Stanley camp's operation, there was a certain degree of coming and going: 'entry was possible if anyone with a pass cared to risk being detained' (35). The internees in the camp hungered for news of the war. Was there a Chinese army on the way? The Eurasian visitor was besieged with questions and requests for food.

Alone, with Billy in the POW camp, her children in Australia, and all her friends and colleagues in the civilian camp, Jean Gittins soon began to doubt the value of her freedom — a wartime freedom that was much sought after by Europeans — but a freedom that had begun to lose its attraction to her as daily survival became harder and harder for a single Eurasian woman in Japanese-occupied Hong Kong.

Ethnic Options: Escape From Freedom

And so, the Chinese stayed, the Eurasians stayed and the dogs stayed, as did overcrowding, and shortage of fuel, food, and everything else.

(Stericker, n.d., Chap. 1, 3–4)

To Jean Gittins the memoirist, the pre-war world of privilege, gentility and cohesion (the life before) is forever separated from the present (life after) by the painful memory of the Japanese internment (life during). The second part of this chapter concentrates on the memory of 'life during', a cataclysmic period of Gittins's life, which breaks her narratives into contrastingly different stages of historical and autobiographical order of realities.

Jean Gittins's first camp narrative, *I Was at Stanley*, was published in 1946, when she was 38 years old and soon after she was released from Stanley. *Eastern Windows* was published in 1969 at the age of 61, 24 years after her internment. *Stanley: Behind Barbed Wire*,[16] her second and more exhaustive camp narrative, was not published until 1982 at the age of 74, 37 years after her internment. These three texts, spread over almost four decades, mark three different stages in the process of recovery from the effects of the Stanley Camp.

The rather brief 22-page memoir *I Was at Stanley* was completed by Christmas 1945, three months after her release from the camp in September.

A long internment, a heavy bereavement, stranger in a strange country, victim of a tropical disease. Any one of them alone might have upset my equilibrium, but a combination of all, within the short space of six weeks proved too shattering a blow for my nerves. My courage failed me: my spirit broke: I was terror stricken, alone — almost insane. I found no comfort in the charm of my children, derived no relief from the kindness of friends. I was spiritually destitute. Living was a hopeless weariness: I prayed for release.

(1946, 22)[17]

The gnawing psychological effects from the internment, the raw emptiness of its aftermath, the belated news of her husband's death, penetrated every struggle to return to normalcy. The memory of the 'life during' continued to exert an overpowering sense of wretched dejection and mental inertia. The narrator expresses an acute consciousness of her own nervousness. The flow of the narrative is often interrupted by the narrator's apologies for her seemingly unbalanced outlook. She appeals to the readers, 'I can only ask of your indulgence, and hope that given time, I might find my way' (19).

Notwithstanding the intense Christian orientation and religious gratitude, there is an unmistakable existential angst in the narrator's voice as she unfolds her camp experiences and how they affect her post-trauma, devastated self in the everyday routine of peacetime. There exist questions that are too painful to confront. Who am I? What is left of me after the three-and-a-half years in the camp? What has Stanley done to me? Two decades later in *Eastern Windows*, the intense existential angst has very much been replaced by a sense of convalescence and recovery in body and spirit. The process of remembering has become less gnawing. There is even a hint of purpose, of didacticism, as compared to the early cathartic surge that inundated *I Was at Stanley*.

Barbed Wire was written in 1982, 37 years from the 'life during'. This 164-page camp narrative offers a much more reflective subject. The wretched sense of spiritual destitution found in *I Was at Stanley* and the sense of convalescence in *Eastern Windows* are gone and in their place, there is a settled sense of reconciliation and moral alertness in *Barbed Wire*. The author says in the Preface,

> … on taking a fresh look at things past their delineation appeared less sharp — the intervening years had softened remembrances of the harsh conditions under which we lived. Clearly the time had come for the facts to be recorded.
>
> (1982, ix)

With the temporal distance from the 'life during', *Barbed Wire* not only expresses a coming to terms with history, but there is a conscious effort in this book to render her camp experience as a distinctly personalized version of historical reality that contributes and complements to the pool of official and semi-official war history. Gittins's strong sense of the autobiographical act as locating one's position in the collective historical continuity is manifested in her inclusion in the Prologue a brief four-page history[18] on the emergence of the Hong Kong society as it was in the 1930s. Her brief historical narrative traces back to the first English trading ship of the East India Company that came to China in the late 1600s, the opium trade, the birth of Hong Kong and all the way to the late 1930s with the inflow of refugees into the colony as a result of the Sino-Japanese war – this display of the autobiographer's acute consciousness of the intersection of her personal life and the larger movement of history was not so strongly felt in her earlier autobiographical works.

The structure of *Barbed Wire*, however, does not abide by the conventional narrative structure of history writing, which operates on the linearity of chronological order. While Irene Cheng's memoir depends a great deal on the whims of memory, Gittins's *Barbed Wire* is shaped 'according to related subject matter and not governed by sequence of time' (1982, ix).

In this late autobiographical act, the process of tracing details which time had dimmed has become an agreeable companion for Jean Gittins. Seemingly trifle mnemonic details become important constituents to be traced in order to construct a half-remembered self. The act of recalling or retrieving becomes an intimate companion to the 74-year-old autobiographer. At the end of *Barbed Wire*, Gittins quotes Edward Gibbon as he finished his first manuscript,

> … a sober melancholy was spread over my mind, by the idea that I had taken an everlasting leave of an old and agreeable companion …
>
> (1982,164; Gibbon, 180)

In the 50 years since the Japanese surrender, there was in fact no lack of camp memoirs/narratives on the Stanley experience. The Japanese occupation had made a painful and humiliating imprint on the collective psyche of colonial Hong Kong. It is true that the Stanley camp has been considered less blatantly gruesome when compared to the conditions of other camps in Hainan or Changi during the Japanese Occupation of the Far East. But the drastic reversal of the colonial condition during the war left painful and unspeakably humiliating memories that could only be redeemed through the healing power of language. Numerous memoirs had been published by ex-internees including Gwen Priestwood, George Baxter, Tanya Lee, Professor W. G. Sewell, as well as John Stericker, the Camp Secretary. Bitter memories of captivity and deprivation by the Japanese masters in Hong Kong had since been told and retold.

Yet what set Gittins's camp narratives apart from all these others is the very important fact that, unlike other Europeans who were herded and forced into the camp in January 1941, Gittins voluntarily submitted herself to internment in Stanley in February 1942. The narrator never really saw herself as a captive but more as someone seeking protection from outside. Her personal perception of her camp status will explain much of the difference in her psychological, emotional, philosophical and political response to camp existence.

Another distinctive feature in Gittins's camp narratives, particularly *Barbed Wire*, is that her narratives are really less an embittered recounting of humiliation but more a celebration of human resourcefulness, resilience, communal spirit, and comradeship forged during three-and-a-half years of hardship. She writes in the Preface, 'It was strange how internment drew out the best in so many, although there were others who reacted in manner so far removed from their normal behaviour that they could scarcely be recognized' (1982, ix). As she remembers it in *Barbed Wire*, the communal closeness between herself and her fellow internees seemed to transcend all her earlier experiences as a member of the elite Eurasian bourgeois. For once, she felt a heightened sense of belonging to a community. The comradely spirit that grew out of the camp, as Gittins says, 'could not possibly have been generated in other ways — certainly not during normal life in Hong Kong ... a greater tolerance towards people ... greater breadth of mind in looking at people of all kinds, all kinds of failings, and all races ...' (Birch, 1979, 32).

The prejudices against her ambiguous ethnic background, which in normal peacetime would evoke certain unease, was now much more diluted with the intimate sense of belonging. With close communal support, she did not feel the need to account for her hybrid racial identity. She no longer considered it as a source of embarrassment. To the Japanese masters, she and everyone else in the camp were all simply enemy aliens. The camp inmates, with a few minimal exceptions, were all Europeans — Europeans of different classes, educational and professional backgrounds.

A strong British patriotism was cultivated during her life in the camp — a patriotism based on her undying faith in Britain as a power that would never abandon Hong Kong. Most of the time, Jean was more like Voltaire's Candide, and was content to tend her malthoid rooftop garden instead of engaging herself in active camp politics. Yet, at other times, we see Jean irrevocably and irresistibly committing herself to the underground mission for the British resistance. The self-representation in *Barbed Wire* shifts between a listless victim of captivity and a patriot who unyieldingly resisted and outsmarted her captors. In many ways, the long years of deprivation and overcrowded conditions had loosened much of the pre-war class and gender constraints in her.

Perhaps most poignantly felt in Gittins's narrative is a sentiment that wavers between gratitude and guilt (a sentiment which cannot be found in other camp narratives). Gratitude — she was able to stay inside the camp where she did not have to worry about her next meal. Had she chosen to remain outside the camp together with the other Eurasians and Chinese, she would have had to worry about her day-to-day survival. Guilt — she was keenly conscious of the plight faced by the local Chinese outside the camp. Unlike the rest of the Ho Tung members, Jean did not claim Chinese nationality. She had, in effect, abandoned all her Chinese connections. There is a prickly guilt-like feeling as the narrator relates the ordeal experienced by her family and the Chinese in town under Japanese rule.

Unlike almost everyone in the camp, and almost everyone outside it, Jean Gittins had a choice by virtue of her Eurasianness and she exercised it, moving from one world to the other where the ordeal was at least less terrible for her. Her circumstances can be read as a classic example of the workings of a situational identity.

No other Ho Tung member was interned in Stanley. Her voluntary internment must have shocked the Ho Tung family — a family, as I discussed in the first part of this chapter, which was self-consciously Chinese in terms of their cultural as well as political identity. In Jason Wordie's interview with Florence Yeo, Florence surmised that her sister Jean's voluntary internment was a reflection of her identification with her European heritage. This issue was never discussed between the sisters (Wordie, 1997, 44). The construction of one's Chinese or European identity was not something that can be discussed openly without any unease in the Ho Tung family. As shall be seen in the Irene Cheng's chapter, the issue of whether one is Chinese or Eurasian was an unspoken taboo shared by many Ho Tungs, including the patriarch himself.

On the Gittins family's side, with the exception of Mabel Gittins and her children, no other member of the large Gittins family was interned. To judge by Jean Gittins's narrative, Mabel might have been a partially voluntary Eurasian internee, as she told Jean one day, 'But I don't regret having come into camp instead of staying out with the others' (1982, 46).[19] The two other Gittins sisters (sisters-in-law of Jean Gittins), Irene and Phyllis, remained outside the camp. They were Jean Gittins's contemporaries at DGS (1969, 85). The Gittins girls, together with the elderly Gittins couple, stayed at Emily Hahn's house on May Road during the initial months after the surrender. They were much against the idea of internment. Irene Gittins reacted quite strongly when Hahn questioned why she did not want to be interned when food and housing were getting scarce in town:

> 'But you look English … The Japanese would intern you if you wanted them to — I know lots of Eurasians who chose to go into Stanley.'
> Irene stuck out her lip. 'I'm Eurasian,' she said. 'I won't go where I'm not supposed to.'
>
> (Hahn, 1946, 102)

Irene Gittins's reply permits a kind of interesting double reading. On one level, 'I'm Eurasian, I won't go where I'm not supposed to' could be read as a kind of ethnic pride that refuses to pass as white. But on another level, it could also be read as a kind of bitterness, of being excluded from a source of survival. Many Eurasians were very much against the idea of being interned as enemy aliens. Joyce Symons, too, has never mentioned the possibility of internment.

In *Barbed Wire*, the narrator devoted much narrative space in justifying her joining the camp. By February 1942, Jean was very much on her own. Her children were now in Australia under the care of Mary King, wife of Professor Gordon King (the Dean of the Faculty of Medicine who later escaped to Free China). Her husband Billy was in the Shamshuipo camp. She had not seen much of the Ho Tung family. Sir Robert had gone to Macau 'as he often did when he needed a rest' (1982, 37).[20]

The narrator recalls how Sir Robert's house(s) on the Peak had been requisitioned by the Hong Kong government during hostilities to station a mule corps, and was extensively damaged. Idlewild, the family town house, was now the refuge of an assortment of family members and friends. The narrator does not mention why she did not go to Idlewild.[21] Two of her sisters, Vic and Grace, who were married to the Lo brothers, M. K. and Horace, also pressed her to make home with them. But they were under much stress and anxiety themselves. M. K. Lo, being a prominent member of the former colonial government, was kept in solitary confinement and his family had been placed under strict surveillance. The narrator admits that her own close associations with the European internees in the Stanley and ShamShuiPo camps 'would only add to their embarrassment' (1982, 38). Relationships and connections with enemy aliens were a constant threat to the security of those outside of the camps. Her youngest sister Florence was in an even less enviable position. Her husband, K. C. Yeo, was a senior medical officer, who was working under the pressure of the Japanese. His loyalty was constantly being questioned and interrogated. Florence, with her husband in constant danger, had little means of support for her three young children. Her situation was quite desperate — joining her was out of the question.

On the practical side, with the cost of even the barest necessities rising each day, Jean Gittins was not sure how she would be able to feed and house herself. As to going back to her own apartment in King's Park, a place which she and Billy had taken after the children had been sent to Australia, that too was out of the question. It was not only badly looted but was also now occupied by Japanese officers. Unlike her sister Irene who eventually worked for a mining-venture in Mukden taken over by the Japanese, Jean Gittins was unwilling to seek employment with the Japanese (38). Speaking as a member of the local Hong Kong community, she says, 'we knew that in spite of all the talk of Utopian conditions, many of its residents, including some of my family, had decided in less than a year after the occupation that co-prosperity was not for them' (127).

Should Jean go into internment, there was also the hope, no matter how slim, that there would be an exchange of prisoners of war. In that event, she could go to Australia to her children. Jean was not unaware of the delicate circumstances surrounding Eurasians and their entry into Stanley Camp. It is a situation where she must assert her choice of identity to be

British, and to temporary camouflage the Chineseness and Eurasianness in her. Dr Selwyn Clark, the Director of Medical Service, at first objected to Jean entering the camp. Sir Robert would never forgive him, he told her. But the director quickly changed his views after Jean's revelation of her part in the escape of Professor Gordon King to China. Her staying outside of camp would greatly increase the chance of being found out by the Japanese. Freedom and safety now lay within the barbed wire, not without. Jean assumed a new identity with the help of Dr Selwyn Clark, who took the precaution of changing her name slightly: instead of Mrs W. M. Gittins, as on the University Relief Hospital staff list, he registered her as Miss Jean Gittins in her admission to the Tweed Bay Hospital in the camp (1969, 136). This gesture would remove any Japanese suspicion about Jean's racial eligibility to be interned. With a European maiden name, she was now more 'authentically' European in the eyes of the Japanese.

The Japanese authorities had, in the beginning, been against admitting Eurasians into the camp. General Myaki of the Gendarmerie was reported to have said that all Eurasians and Chinese would be required to leave the camp (Stericker, n.d. Chap. 4, 3). But their policy towards Eurasians was not consistent. As discussed in the last chapter, some Eurasians were already ejected from the Chinese brothels/boarding houses on the Western waterfront where the Europeans were first incarcerated. Inside Stanley camp, the Eurasians and the few Chinese British (mostly wives of British internees) remained. The attitude of the Japanese authorities towards the interned Eurasians varied from time to time and from camp to camp. There was the constant question of what to do with the Eurasians and how to fit them into the racial hierarchy under the New Order. In George Hall's entry dated 7 September 1942, written while he was interned at the Shamshuipo POW camp, he wrote:

> ... All Eurasians are to report at once to the Camp Office. There we (about 60) were asked by the chief Japanese interpreter why we were not registered as Chinese, but British. I replied that our respective C.O.'s had commanded us to do so last January when filling in the form as BRITISH - WHITE, I added that, under remarks, I had written *'Hong Kong born, British Eurasian'*.

> (Hall, 1992, 65)

Seven months later in February 1943, three Eurasian brothers were released from the camp (65). These sudden unpredictable changes in policy and attitude towards interned Eurasians were quite common during the Occupation. The arbitrary decisions of deciding who is European and who is not clearly illustrate the instability of category frontiers in a discourse about 'race' which was supposed to be on a scientific and objective footing. (The Japanese, however, had themselves invoked Western scientific racism to declare themselves ethnically and culturally superior to their Asian neighbours [Clemons, 217].)

Within the community of the camp inmates, this issue of whether the Chinese and Eurasians should stay or not had been discussed at various meetings of the Temporary Camp Committee (later the British Communal Council). John Stericker, the Camp Secretary, wrote in his diary not without some cynicism how the issue was settled. 'And so, the Chinese stayed, the Eurasians stayed and the dogs stayed, as did overcrowding, and shortage of fuel, food, and everything else' (n.d. Chap. 1, 3–4). The more conservative elements of the community were evidently quite contemptuous towards the Eurasians, who had taken up places where they did not belong. This decision reached by the British Communal Council again drew out the conflicting inclusionary/exclusionary tendencies in the British colonial sentiments discussed in the last chapter. The liberal inclusionary principle of the British colonials might want to include the Eurasians, but at times their attitude towards the actual Eurasian presence in the camp, spoke quite the opposite.

⊶⊷○⊶⊷

Jean Gittins was admitted into the Stanley Camp on 20 February 1942. Looking back to that three-and-a-half years of her interned life, the narrator writes, 'I cannot remember a single occasion when I experienced real regret' (1982, 41).

The Stanley camp that she had joined was no exclusive European reserve. There were 2,700 internees (2,325 British, 290 Americans, 60 Dutch, and later the group of Norwegians left in Hong Kong[22] after the Americans had been repatriated). The number of British internees was many more than expected (Endacott, 1978, 199–200). The Japanese intended the term 'British Nationals' to mean Europeans and were surprised at the number of Asians who claimed to be British. The Japanese authorities evidently seemed to have difficulty in separating race and nationality. The British section included Chinese, Portuguese, Eurasians and people of various other origins, many being families of prisoners of war (199–200).

Life for these internees, as described by Stericker, was very much like the life of a group of passengers from a large ocean liner wrecked on a desert island, out of contact with the world for years on end. Everyone is stranded, from first class passengers to the steerage (Stericker, n.d., Author's Note, 2). Everyone is suddenly reduced to a certain equality — equality based on hunger, deprivation and isolation. Brown recalls what he witnessed in the early days of the camp. A millionaire businessman and a university professor were scrounging in a refuse pile. Both were bearded and dressed in ragged clothes. An old shoe turned up. It had a great hole in the sole and no heel, but it contained a serviceable piece of leather. These two dignified men quarreled, screamed and shouted at each other, bitterly denounced each other as thieves, and nearly came to blows in an acrimonious dispute over the old shoe (Brown, 12).[23] This was the state of existence for the once respected and distinguished Europeans in the colony. As Gittins says, 'internment certainly reduced us to a state of pauperism compared to what we had been used to ...' (1982, 149). She recalls numerous cases where people would completely depart from their normal behavior. A clergyman and his wife had occupied the cubicle of a widow and her baby and no amount of pleading would budge them (47). The police force abandoned its law enforcement duty and became a law-breaking racket within the camp. They resorted to stealing supplies at the godowns and selling them at black market price to the internees (60).

Jean's consciousness in the camp can now basically be read on three levels. On one level, she remained the Eurasian female. She remained very much connected with her role as a wife now separated from her husband. She was constantly worrying whether her husband Billy would approve of her decision of joining the camp. She made winter wear for Billy from old clothes that her sister sent her. She formed a kind of female and ethnic solidarity with her Eurasian sister-in-law Mabel Gittins, helping her with her three children, such as giving Cantonese lessons to the 11-year-old Michael, thus resuming the nurturing role of a female as culturally expected. She engaged in daily domestic chores such as picking out weevils from food, grinding rice, gathering bits of fuel, rolling cigarettes out of ends mixed with dried leaves, killing cockroaches, debugging beds and queuing for water and food (Gittins, 1969, 152).

On another level, Gittins saw herself as an utterly de-classed and, in some ways, de-gendered individual completely cut off from her family, husband and children. With the deterioration in diet, many women like Jean suffered severe hormonal dysfunction, which resulted in a cessation of menstruation (Gittins, 1982, 92). Her earlier identities as wife, mother, daughter became blurred, abstracted, almost obliterated in her mental and physical isolation wherein she found herself leading 'a vague, perplexing and debilitating existence' (149). Sensitive to her local ties outside the camp, she kept to herself and devoted her time to nurturing her rooftop garden, staying away from camp politics. But most of the time, like the rest of the 3,000 odd inmates, her consciousness was that of someone in captivity, in isolation, completely severed and disconnected from the outside world, from the progress of civilization, from the flow of time and history. It is an existence of 'not knowing where we were headed nor what the next day would bring' (149). (The collective 'we' is always used in her camp narrative, which suggests that amid the despair and apathy, the sense of community remained strong).

On the third level of consciousness, she felt very much a patriot and loyalist, eagerly participating in the communal activities of the British internees, and even involved in the British resistance underground movement; a Eurasian who had proved again trustworthiness as interpreter and loyalist for the colonial government. Jean was involved several times in the translation into Chinese messages for the underground movement. On one of these occasions, it was a request for immediate intervention by the British Ambassador in Chungking. Jean was warned of the risks involved by the former CID Superintendent. The narrator recalls how the superintendent said, "'I don't have to tell you the consequences, but I am duty bound to warn you of the risk." He ran his forefinger across his neck. "There are not many who would be willing to accept the challenge. Do you still want to do it?'" (144) It was a patriotic call for Jean as a British subject. By accepting the risk of punishment and death, she had abandoned her personal responsibility to stay alive for her husband interned in Shamshuipo and her children in Australia. It is in a way the great vindication of her Eurasianness, both interpreter and loyalist.

On the whole, Gittins's camp narratives emphasize very little on humiliation and indignation. Her narratives are suffused with memory of the close communal feeling and a strong patriotism she grew to embrace.

Within the British community, efforts were made to maintain a kind of normalcy. Classes of different sorts were organized. Jean took Mandarin classes. (The irony is that instead of learning the language from a Chinese master like she did when she was young, she was now learning it from a British Sinologist). The author has in fact included in *Eastern Windows* an illustration of her closely packed Chinese writings. Both Jean Gittins and Joyce Symons tend to show mnemonic pride in their re-connection with the Chinese language during the war years — a language and a culture which both of them, in their own different ways, had felt alienated from.

Plays and public performances were also organized by the British internees. The Japanese authorities had asked the internees to prepare a performance for some important visitors. *The Death of Nelson*[24] was staged. The Japanese visitors seemed to understand sufficient English to follow the gist of the story. However, Gittins recalls with amusement how they seemed to be in some doubt as to whether or not to join in the applause. She writes:

> When the audience rose to sing, 'Land of Hope and Glory' at the conclusion (we weren't allowed to sing 'God Save the King') they stood to attention. They must have regretted this later because, unable to find any reasonable excuse to fault the performance, they punished us just the same.
>
> (1982, 115)

The narrator relishes very much the memory of how she and the British internees managed to perplex and annoy their Japanese masters by their subtle display of British patriotism.[25] In fact, Gittins seems critical towards the Japanese not only in their general control of the camp and the colony at large, but in their tendency of hankering after British ways. 'Wittingly or unwittingly they aped British customs. Even observance of the anniversary of the Mikado's birth was organized on similar lines to those which previously marked our King's Birthday celebrations' (1982, 121). In Gittins's eyes, the Japanese seemed to be appropriating a colonial 'whiteness' in their emulating the British and their colonial ways. Gittins is trying to distinguish between an authentic hegemonic colonialism (good) and an inauthentic enforced colonialism (bad), though both powers actually do similar things (celebrate their monarch's birthday, name streets in their own language, etc.). Yet despite what Gittins believes to be the authentic hegemonic colonialism, there was in fact very little loyalty to the British colonial government at that time, whether outside the camp amongst the Chinese population, or within the British internees.[26] Ironically, people like herself, who had never been fully accepted by the British, continued to demonstrate a strong loyalty for a disgraced and defeated colonial government.

The Eurasian internee came to identify strongly with England — a place that she had only briefly visited at the age of 16 when she went for a medical operation in 1924. Her bond with her fellow captives had forged in her a British patriotism that did not require any actual association and connection with the geographical fatherland. Jean's patriotism here could perhaps be seen as another form of what Wang Gungwu describes as 'marginal nationalism' (2001).

In most camp narratives by British internees, the issue of repatriation is often remembered with bitterness and anger. Yet in Gittins's memoir, in place of bitterness, we have resignation — a resignation that is supported through her constant use of the pronoun 'we' and 'us'.

The reluctance of the interned Colonial Secretary, F. C. Gimson, to endorse the principle of repatriation on the grounds that the initiative for repatriation must come from the Imperial government in London and not from him (Emerson, 66) had a very demoralizing effect on the British internees. Many argued that their residence in the colony was temporary; they were citizens of the United Kingdom and so had no allegiance to the Hong Kong government. Repatriation, they maintained, was their right …(Lindsay, 1981, 40). But Gimson insisted that it was for the interest of the Imperial government 'to maintain a nucleus of British residents in Hong Kong, not only as a matter of principle, but because it was felt that the morale of the Chinese in town and their interest in the Allied cause, would be more fully maintained by the continued nearness of the British civilians and the former Hong Kong government …' (Stericker, n.d., Chap. 8, 5).

Watching the repatriation of the Americans in 1942 and the Canadians in 1943 had left the remaining British inmates with a paralyzed reality of being forsaken and forgotten. A sense of fatalism pervades Gittins's memory as she recalls the series of repatriations they witnessed:

> I think that repeated disappointments had made us lose interest — it almost seemed as if we no longer cared. As we went up to the cemetery and sat by the casuarina trees to watch them board the *Tei-a-Maru*, which was to take them to Goa for exchange, we knew that nothing more substantial than the verbal messages they carried would ever reach the outside world. Perhaps we had become conditioned into believing that direct contact was not so important after all — we did not even question why no Britisher had been included.
>
> (1982, 133)

What puzzles the reader in the case of Jean is her perception of repatriation. Did it really apply to her? Was repatriation her right considering her status as a Hong Kong resident and her voluntary internment? And besides, strictly speaking, what would be her home country? For Jean, Hong Kong was her home. Up till then, she had not known any other home outside of Hong Kong. Her children had been shipped to Australia passing as 'pures'. Billy was in Shamshuipo camp. Jean Gittins does not comment on the issue.

Whatever hardship Jean had endured in the camp, it is always remembered and allayed with a redeeming sense of comradeship she felt in the British community. Yet her story of camaraderie, of collective human resourcefulness, resilience and mutual support is interspersed with occasional voices of despair, loneliness and awkwardness as a single Eurasian female. The unvanquishable collective voice of the 'we' the British is often interrupted by the lonely voice of the 'I' the Eurasian.

As their first Easter approached, a limited number of parcels were permitted to be sent over to the Shamshuipo Camp through the Welfare Office. This was known only to a favoured few of which Jean was included. As a way to help the Shamshuipo internees to know the whereabouts of their wives and families, Jean had ingeniously compiled a list of all the Stanley internees and concealed them in the folds of a toilet paper roll. But ingenuity was no match for envy and malice. Her scheme was discovered and her desire to help was looked upon with suspicion and interpreted as betrayal.

> There must have been someone who resented my being included
> — or perhaps my look of satisfaction had antagonized them.
> Early the following morning I was summoned to appear before
> the former Colonial Secretary, now the Representative of
> Internees.
>
> (1982, 131)

The narrator does not explain why some people resented her being included in the parcel day for Easter. It could very well be something to do with the Eurasianness on her face, which automatically reminded them of her taking up the space and resources in a crowded camp. A Eurasian being one of the favoured few to send a parcel to Shamshuipo clearly would invoke certain resentment. The narrator recalls how the Representative of Internees reprimanded her on how she could be so selfish as to expose the entire camp to possible reprisals in the event of discovery. Had she no consideration for the women and children who were suffering enough without her adding to it? Since it was her first offence, Jean was let off with a caution. The narrator says, 'I was in disgrace, but I was unrepentant' (131). She was no doubt sensitive too — given the conditions of her arrival — to the reproach of not showing proper regard for the interests of the community she had voluntarily joined. Her loyalty and desire to relieve the anxiety of the interned families was interpreted as betrayal by the camp committees. Her camp memories seem inevitably to turn at every point into a story of identity, loyalty, and betrayal.

⊱━◆━○━◆━⊰

Gittins has only once mentioned the Eurasian community within the camp. It is not narrated with the collective pronoun of 'we', but more as someone observing the racialist sentiments that existed within the camp. With her local connections as a member of the Ho Tung family, Jean enjoyed certain privileges over other internees. Her sisters continued to send parcels to her. And before she went into camp, she had left a number of signed cheques with the Russian students so that they could use the proceeds to procure food and supplies to be sent to Billy in Shamshuipo camp and to her in Stanley camp (1982, 34). Like the Portuguese and other non-European British Nationals, the Eurasian presence in the camp was seen very much as a kind of colonial burden to be borne grudgingly:

> Some of the British felt that were it not for the many Eurasians in the camp there would be sufficient food for them. Racial discrimination had by no means moderated in the face of general adversity, and some people were too bigoted to understand that the food was provided, not in lump quantity, but rationed by the Japanese according to the number of mouths to be fed. ... They were envious not of the large business houses whose parcels came regularly and had to be paid for at the end of the war — the main target of their resentment was against the Eurasian community whose relatives in town sent parcels from sheer solicitude and often at much personal sacrifice.
>
> (1982, 66)

This racist treatment can, of course, also be attributed to the reversal of class and privilege within the camp. While most European internees found themselves losing their privilege they once possessed over their Chinese and Eurasian subjects, the Eurasians inside the camp were still able to retain their middleman privilege of resorting to their Chinese connection outside the camp.

＞━╌━━━━○━━━━╌━＜

When the lonely voice of the Eurasian captive speaks, the voice of communal strength recedes to the background. The departure of the Americans and Canadians did not seem to have such a demoralizing effect for her as for other British internees. However, when she received the information about the departure of her closest sister Grace into Free China, her voice retrieving the incident is suffused with a crippling sense of being abandoned, of being utterly alone.

One day, Jean received a parcel that contained Grace's padded Chinese gown — a *mien-po [mian pao]*. A few days later a stranger approached her without a word at the Indian quarters and handed her a letter from Grace telling her of their departure.

> The world grew suddenly bleak and empty: as long as Grace was in
> Hong Kong, I had at least a psychological prop. With her in China,
> I was completely on my own.
>
>   (1982, 128)

Since hostilities began, some of her siblings such as Eva, Vic and Grace had
become important emotional sources of support for Jean. Eva, who worked
for the Red Cross in China, was stranded in Hong Kong after the outbreak
of the war. She had gone over to the Shamshuipo camp herself and sighted
Billy on the other side of the fence. Vic and Grace willingly risked their
own safety to send parcels to Jean in the Stanley camp, when associations
with enemy aliens were not encouraged (65). The joy of receiving parcels
from her family meant much more to Jean than the actual food supplies
received (64). It was a physical reminder of her identity as a member of the
powerful Ho Tung family network and a member of the local elite, which
had seemed at times so remote to her during her internment. As Grace and
the other Ho Tung members left for Free China, Jean felt, for the first time
in her life, completely cut off from the Ho Tung kinship. She was completely
alone.

━━◆━○━◆━━

One common image found in camp narratives is that of a ragged and
half-starved European furtively following a Japanese soldier for the cigarette
butt. W. Brown explains that this business of scrounging for discarded
cigarette butts had long been a recognized business in China. Ragged Chinese
roamed the streets of pre-war Hong Kong assiduously collecting butts and
storing them in stained paper bags. When a bagful had been gathered it was
taken to a cigarette maker and sold for a penny (Brown, 132). But for the
ruling class to assume this lowly business was a collectively humiliating
experience on the colonial consciousness.

Brown recalls how gradually the self-conscious degradation involved
in diving for cigarette butts were abandoned:

> I have seen women who had been my gracious hostesses in their
> homes on the Peak, who had served the most elaborate of meals,
> fighting grimly for possession of a wasted cigarette end. The Jap

soldiers delighted in smoking in our presence and observing Englishmen and Americans watching the curling smoke like hungry dogs eyeing a meaty bone. A soldier would throw away a half-burned cigarette contemptuously. The watching men would be torn between pride and greed, and finally one would step forward furtively and slip the long end into his pocket.

(Brown, 133)

These images are also recalled and described in the personal narratives of Jean Gittins and two other Eurasian internees. However each has a different reaction and interpretation to this humiliating image of the once-dignified colonial ruling class. Their responses reflect their respective pre-war attitude towards the colonial rulers and their sociopolitical position within the hierarchy. Tanya Lee, a Eurasian secretary (who attended DGS and later Maryknoll Convent), expresses her utter shock and horror at the unseemly compromise in her memoir:

I thought about the senior British Government official I had seen on more than one occasion, trailing at a safe distance behind a Jap sentry, eyes darting and furtive, waiting to pounce on a cast-off cigarette butt tossed away, at times half-smoked by the Jap, who then revelled at the grovelling in the gutter of this desperate Englishman. Such degradation, and the ultimate humiliation, all for the craving for a fag-end. Once, a sentry had sneered, laughed, then slammed his rubber-soled boot on to the hand reaching down for the butt, but the middle-aged Englishman did not let go and, with a Jap kick on his backside, he clutched the stub and fled.

(Lee, 173)

Jean Gittins remembers how colonial officers had scrounged around for discarded cigarettes butts. Yet, the narrator deems it necessary to present their side of the picture to prevent the readers from judging them too harshly. She is more ready to defend them than Lee:

They claimed that a meal which did not satisfy only made them feel hungrier, whereas a cigarette would act as an antidote to their craving for food. All butts were saved, even those discarded by other people and normally respectable citizens and former senior government officers would think nothing of stooping to pick up a butt from the roadside in camp.

(1982, 79)

Clifford Matthews, a Eurasian who was interned at the Shamshiupo camp, sees the humiliating act of picking up cigarette butts as a prefiguration to the end of imperialism. He says in an interview:

> I remember in Sham Shui Po I saw a line up of all Chinese outside the camp, and I could see it was the end of Imperialism in the Far East. They['ve] seen the foreigners [English etc.] being humiliated[:] Some of us picking up cigarettes butt [sic] which were thrown down by the Japanese sentry. Even there and [I] saw it [:] obviously this was the end of the whole superior attitude. Afterward, it got to be different, it got to be something else, I think that's happened because it had to. I just said that there [sic], [the Chinese were] standing there watching us and there we were humiliated. The Japanese, obviously could shout at us and kicked [sic] us around. They just did that, so there we were humiliated. All of them, they could see that we were nothing special, we were just human beings. That was clear to me that there will be another world after the war.
>
> (Matthews, Track 4, 1996)

These three Eurasian internees had very different reactions to the image of scrounging for cigarette butts. Jean Gittins, closely connected with the colonial elite, sees it as an essential antidote and a temporary compromise rather than degradation. She sees it as a fully understandable and perhaps necessary behavior in the normal conditions of the camp. Tanya Lee was less sympathetic. She could not accept such a drastic reversal of behaviour from British colonials. Being a witness to their degradation had seriously affected her earlier admiration for the dignity of this ruling class. Matthews, a Eurasian POW in Hong Kong and Japan and subsequently an emeritus Professor of Chemistry at the University of Illinois, sees it as a prefiguration of the end of the colonial era. His use of first person plural suggests a strong identification with the European ruling class. His consciousness of watching Chinese eyes clearly betrays an early colonial anxiety towards a world without colonial divide. This juxtaposition of the different views demonstrates how members of the same ethnic group could respond very differently in internment where the former colonial structures were no longer in force. Ideology cuts across class and ethnic group solidarity. Tanya Lee and Clifford Matthews had lost their confidence and respect for the formerly formidable colonial power. Jean Gittins, however, remained the loyalist to the end.

The end of internment means hope, freedom and a new beginning in most camp narratives. But in Jean Gittins's memoirs, the end of internment means a freedom that brings with it fear and loneliness.

The fall of Manila in July 1945 had a very strong impact on the internees because the Philippine Islands were only hours away. It was at this time that the Japanese attitude changed dramatically:

> Arrogance gradually gave way to an apologetic attempt at friendliness. They blamed one another openly: 'Very sorry, but we are not responsible for your treatment, you know.'
>
> (1982, 148)

A copy of the *Hong Kong News*, dated Thursday, 16 August 1945, was smuggled in by the Formosan guards[27] who had now became very friendly with the inmates; it reported a broadcast by the Emperor of Japan where his Imperial Highness had decided to end hostilities (50). Franklin Gimson, the interned Colonial Secretary and the most senior internee at Stanley, quickly declared himself as Acting Governor. Like Captain Elliot a century before, he took this step without any authority from London, created a kind of *fait accompli* which no body felt able to reverse (Morris, 1988, 258).

Visitors from town and other camps came pouring in. The police officers donned what was left of their uniforms. The colonial government salvaged their tattered remains. Jean Gittins's sister Vic and brother-in-law M. K. were among the first to come into the camp to see her. 'Their smiles broadened as we shouted a greeting, but the pallor of their complexion spoke more eloquently than words could have done' (Gittins, 1982, 151). Jean had no lack of visitors. Her sister Florence and brother-in-law K. C. came to visit her as well as some of the family servants (152). The Russian student, Sergei Hohlov, whom she was eventually to marry, walked the long miles from the university to Stanley to bring her a pan of curried chicken (152).[28]

The release from physical internment, however, was replaced by a new mental and spiritual internment. The narrator recalls having a strange sense of depression during her departure from the camp:

> Now that I was leaving, I felt conscious of a tinge of regret. The years had been filled with hardship and sorrow, but we had found

compensation in shared troubles which had bonded us through every
crisis. The years held memories I would not want entirely to forget.
(155)

In the three-and-a-half years of material and physical privation, the
emotional bond between her and the inmates had provided her with a strong
sense of security of belonging to a community, albeit a community in
captivity. It is perhaps a sense of belonging that she never had so intimately
felt. The parting with this community suddenly created a vacuum which
she had to deal with. The Ho Tung family had scattered. Billy had been
drafted to Japan. The children were in Australia. Jean was quite apprehensive
about this new freedom.

She wanted to wait in Hong Kong for the news of Billy. However, a
new regulation required all former internees to produce certificates of fitness
before they were permitted to stay (159). Unable to clear the health
regulation, Jean was required to leave for Australia immediately. She was at
that time completely ignorant of what happened to Billy Gittins while Dr
Selwyn Clark and Vice Chancellor Sloss had already heard that he had not
survived. In the absence of any official confirmation, they kept quiet and
arranged for the immediate repatriation of Jean to Australia where she would
at least be near her children when the ordeal of coping with Billy's death
came.

Filled with optimism at resuming her pre-camp identities as wife and mother
and the interrupted life as member of the privileged Eurasian network, the
narrator recalls, 'I did not think I would be away for long; it would only be
a matter of meeting up with Billy and the children — perhaps a brief holiday
with them — and we would all be home again' (160). The narrator's memory
of that dolorous innocence and woeful ignorance of her own widowhood
had quite darkened her memory of those early days of release. Her hopeful
expectation of family union was a painful irony to what was awaiting her.
This dramatic split between the two voices — the knowing narrating voice
and the innocent narrated voice is an intense and dramatic autobiographical
moment. Her ignorance during those early days of release becomes the
ironical harbinger of the 'life after'.

Joyce Symons's honeymoon 'repatriation' provides a powerful contrast to Jean Gittins's shattering 'repatriation'. The narrator recalls the moment the HMS *Vindex* sailed into Sydney Harbour. Cheers and sirens greeted them from every side. Small craft of every description had come out to meet them, following them like the fleet of an armada. 'Hope and expectation ran high but to many it was tinged with a natural trepidation. But my own part, I brushed aside my fears and looked towards the future in blind faith' (162).

The crushing blow of cruel reality was waiting for Jean in the beautiful Sydney harbour. The narrator recalls, 'A military band played for us while representatives of the Australian Red Cross Society and the Department of Social Services attended to the more mundane matters of our welfare'. She saw Billy's sister Charlotte at the pier breathlessly running towards her. The narrator recalls, 'She now threw her arms around me and began to weep' (1969, 161). The universe collapsed for Jean at that moment — an emotionally shocked ex-internee and a single mother in a strange land.

Peace brought to Jean Gittins a new form of spiritual internment. It was a period of destitute, acute melancholia and hopeless weariness in Australia (69).

Despite the fact that the Hong Kong government representative in Sydney had been giving a 'resume of conditions in the Colony' to discourage intending repatriates to return, the Eurasian ex-internee was too homesick and heartsick to be deterred. In less than a year after that woeful landing in Sydney, Jean returned to Hong Kong on a 'health trip' for 35 days. She sailed on M.V. *Nellore*, which was carrying repatriates to Hong Kong.

> At first glance, Kowloon seemed fairly normal. But, instead of a fleet of modern buses at the pier by the Star Ferry, we were met by a host of rickshaws, tricycles and bicycles, all clamouring for patronage. Again we were independent. Horace's car was standing waiting. In ten minutes we were home.
>
> (90)

Jean felt like 'the returning prodigal' for the moment (160). The tumultuous crowds of jostling Chinese rickshaw pullers and tricycle drivers once more became some noisy Chinese crowds in the background. The 'life before' had suddenly come back to her as she came back to Hong Kong. She had once again become the privileged member of the Eurasian elite in Hong Kong.

Her visit to Hong Kong had the emotionally reinvigorating power to help her in settling as a new immigrant in Australia. Yet, after her dream-like visit to Hong Kong in the summer of 1946, her re-entry into Australia rendered her acutely conscious of her ambiguous ethnicity in her new homeland.

> "'You are partly Chinese, are you not, Mrs. Gittins?' And without waiting for me to reply he added: 'What percentage?'
> 'Fifty per cent. But what has this to do with my passport?'
> 'It has a great deal to do with your entry into Australia. Are you sure that it is fifty per cent? Couldn't you make it a little less?'
> 'I am sorry, officer. Not forty-eight per cent nor yet forty-nine per cent but fifty per cent.'"
>
> (201)

It is very probable that Jean herself might not know the exact racial distribution of her genealogy and indeed her quixotic insistence on claiming exactly an equal percentage of Chinese and non-Chinese 'blood' just points up to the fatuity of thinking in terms of a constitutively divisible identity. The narrator seems to enjoy a kind of moral and ethnic satisfaction as she recalls how she had refused to compromise her Chinese heritage. In doing so, Jean was upholding her childhood vision of Utopian hybridity — a harmonious, equal and non-hierarchal blend of two races — indivisible and inalienable from each other. The two antitheses have synthesized in her and neither one can be separated or singled out from or privileged over the other. Jean wanted to be a non-divisible Eurasian.

Her answer, of course, had the unwelcome consequence of obliging her to report at regular intervals to the Immigration Office in Melbourne if she wished to remain in Australia.[29] She and her children were summoned to report to the Immigration Office eventually to be assured of their eligibility to stay. But why did the Australian officials want to see the children?

> I gathered that the children's presence was required so that a check could be made of their appearance. If they were to remain in the country and possibly become Australians, they had to look the part!
>
> (1969, 202)

The children passed again the racial test that they had took six years ago when they came to Australia as evacuees.

This incident as experienced by Jean quite dramatically calls into question again the arbitrariness of 'race' as a category and as a dividing standard to distinguish people from one another.

The White Australia Policy was a racial discourse based on the assumption that racial distribution within a person is something mathematically computable and divisible. On the surface, the Immigration Officer, was affirming this Australian racial discourse in carrying out his duty to ascertain Jean's racial constitution. However, in his kindly prompting to Jean to make her Chinese 'blood' less than fifty percent, he was in a way interrogating this very racial discourse or at least admitting it to be in fact a matter of discourse, of which words to use. By his appeal to Jean, he was also acknowledging the fact that these exact racial percentages were not real, no matter how hard all the racial 'science' of the nineteenth and twentieth centuries had tried to make them exist.

Jean, on the other hand, in her refusal to comply with the officer's suggestion to lessen the percentage of her Chinese blood, was deliberately and ironically subscribing to a racial discourse that believes in the essential biological differentiation of race computable in a person. She was exactly fifty percent Chinese if she said so. Yet, the very fact that she could fix her own racial identity by the assertion of a percentage number to the Officer deconstructs and exposes the inanity of the White Australia policy and the race discourse that supported it.

Her identity at this stage is no longer situational or strategic, but a willful choice to be neither, nor is it a refusal to be fixed, labelled into any racial category. It is a decision in favour of undecidability and indeterminacy.

Excerpt From *Stanley: Behind Barbed Wire*

Plate 5 Jean Gittins,
author of *Stanley:*
Behind Barbed Wire, courtesy of
Hong Kong University Press.

When the Second World War broke out in Europe in 1939, it did little to disrupt Hong Kong's normal routine, but after the Allied retreat from Dunkirk in May 1940, the realization came that if, or rather when, trouble reached the colony no help from Britain could be expected.

Preparations against such an emergency, begun in a somewhat desultory fashion after the Munich crisis and the fall of Canton in 1938, assumed a more urgent note. Four regiments of regular troops were stationed in the colony but many of its residents, eager to help in the defence of their home and country, now enlisted in the Hong Kong Volunteer Defence Corps (HKVDC) which adopted a more active training programme. My husband, Billy, had joined a year before. Always a realist, he said he wished to be ready when the time came. A great deal of publicity had been drawn to air-raid precautions. Renewed lectures were given, practical training sessions intensified, and work on the construction of tunnels for shelters for the masses was speeded up. The Medical Department was deeply involved in an extensive programme. A scheme for the clearing of major government hospitals for the treatment of mass casualties necessitated planning for large institutions to be converted into relief hospitals at a moment's notice to take care of patients who were not casualties. Other institutions nearer the expected fields of action were to be casualty clearing stations. Staffing and equipment and related supportive bodies had to be worked out. Organizations for the control of transport, supplies and general civilian care were formed. Most urgent of all was a sudden announcement by the government in July ordering the registration of British women and children for immediate departure to Australia. The order was addressed to civilians as well as to service personnel; only persons engaged in the essential services were exempt. This made no secret of the view taken by those in authority of the seriousness of the situation. The colony was really shaken out of its complacency but, as few wished to be evacuated, there was an immediate rush to join any organization which might provide an excuse to stay.

The question of who was 'British' created doubt in some quarters and downright dismay in others. Although anyone born in the colony was legally entitled to British nationality and was eligible for a British passport, mention of Australia raised at once the question of her White Australia policy and enquiries at registration centres threw no light on the matter. Official announcements were purposely camouflaged to give us to understand that it concerned everyone but, in actual fact, the order applied only to those of 'pure' British descent. And yet the Volunteers, for instance, had been told specifically that, in the event of hostilities, they would be regarded as service personnel and promises had been made that their families would be taken care of in the same way as those of regular troops. However, the fact remained that a large number did not come under the heading of *pure* British descent.

Of Hong Kong's one and a half million cosmopolitan population* the Chinese comprised ninety-eight per cent. For the rest, European nationals, including Americans, totalled about 11,500, with over 7,000 Indians, 3,000 Macau Portuguese and about 1,000 others. Included among the Chinese and Europeans was the local Eurasian community, people of a mixed Anglo-Chinese heritage, most of whom claimed Chinese nationality whilst many regarded themselves as British. The tragedy of it all was that until after the Second World War, when so many of the local community died for the Allied cause, racial discrimination was such that they were accepted by neither British nor Chinese, although the Chinese were not so discourteous as to disclaim them.

---

* Davis, S. G., *Hong Kong in its Geographical Setting* (London, Collins, 1949).

Both Billy's family and mine were of this community. My father, although a British knight of many years' standing, held very strong views on the subject. He and others who thought likewise threw in their lot wholeheartedly with the Chinese. The Gittinses, on the other hand, took a more tolerant attitude. Other people's opinions did not worry them — they accepted the situation of their birth, lived their own lives and were the happier for it. Neither Billy's sisters, three of whom had husbands in the HKVDC, nor I regarded the registration order as being applicable to us, but many of our friends adopted the view that they were families of service personnel, obeyed the summons to register and within a few days had sailed. On reaching Manila, evacuees were divided into two groups: those of pure European descent were sent on to Australia; the Eurasian families were returned to Hong Kong. It was then explained that Australia could not be persuaded to give them refuge even in the event of open war. Thus a delicate situation was handled with bungling indelicacy. It did much to damage the morale of the local Volunteers.

My own position as far as the registration problem was concerned had been perfectly clear. I knew that as family of a member of the HKVDC our children and I would become the responsibility of the British government in the event of hostilities but, until such a situation occurred, we were entirely responsible for ourselves. Moreover, I was my father's daughter and, irrespective of any influence he might have in Hong Kong, the fact of his claim to Chinese nationality would automatically rule out the possibility of my entry into Australia.

My father, Sir Robert Ho Tung, was born into a family of humble circumstances when Hong Kong had been a British colony for over two decades. It had overcome its early difficulties and was on the way to being Britain's principal outpost in the Far East. The early years had been a period of preparation: public utilities and medical and health services were developed; schools, hospitals, police stations and churches were built; banking, shipping, dockyard, and even shipbuilding facilities had been established. In this healthy economic climate commercial enterprises flourished.

As a boy my father attended the Central School, the leading educational institution which was later renamed Queen's College. He had a Chinese upbringing but learnt English at school. He told us that lessons began at 6 a.m. in the summer and at 6.30 during the winter months. His mother gave him five cash (half of one cent) each day for his lunch. He would spend two or three cash only on some small bite to allay his hunger — the rest would be saved. This habit of resolute frugality was to remain a guiding principle in future business dealings.

He began adult life as a schoolteacher but soon left to join the Chinese Maritime Customs in Canton where he first came into contact with foreign business community. He was at once interested in and greatly attracted to the world of commerce for which he seemed to have a natural propensity. Leaving the Chinese Maritime Customs, he accepted a junior position with Jardine, Matheson and Company, a firm which had led the foreign traders for half a century. Father's knowledge of English together with his innate intelligence proved invaluable as a liaison between the Company and the Chinese. He rose to be Chinese Manager before he was thirty, and, indeed, his association with the 'Princely Hong' (*hong* is the Chinese name for a large firm) lasted throughout his long career.

Father knew what he wanted from life and possessed the ability and perseverance to get it. Besides, his connection with Jardine's offered plenty of scope for foresight and judgment — it was a time when opportunity begged at one's door. From his humble background he became the doyen of the Eurasian community and was made a Justice of the Peace in 1899 at the age of 35. The onset of poor health at this stage curtailed his activities. He developed a mysterious digestive ailment — a form of sprue — which was thought to have been caused by prolonged deprivation of a proper diet during adolescence. It was almost to cost him his life. However, with Mother's care and devotion, and his own indomitable spirit, he recovered sufficiently to carry out business commitments, although he was forced to lead the rest of his life as a semi-invalid.

As a result of this curtailment of activities he declined to serve on the Legislative Council when invited to do so, but gave his services liberally whenever they were sought at top-level conferences, or he would act as personal adviser to the Governor-in-Council. The wealth which came to him at an early age made him a ready and generous benefactor to the community generally. He was the first private citizen to donate a school for children of mixed parentage. Other educational institutions, including the University of Hong Kong, benefited from his philanthropy. He was human enough to take pleasure in any recognition given to him and one of his more satisfying honours was a degree of Doctor of Laws *honoris causa* from the University. For his services to Britain he was created Knight Bachelor by King George V in 1915, and later in 1955 Queen Elizabeth II conferred on him the further honour of Knight of the British Empire. Nor did his donations to relief work in China and his help to the Portuguese administration in Macau escape recognition by their respective governments. In business, his acumen ensured success in his dealings, yet he was esteemed and respected by all friends and associates; he held directorships in many of the leading business houses where his foresight and judgment were keenly sought.

My mother, Lady Clara, was a remarkable woman and a most conscientious parent. Father had a large house on the mid-levels overlooking the harbour, but as the children arrived Mother was not at all happy about the prospect of their growing up in the heat of Hong Kong's summer months. Someone had told her that there was nothing to match the health-giving properties of the Peak air for young children, so Father had no rest until he had obtained special permission from the Governor-in-Council (necessary until after the Second World War) for a Chinese family to live in that exclusive residential district. Father bought a cluster of three houses from a retiring businessman: two, separated by tennis courts on two levels, for the family and a large staff of servants, and one for his own use. The move was made in 1907. There were altogether ten children in our family, seven girls and three boys, one of whom died in infancy. The last three, including myself, were born after moving to the Peak.

In spite of the fresh air and exclusiveness, living facilities on the Peak were understandably primitive. Braving these conditions would have tried the spirit of anyone, but for a woman with a large family of young children it needed true courage. The isolation alone must have been frightening, for access, other than walking, was by the funicular railway which gave an infrequent service. Here the amenities stopped. Roads were little more than footpaths and travel between tram terminus and home was made by sedan chair for which we kept our own staff of coolies. There was not a single shop or even a small store in the entire district so that every simple need had to be procured from town. Refrigeration and sewerage were dreams of the future; cooking was done by wood or by coal and gas was used for all lighting including street lamps. Added to this was the problem of fog which was particularly heavy during the summer months and sometimes, for days on end, humidity would remain at saturation point and visibility reduced to no more than a few feet.

But no problem proved insuperable nor task too great for Mother if it meant that our health or education would benefit. She aimed at giving us the best of both cultures. To help her achieve this she brought into the family a Chinese master and an English governess. These two exerted a strong influence on our daily lives and we grew up in pleasant rural surroundings, spending our time between learning the rudiments of a general English education as dispensed by our governess and studying elementary Chinese classics under the Old Master. Twice a week we had piano lessons from a French lady who spent Wednesday and Saturday afternoons devoting a half hour to each child.

Life was not all work and no play. Even though we were the only Chinese family to live on the Peak, with so many of us, we never felt lonely. We had cats and a dog each and kept a pair of goats — they were to have been slaughtered but Mother, being a devout Buddhist and against killing, offered them a home. Someone told her that riding was good for posture so she imported two donkeys from north China. On arrival they were fitted with saddles and bridles at the Hong Kong Jockey Club stables. Whenever we

Excerpt From *Stanley: Behind Barbed Wire*

went riding we were the envy of the other children on the Peak. The donkeys were often lent to charitable organizations where they were a special attraction at garden fêtes.

We had little contact with the neighbouring children and only met those whose governesses were friends of ours. During our afternoon walks the governesses would sit together while we children played hopscotch on the pavement or games on the hillside not far away. I do not remember ever having been invited to any of their homes. They had no intention, I am sure, of being unkind, although they would on occasion suddenly refuse to play with us because we were Chinese, or they might tell us we shouldn't be living on the Peak. Whenever this happened, our governess would pick up her knitting and take us home, telling us stories on the way, hoping to soothe any hurt we might have suffered.

There were day-long walking picnics organized by the Old Master, outings in which Mother sometimes joined. These hikes were entertaining and instructive as the Old Master rather prided himself on his knowledge of natural history, on which he expounded as we went along. His ability to forecast weather conditions was quite remarkable and, indeed, I cannot recall a single occasion when we were caught in the rain. We were always accompanied on these outings by two coolies who carried the lunches, raincoats and extra woollies as well as a light chairlift in case of accidents or if Mother or one of us younger ones could not quite make the distance and had to be assisted.

The older children played tennis. When the court was not in use we roller-skated. Mother had been advised that the best exercise of all was swimming, so Father had to borrow the company launch for her to take us to some nearby beach. Later she had a motor yacht built to her own requirements and we would spend weekends on board. After the tragic sinking of a Macau ferry, with heavy loss of life, she arranged for a professional to give us swimming lessons. However, the highlight of our activities was Chinese opera of which Mother herself was passionately fond. We would be taken to a matinée or to a Saturday night performance and would find ourselves thoroughly fascinated by some historical or legendary presentation in which virtue always triumphed over evil. The cast was usually all male but occasionally there would be a female troupe. The impersonation in either case was superb, the costumes consistently extravagant and always in the correct style of the period. Each troupe carried its own orchestra and instruments — gongs, drums, cymbals, bells and various strings. The noise, especially when depicting something exciting like a battle scene, would be deafening. There would be little or no scenery, but from the perfect action of the players little imagination was needed on the part of the audience to know what it was all about.

The Peak houses were built of timber and simply designed with wide enclosed verandahs, the windows of which rattled at the slightest breeze throughout the night — and yet they were strong enough to withstand the typhoons. These came with terrific force and steady regularity from June until November each year. The summers were long and very trying and, especially during our early years, Mother would take us away to one of the seaside resorts in the north to escape the heat, until the First World War and German raiders on the China Sea put an end to this type of holiday.

We lived on the south side of the Island overlooking Deep Water Bay and Repulse Bay. Our view may not have been as exciting as that of houses facing the harbour where there was a constant movement of ships, but to us on the ocean side, with its magnificent panorama, each variation in shade and colour of land, sea and sky brought fresh and unending interest. At dusk and in the moonlight the outlines of bays and islands were strangely softened yet clearly defined and we would linger on the lawn until fishing lights shone in the calm waters below us like earthly stars.

Because of Father's business commitments and his indifferent health, Mother had the main responsibility of our upbringing. We had to practise humbleness and courtesy to all people at all times and were taught to be frugal because, she often said, our future husbands might not be as well off as Father and she did not want us to feel the difference. I don't know about the others but I, for one, was totally unaware of Father's financial status

Excerpt From *Stanley: Behind Barbed Wire*

and, as we were given all we needed, there was no reason to think about such things. The result was that I never learnt the value of money, although our frugal upbringing certainly taught me how to make a little go a long way in later life.

We saw little of Father during these years, but sometimes on a Sunday he would send for us and, when we were assembled in his drawing room, he would come in and sit down. As we approached him in single file, we would be shaken gently by the hand and given a parental kiss. He always accorded us the same courtesy he gave to visitors. I can still recall the slim elegant figure of those days, the frailness of his physique, his long blue Chinese gown and short black jacket with jade buttons, and his delicate and very smooth hands. If at any time he was displeased with us he would not show it but left it to Mother to correct us. I can remember only one occasion when he disciplined anyone himself. He had received a complaint from the Peak tram inspector about my brother Robbie having been rude to him. Father took this very much to heart. He sent for us all, lectured us on propriety in conduct and then, to our amazement, he picked up a cane and gave Robbie several strokes on each hand.

The time came in 1917 when Grace, two years my junior, and I joined our elder sisters in their daily journey to school in Kowloon. Kowloon was being developed and the Diocesan Girls' School had moved over there in 1913, when space still allowed unhampered expansion in as yet rural surroundings. The school had been established in 1860 by the Church Missionary Society for European and Eurasian girls. By 1904 it had so prospered that it was mentioned in the Government Report of that year as being one of the five most important grant-in-aid schools in the colony.

Going to school in Kowloon meant leaving home at 7.30 a.m. with several changes in transport. The Peak roads had been improved sufficiently to take light vehicular traffic and rickshaws were replacing the sedan chair, but it was still a long journey by rickshaw, Peak tram, ferry and rickshaw again for the last mile along tree-lined Nathan Road on Kowloon side. When the weather was good, we would travel to and from the Peak tram terminus by donkey. We could possibly have gone to the Peak School nearby: although it did not normally admit Chinese children, Father might have been granted special permission to send us there had Mother wished it. Our cousins attended St Stephen's Girls' College in Hong Kong. It was *the* school for daughters of Chinese gentlemen, but Mother chose the Diocesan Girls' School in Kowloon because she thought it would give us the best English education.

We must have presented an unusual spectacle to our travelling companions on the Peak tram. Mother liked to dress us to match. Unfortunately, she had little idea of what was suitable and, even though our frocks were sometimes made by a dressmaker in town and there were two tailors permanently employed at home, I have since been told that our general appearance was a source of great amusement to the other passengers. No wonder, for I can remember wearing a voile dress trimmed with a pink ribbon in the middle of winter. This was reinforced by a woollen singlet underneath, which had the annoying habit of peeping out from under the voile neckline. To complete the incongruity of the ensemble, I wore brown woollen stockings, held up by garters which were slack enough to allow proper circulation of blood to my legs, inside brown leather boots! Boots were considered necessary because they were good support for our ankles. Hats, whether or not they suited us, were always worn, these being substituted in the summer by sun topees with embroidered linen covers also trimmed with ribbon to match our dresses. Poor Mother, to have been so well intentioned and to have achieved so unfortunate a result. We would not have been so conspicuous had there been only one or two of us but, with four and sometimes more travelling together, we could not fail to attract a good deal of attention and comment.

I enjoyed my schooldays immensely. There were naturally subjects such as Biblical Knowledge about which I knew nothing, but I soon caught up. As well as lessons there were team games like hockey and also the Girl Guides. I left at the end of 1923 having passed the senior examination conducted by the University of Hong Kong. I was naturally anxious to go on to further studies at the University, but as Chinese was not taught at the Diocesan Girls' School my knowledge of the language was not of sufficiently high standard to pass the examination in Chinese literature, and this was a prerequisite for matriculation for students of Chinese nationality. I had to make up for this by attending a Chinese secondary school for two years. Before this, though, there was a trip to London where Father was a Hong Kong delegate to the British Empire Exhibition at Wembley, as well as a short visit into China with Mother.

In 1927 Grace and I joined the University. By this time, motor cars could be driven to the Peak although our houses were still beyond the range of the new motor road. Nevertheless, Father gave us a car which we garaged at the Peak tram station, before going on home by rickshaw. Two years later, Father's new house when completed had a special approach road and we could drive right to its door. The two years I spent at the University were the happiest and most carefree of my life, in spite of the fact that it fell to my lot to run the Peak household. Mother had gone to England with our two elder sisters and the others, except Florence, the youngest, were either away or married. But housekeeping was only a nominal duty because the servants who had been with us for many years took over the responsibility and all I had to do was to draw the money from Father's office for wages and general running expenses.

The University of Hong Kong was founded in 1911, but the importance of providing facilities for educating local aspirants in Western medicine had been recognized in the previous century, and the 1880s had seen the establishment of the Hong Kong College of Medicine from which Dr Sun Yat-sen, founder of the Chinese Republic, had graduated. The College became the new University's Faculty of Medicine. There were also Faculties of Engineering and Arts. Grace and I both enrolled as Arts students, reading Letters and Philosophy.

We went through our first year without difficulty. Because of our good grounding at the Diocesan Girls' School we were rather ahead of our contemporaries, so it was possible to indulge in all the extra-mural activities which made those days so memorable. We played a lot of tennis, attended all the dances, and the car gave us easy access to all of Hong Kong's lovely bathing beaches. Throughout the long vacation, swimming was a daily, if not twice-daily, event.

Most memorable of all, I met Billy Gittins.

Billy was on the staff of the Faculty of Engineering and was one of the University's own graduates. As a student he had been an outstanding athlete, having won the championship title in successive years. He had played for the University in both cricket and football and was still in the Second Eleven in cricket. Being on the Committee of the Athletic Association, he was very keen to promote sporting activities among the student body. Whenever we played tennis at the sports pavilion he was always there and somehow managed always to get into our foursome for mixed doubles. Grace observed that he was interested in me, but I was determined not to get involved with a member of the teaching staff. Somehow, though, my prejudice was overcome — perhaps he was just persistent. It was not long before I fell deeply in love.

I was soon taken home to meet his family. Billy's parents, Mr and Mrs Henry Gittins, lived in Kowloon. He had five sisters and a brother. They were friendly and easy-going and accepted me into their circle without question. Billy's mother in particular showed a special liking for me, a liking which grew into a deep affection as the years went by. I had known the three younger sisters at school and had on occasion brought one of them home to the Peak where Mother had treated her with the usual courtesy she afforded our friends. I could not possibly have known that beneath her apparent friendliness there lurked the shadow of a bitter family feud which had not diminished in intensity in almost twenty years.

When Mother returned from England she showed her hostility in no uncertain manner. She refused to discuss the rights or wrongs of the feud but just demanded that I stop having anything further to do with Billy. Actually I had not even known about the incident until shortly before her return, when my eldest sister Victoria, who remembered it quite clearly, told me the story. It appeared that, seventeen or more years before, the Gittinses had occupied a house on the mid-levels, which the owner suddenly wanted to repossess in order to let it to my mother's brother. A smaller house next door was offered in exchange and, although Mrs Gittins had not welcomed the idea, the move had been made. Unfortunately, only a few weeks after the move my maternal grandmother had suddenly died and shortly after that Mother's brother had failed in business. Less than a year later his wife had succumbed to a serious operation. The hardest blow of all seemed to be the fact that, although my aunt died, Mrs Gittins, who had the same operation at the same time, recovered. Vic told me that Mother, who was rather superstitious, had laid all the blame at the time on the Gittinses and the years had not lessened her bitterness, but my sister promised that she and her husband, who had some influence with Mother, would help smooth the way for me. Mother, however, having nursed her grief for so long, would not heed any reasoning whatsoever. She simply could not believe, she told me bitterly, that any child of hers could be so disloyal and lacking in consideration as to contemplate marrying into a family which had caused her so much sorrow. I felt the greatest sympathy for her but saw no reason for her continued bitterness.

Although Father did not actually show his displeasure, I felt that he, too, was not entirely happy at the prospect. Billy had asked for an interview at which he explained that he hoped to marry me when I had completed my studies at the University and had formally requested Father's permission to court me. Father replied that he could make no promises in my mother's absence but he had given his consent for Billy to take me out. I should have known that he would have been against any daughter of his marrying into an Eurasian family which did not subscribe to his view and adopt Chinese nationality, because he felt that they would not be accepted into any community. I was not certain of this but decided that there was no point in arguing either with him or with Mother, so I quietly went on seeing Billy. By this time, he was no longer at the University but had joined his friend James Mackenzie Jack, who was manager of his family's firm of electrical engineers, William C. Jack and Company.

At the end of a most satisfactory second year at the University my parents dropped a bombshell. To my astonishment and utter dismay, they gave me the alternative of either discontinuing my association with Billy or giving up my course of study to be married. To do them justice, I am certain now that they did not for one moment think that I would take their ultimatum literally, but I was too young, too inexperienced and too rigid in nature to consider compromise. It was not an easy decision, but I gave up my course at the University and Billy and I were married the following March.

Father's new house, planned for many years, was at last ready for occupation although it was by no means completed. We moved in at the beginning of 1929 shortly before I was married. It had the same lovely view, though slightly angled, of bays and islands and the sea beyond. It was Mother's dream — a home large enough to hold the family under one roof, fitted with all the comforts that Father's means could afford, and lavishly yet tastefully furnished in appropriate Eastern and Western styles. By this time, however, the family had grown up: two of my elder sisters were married, the other two were overseas; both brothers had homes and families of their own; and now I, one of the younger group, was about to leave. In another four years both Grace and Florence had married.

Mother was left alone in a house too large for her and built too late to fulfil her desire of having the family under one roof. She became increasingly involved with the Buddhist religion and, interested in promoting education for poor Chinese girls, established a free school for them in one of Hong Kong's less salubrious districts. Her selfless devotion to these interests culminated in the building of a magnificent temple-school complex during the last years of her life. We spent about two months of each summer with her. The children gave her immeasurable pleasure and I was able to help with the planning of her new garden which she wanted to extend in terraces down the hillside.

Ever since Elizabeth's birth when Mother stayed in the hospital to be with me, her views had undergone a change. She had seen more of Billy

Excerpt From *Stanley: Behind Barbed Wire*

and his mother. Billy had a natural charm of manner which endeared him to elderly women and his mother certainly went out of her way to heal the breach. Mother's resentment gradually wore off and in its place a firm friendship and mutual respect grew between them. She found Billy's wide knowledge of engineering and construction work invaluable and leaned heavily on him for advice in her building project. Mother was a well-known, well-loved figure. When she died suddenly in 1938 many mourned her passing. The temple-school stands as a lasting monument to her deep devotion and her concern for the welfare of those less fortunate than herself.

Billy and I enjoyed ten completely happy years before the Second World War cast its shadow over us. Kowloon Tong was a new suburb designed especially for young families. We brought up our children in pleasant surroundings in an atmosphere as yet unspoiled and unpolluted. I spent a great deal of time in the garden, which we had to make from land reclaimed by developers. Billy was working on the electrification of the New Territories at that time and brought home each day a large bag of good soil to enrich the new flower and vegetable beds. I had the loan of a three-volume encyclopaedia of gardening which I studied assiduously and this, together with practical application gained from Mother's garden and our own (although gardeners did the actual work), endowed me with the knowledge and experience which were to prove so invaluable later on.

When John began attending junior school in 1939, I found time on my hands. I had no desire to spend my days at lunch or afternoon tea parties or at games of bridge or mah jong. I had attended a course of lectures on air-raid precautions and had sat and passsed a three-hour paper with credit. It occurred to me that I could still study and, rather than return to the University to complete my Arts course (which was probably what I should have done), I decided to take a secretarial course with a view to working at the University instead. By early 1940 I had joined its administrative staff as Secretary to the Dean of Medicine, Professor Gordon King. The Registrar had been happy to welcome me back as a staff member and I was soon thoroughly engrossed in the administration of medical students and, at the same time, taking part in the University's preparations for war.

It had been planned that in an emergency the University would immediately become the University Relief Hospital under the Medical Department to provide for a possible 750 beds. Professor Gordon King would be Medical Officer-in-Charge and Professor W. Faid, head of the Department of Physics, Lay Superintendent. I was to take over the hospital secretaryship. I was sent to the Queen Mary Hospital for training in hospital administration, with special attention to details of admission and discharge of patients so important to the function of a relief hospital.

At the evacuation order in 1940 Professor King's wife, Dr Mary King, left with their daughters for Melbourne. She offered to take our children with her, an offer which we accepted a year later. By this time the situation in Europe and China had so deteriorated that families returning from leave were not allowed to land unless they undertook to leave again after a brief visit. Billy was very anxious to get the children away, especially when it was pointed out to us that there would be no problem about their entry into Australia were they to travel on their own passports. This was because Gittins was an English name and they looked foreign enough. It was at this juncture that the Jack family, returning from England, were ordered to leave immediately for Australia. It was a heaven-sent opportunity for us to send Elizabeth and John with them to join the Kings in Melbourne.

Reprinted from Jean Gittins, *Stanley: Behind Barbed Wire* (Ch. 1, pp. 7–20), with the permission of Hong Kong Unversity Press.

7

$$\succ\!\!-\!\!|\!\!-\!\!\blacklozenge\!\!\succ\!\!-\!\!\bigcirc\!\!-\!\!\prec\!\!\blacklozenge\!\!-\!\!|\!\!-\!\!\prec$$

Irene Cheng

The Old World: The Chinese Girl Behind a Eurasian Face

All she's trying to do is to keep things straight in her head. To keep the weight of her memories evenly distributed. To hold the chapters of her life in order. She feels a new tenderness growing for certain moments; they're like beads on a string, and the string is wearing out. At the same time she know that what lies ahead of her must be concluded by the efforts of her imagination and not by the straight-faced recital of a throttled and unlit history. Words are more and more required. And the question arises: what is the story of a life? A chronicle of fact or a skillfully wrought impression?

(Shields, 340)

'I retain a memory of Irene, stately and sprightly still, and rather the Grande Dame, not quite Chinese, though fluent in Cantonese to her amah, not quite English, though fluent in English to me ... .'

(Hoe, 233)

Irene Cheng is one of the older sisters of Jean Gittins. This chapter, apart from looking closely at Cheng's own self-writing, will bring together and juxtapose the memoirs of the Ho Tung sisters, namely, Irene Cheng, Jean Gittins, and occasionally Florence Yeo. It will also examine their respective autobiographical representations as members of the Ho Tung family. The purpose here is not to ascertain the veracity or the referentiality of these memoirs. But by putting together these autobiographical writings, this chapter considers how memory and the retranslation of memory in a narrative reflect the sisters' ideological orientations, cultural propensities, and political loyalties, which in turn, contribute to their very different constructions of their own ethnic identities. Irene Cheng's and Jean Gittins's memoirs offer two very distinctly different versions of the Ho Tung family. In fact, looking at the childhood memories of Cheng and Gittins, it seems the two could hardly have belonged to the same family. Young Irene was like a Chinese girl who found herself discovering new things in a Western environment. Young Jean was a Eurasian girl who found herself trapped in a Chinese family. The sisters might have experienced the same events, yet their outlooks and reactions at the time of the event and at the moment of recalling are diametrically different.

The two major autobiographical works of Irene Cheng are: *Clara Ho Tung: A Hong Kong Lady, Her Family and her Times*[1] published by the Chinese University of Hong Kong in 1976, and *Intercultural Reminiscences*, published by Baptist University of Hong Kong in 1997.[2]

Though *Clara* claims to be a biography of Lady Clara, it is in effect an amalgam of biography, part-autobiography and history, with the autobiographical part prefiguring her later memoir. Much of *Clara* deals with the history of the Ho Tungs as a Hong Kong family.

Conscious of the fact that she is about to present a story of the family which had previously been written about by her sister Jean six years before, and keenly aware of their respective ownership of experience, Irene Cheng says in the Introduction of her 1976 book that:

> Later, when I had begun this book, I learned that my sister, Jean Gittins, was writing her autobiography. This was published in 1969 by the *South China Morning Post* of Hong Kong under the title *Eastern Windows – Western Skies*. Inevitably, the descriptions of our childhood years overlap, but our viewpoints sometimes differed and it is evident that we were often interested in different things.

(xii)

Clara, as Irene Cheng claims, was written at the urging of Margaret Mead who gave her much encouragement in her book on Lady Clara. Both Cheng and Margaret Mead were members of the Executive Board of the World

Federation for Mental Health from 1956 to 1959. During this period when they met, they often talked about 'the interracial and inter-cultural characteristics of Hong Kong ... a prototype of the meeting of East and West' (x). According to Alexander Grantham (Hong Kong Governor, 1947–57) who contributed the Foreword to *Clara*, Cheng has 'painted a picture of a Hong Kong family in all its intimate detail, which is in itself a chapter of Anglo-Chinese history' (Cheng, 1976, vii).

A decade after the publication of *Clara* and a decade-and-a-half after the publication of her sister Jean's memoir, Irene Cheng embarked on her very own autobiographical venture in 1984. The autobiographical project took 14 years of incubation and *Reminiscences* was not published until 1997 — the year that officially marked the change of Hong Kong's sovereignty from British to Chinese. By then, Cheng was in her 90s and had left Hong Kong for San Diego, US, almost three decades before.

In *Reminiscences*, the aged narrator complains about 'the trouble with growing old' is when 'you inevitably lose the ability to get around as much as you would like and end up spending too much time with your memories' (1997, 449). However, with her fascinated discovery of the personal computer at the age of 80, she 'felt compelled to tell the younger generation something of what she had experienced and what she thought and felt at the time and thereafter' (ix). So, as her editors Frank Murdoch and Ian Watson say, Irene Cheng had embarked 'on possibly the final stage of life's great adventure' — the autobiographical act — an act that two of her younger sisters[3] had already performed by the time this second book was published.

Reminiscences is a massive text covering the period from the time Ho Tung and Lady Margaret were married in the late 1880s, to the 1980s. This book does not purport, like in her previous one, to represent a chapter of Hong Kong Anglo-Chinese history, but is more a personal 'compilation of recollections' (ix).

Notwithstanding the claim of the title, the inter-cultural or inter-racial aspects of her story are in fact very much blurred in the background. The book is in effect about Cheng's own recollection of herself, brought up in the Chinese tradition where she was taught to act and think as a Chinese. The notion of Eurasianness is very much obscured by her ethnographical emphasis on Chinese heritage.

Reminiscences is introduced more as a Hong Kong Chinese cultural experience through the personal narrative of Irene Cheng. As Daniel Tse, Vice-Chancellor of Hong Kong Baptist University, says in the Preface:

> To Hong Kong Chinese readers, the book offers many intriguing stories and familiar scenes, and it quietly stirs the nostalgic sentiments of those who have made the territory their home. To Westerners, I believe the book provides a very interesting and informative account of Chinese customs and beliefs. It serves as a bridge that links East and West and hopefully enables Westerners to gain a better understanding and appreciation of Chinese culture. It can also be seen as a bridge linking the past and the present though the life and experiences of the author.
>
> (iv)

Reading the voluminous *Reminiscences* requires a certain amount of readerly effort. The narrator's sketches from memory are not always connected in a sequenced narrative order. The relationship of significance between events is often arbitrary. Events narrated within a chapter might have very little to do with what the title suggests and the events might not be necessarily connected thematically, temporally or spatially. A great part of the DGS chapter is devoted to the author recalling her 1917 Tsingtao sojourn, Florence's inferiority complex that lasted until the 1930s, Robbie being disciplined by Ho Tung and Vic's romance with Dr Thomas. Her narrative, at times, tends to be slightly repetitive and reiterative. The reader very often has to re-assemble the bits of repeated narratives interrupted through her memory maze. Interruption is a norm in the textual rhythm of *Reminiscences*. Her introduction of her husband's connection with Imperial Commissioner Lin is itself interrupted with paragraphs of explanation on the Chinese concept of *chin jia [qin jia]* or in-laws. Although Jean Gittins sometimes interrupts her own story as well, she seems more aware of the fact; when she feels her narrative is digressing, she would simply say, 'But I am digressing' (1945, 18). Still, a patient reader may recognize and appreciate in the desultory rhythms of Cheng's narrative, the authentic movements of memory in late-life ruminations, which a tidier storytelling would have lost.

In terms of narrative style, Cheng seldom resorts to the traditional literary techniques and narrative flow found in Gittins. Her prose, compared to Gittins, tends to be prosaic and unadorned. *Reminiscences* is also very mixed in mode and at times it is like a kind of collage with different narrative styles and strategies. The author is inclined to interrupt her narrative at every turn to make room for whatever background information that comes to her mind. She includes in her text elaborate family genealogies, anthropological details on Chinese customs and rituals, a survey of Chinese literature and folk tales, travel writing in different parts of China and Europe, extracts from Confucian classics, aphoristic Chinese statements, praise for modern Chinese sociopolitical systems, circular letters written by herself to relatives and friends, inter-textual insertion of passages from her sisters' memoirs, educational reports from international conferences, etc. It could be described as a modernist composition without the modernist irony.

Cheng's intense identification with her Chinese ancestry has all the fervor of an eager teacher explaining her Chinese ways to Western readers or Westernized Chinese readers. She sees the need to present her reminiscences as sociologically informative and edifying. As Sau-Ling Cynthia Wong says of an earlier Chinese memoir (*When I Was a Boy in China* [1887] by Lee Yan Phou), 'the individual's life serves the function of conveying anthropological information; the freight, in fact, frequently outweighs the vehicle' (40). The narrator in *Reminiscences* is very much like the narrator in *When I Was a Boy in China*, which Wong describes as one who 'consciously assumes the persona of a tour guide' (40). In Cheng's efforts to explain Confucian practices in funerals, anniversaries, and festivals, she too is consciously assuming the role of a cultural interpreter to her Western audience. In a way, her memoir is very much a kind of ethnic autobiography, or 'autoethnography'.[4]

⊶•◆〉─○─〈◆•⊷

Cheng's ebullience as cultural interpreter can be somewhat overwhelming, in dramatic contrast to her sister Jean Gittins's inclination to avoid the role of cultural interpreter. Whenever Gittins describes some Chinese custom practiced in the Ho Tung family, it is presented somewhat gropingly as if half-acknowledging her own cultural ignorance and haphazard understanding. To Gittins, the Chinese almanac with all its calculations is referred to as the 'Red Book' — a book which she obviously had very little usage and knowledge of and which she identifies by the colour of its cover. Cheng recalls how she has her own personal copy of the almanac. She also expertly identifies to her readers which lunar years were the Blind Years versus those with Lap Chun *[li ch'un]* days (1997, 11). Symons, of course, never pretends to be familiar with Chinese customs. Cheng's explanations of Chinese customs and practices tend to be very detailed and elaborate. To use Cynthia Wong's terms as she describes the interethnic perspective in an autobiography, the element of *display*, whether intentional or not, is unavoidable (42).

Looking at the very different cultural orientations of the two sisters, the most crucial issue to be addressed in this chapter is this — how can we explain the contrasting differences between the two Eurasian sisters, in terms of ethnic identification, cultural assimilation, sociopolitical aspirations and even national allegiance?

Both Irene Cheng and Jean Gittins were of the same parents. They grew up together in the same Ho Tung household at the Peak, went to the same English Anglican school, the same Chinese *si-shu*, and both attended Hong Kong University, yet their personal perception of their social and ethnic identities are in opposing difference on almost every level.

One major objective in this chapter, therefore, is to challenge the absolute position of cultural and historical determinism. How can we explain two sisters, who grew up in an identical socioeconomic environment, sharing the same cultural and political contexts, can have such utterly contrasting notions of their own social and ethnic identities and articulate such willfully chosen categories of race and ethnicity? In the Symons chapter, we have seen her representation of the Eurasian's grafting of European culture as he or she moves up the economic scale. This allows us to draw on the importance of economic determinism in the construction of ethnic identity. But the concept of economic determinism is not much help in explaining the differences between the sisters so similarly brought up.

Antonio Gramsci in his *Prison Notebooks* written in 1929 and 1935 has shown how ideologies can cut across different classes, and how, also, the same class can hold many, even contradictory ideologies (Loomba, 28). Gramsci also questions the primacy of the economic over the ideological. He does not believe that economic factors alone create historical events, but that they can only create conditions which are favourable for certain kinds of ideologies to flourish (Loomba, 28). Gramsci has expanded the meaning of ideology as 'more than just reflections of material reality. Rather, ideologies are conceptions of life that are manifest in all aspects of individual and collective existence. Ideologies therefore animate social relations, organize human masses, and create the terrain on which men move, acquire consciousness of their position, struggle ...' (Gramsci, 1971, 324, 377). Hence, in order to understand the sisters' very different conceptions of their ethnic identities, one must look closely at the ideological configurations behind such differences.

Accepting the Gramscian understanding of ideology, Irene Cheng's construction of her social and ethnic identity(ies) can be seen as closely hinged upon two major ideological discourses operating in her memoir. One of these expresses the dominant colonial interests or the colonial discourse of the Hong Kong elite, which is overwhelmingly strong in Symons's text and can also be substantially felt in Gittins's text too. It is a discourse based on exclusive collaboration and identification with the British rulers, and on maintaining a status quo and a kind of distance from the Chinese populace in the background. In *Reminiscences*, this elitist colonial discourse can at times be felt very strongly, yet operating apart from it is a staunch Chinese Confucian discourse that dominates much of the discursive pattern in the text and which articulates, justifies and explicates Cheng's conception of the individual and collective experience. These two discourses seem to operate and co-exist simultaneously; sometimes with the Confucian discourse occupying the foreground, casting into shadow the colonial discourse in the background, sometimes vice versa. The two discourses of colonialism and Confucianism and the worlds that they respectively invoked are like watertight compartments; neither interferes with the other and they remain securely separate. As Amy Ling pointed out W. E. B. Du Bois's description of the consciousness of the African Americans, in Irene Cheng, we feel the same double consciousness with 'vision bifocal and fluctuating' (Du Bois quoted in Ling, 137). The two consciousnesses seem to be progressing like two lines in the same direction that seldom disturb or cross over each other's path.

The notion of Eurasianness in *Reminiscences* is a very elusive phenomenon that surfaces sporadically in a somewhat apologetic tone. On the personal level, Cheng's own Eurasianness is for her a kind of biological accident. She sees herself as essentially Chinese except for the contingent Eurasian heritage in her. On the collective level, the Eurasian community[5] as described by the narrator was very much *a part* of the Hong Kong Chinese community, as opposed to being *apart from* the Hong Kong Chinese community — a perception strongly held by Symons and occasionally by Gittins. Throughout Cheng's text and discourses, the word 'Eurasian' seems readily interchangeable with the word 'Chinese'. Her sense of *sinocized* Eurasianness is therefore at the other extreme from Symons, whose construction of Eurasianness is based heavily on her identification with her European heritage and dis-identification with her Chinese heritage.

Cheng's consciousness of the existence of her sisters' autobiographical works that came before her own remains strong on a subterranean level. We feel the author's need to establish her place as the more informed family historian — the family bard who has more faithfully and truthfully preserved shreds of forgotten stories and buried events in the large Ho Tung family. There is a strong desire to portrait her family as a traditional Chinese family as she remembers it — that is, different from her sisters' depictions. Her personal narrative, therefore, can be read as a counter-narrative to the more Westernized portraits of the family offered by her sisters.

The two versions of the Ho Tung family (recalled by Gittins and Cheng) whether in terms of the family ethos, the constituents, the complex system of human relations within it, have in fact very little in common. The family which Jean Gittins represented is a very bourgeois, Western-oriented family of the compradore class. The family which Cheng describes is an extremely Confucian, patriarchal and anachronistic Chinese extended family, giving the impression of a miniature kingdom.

⊱┈◆┈○┈◆┈⊰

Irene Cheng's *Reminiscences* can be divided into three phases. The first phase deals with her negotiations with the patriarchal power during the pre-war period, as an unmarried daughter who tried to reconcile an unconventional identity in her professional ambitions with her profound loyalty to the Confucian demands on a Chinese unmarried daughter. The second phase marks the newly widowed Cheng with a young infant and her gradual ascendance in her public career in Hong Kong. The third phase deals with her migration and settlement in San Diego, US and the awakening of her renewed loyalty to China.

Placing *Reminiscences* next to all the other memoirs examined here, Cheng's text offers a perfect example of a 'relational self' — a concept of the self as being primarily dependent on the self's relations to the others. In autobiographical writings, this concept of relational selfhood comes into operation where the 'I' is often subordinated to the story of some other for whom the self serves as privileged witness (Eakin, 1999, 58).[6]

This concept of the relational self had often been seen as a common feature in the autobiographical writings of women. Yet, in reading the written lives of Symons and Gittins, even though both are women's autobiographical writings, there is scant evidence for seeing the self as being constructed on a relational basis. Their respective life and sense of identity are written out more or less as single and isolated individual selves, grappling with different social identities under different circumstances. But in looking at Cheng's life, her sense of being an individual single self is not so strong. Her sense of self and identity is founded and defined very much by her relationship with her three illustrious parents. Her identity as a Confucian filial daughter and a privileged witness to their lives becomes a kind of core identity, which sometimes takes precedence over all other social identities, hierarchies or loyalties.

Irene Cheng, the oldest amongst the three Ho Tung autobiographers, had spent the longest time living in the family home. Her account is often laced with a tone of authority and representativeness in speaking on behalf of the family. Cheng begins her memoir not with the subject 'I' but with the collective 'we':

> Although we were Eurasians, ostensibly we were brought up in the Chinese tradition. We spoke Cantonese at home, honoured Chinese festivals, and lived according to the lunar calendar.
>
> (1997, 1)

To Cheng, the Ho Tungs' Eurasianness is a kind of phenotypical façade behind which lies their Chinese essence. The Eurasianness in her case is given as a grammatical concession: Chinese culture occupies the main clause of the Ho Tung family.

Cheng's story opens by presenting to the reader the senior figures of the large Ho Tung clan, starting with Ho Tung's mother, Ho Tung's numerous named and anonymous siblings, Sir Robert's spouses, followed by the introduction of her twelve siblings, then proceeding downwards in the family hierarchy to the butlers, amah-companions and the array of *muitsai* with their fanciful Chinese names. Cheng seems inclined to intersperse her clan narrative with obscure bits of family history — how Ho Tung's mother gave away her fourth son to a passenger on a boat coming back from Shanghai to Hong Kong, how Ho Tung's youngest sister who married against the advice of Lady Margaret was cut off from the family. The inclusion of these shreds of forgotten family history can, of course, be read as Cheng's assertion of her position as a family historian with the exclusive ownership of these stories. But the narrator, as if to prevent any query about her sources, always wisely and cautiously keeps her distance from these family tales, by attributing them as stories she heard from Lady Clara.

Plate 6   Ho Tung, around 1910, reprinted from Feldwick, *Present Day Impressions of the Far East* (1917).

Cheng's gusto in her introduction of the Ho Tung senior members becomes somewhat inhibited at certain points in her narrative, for what is conspicuously absent from the narrative is the father of Sir Robert — the most important figurehead and most recent patriarch who passed on the lineage name to all members of the existing Ho Tung clan. Patrilineality is one of the fundamental principles of the Chinese family system. The use of patrilineal surname is a kind of identification of one's lineage and one's origin. The worship of recent patrilineal ancestors is 'an expression of gratitude towards the originators and recall[s] the beginnings' (Yang, 1970, 44).

Plate 7 Lady Clara in Western attire, from *My Memories*, courtesy of Florence Yeo.

Plate 8 Lady Clara in Chinese ceremonial gown, from *My Memories*, courtesy of Florence Yeo.

In Cheng's narrative, the Ho Tung ancestral community includes only matrilineal ancestors, namely, Sir Robert's mother's ancestors, Lady Margaret's maternal ancestors, the Changs or Cheungs. Since Lady Margaret and Lady Clara are first cousins, their common ancestors are represented through the Changs' ancestors. Lady Margaret's father, Hector Mclean (Keswick, 94), as well as Sir Robert's father, Henri Bosman (Hall, 1992, 181) are omitted from the narrative. The Ho Tung ancestor worship is therefore based upon an unusual shift away from the Confucian tradition of patrilineal or agnate ancestors to the matrilineal ancestors. In other words, only the Chinese and Eurasian ancestors are worshipped. All European ancestors are excluded. In *Clara*, Cheng explains how in some Hong Kong Eurasian families, 'the rarely seen European parents of Eurasian children were provided with Chinese names to be used on family ancestral tablets and on tombstones' (1976, xvi). But in *Reminiscences*, her description of the Ho Tung ancestor worship does not include any of her European ancestors or their tablets.

With the absence of the major patrilineal ancestors, where does the patrilineal surname come from? Sir Robert's mother is introduced as having a last name 'Shi' (1997, 31). If the last name 'Ho' was not inherited through Shi, where does it come from? 'Ho' does not sound very much like a phonetic translation from 'Bosman'.

Cheng, as narrator, simply decides to remain silent on the identity of Sir Robert's European father or the origin of the Ho Tung family name. With Cheng's zeal to explicate the importance of Confucian ancestral worship, which is based fundamentally on patrilineal continuity, this strained silence and dismissal of the patrilineal figureheads of the Ho Tung clan seems incongruous. This silence can perhaps be read as the first sign of the narrator's own discomfort in dealing with the family's Eurasian heritage.

Jean Gittins never mentioned any of her ancestors, whether European or Chinese. Her sense of identity is more fluid and depends less on her ties with her Chinese or European ancestors. For Irene Cheng, her identity is very much based on her filial connection to and pious remembrance of her Chinese ancestors. Her refusal to acknowledge her European ancestors creates a kind of genealogical void and a problematic construction of her ethnic identity.

Cheng also seems equally inhibited when alluding to the Eurasian background of her mother Lady Clara. Lady Clara's father Cheung Tak Fai was a first generation Eurasian (Cheng, 1976, 7).[7] As if to assure the reader of their Chineseness, the narrator says, 'although both of Mamma's parents were first generation Eurasians, they identified themselves with the Chinese and their children regarded themselves as such' (133). There is also no reference to any European ancestor of Lady Clara. Florence Ho Tung Yeo is the only one amongst the sisters to break the silent complicity by revealing and identifying the racial identities of the Ho Tung parents. Her father, she says,

> was the eldest son of a large family; a first generation Eurasian — his father was Dutch and his mother Chinese. He was brought up by his mother according to Chinese customs. Eurasians were not accepted well in society in those days, and to be successful one had to make a choice to be Chinese or European. Father chose to be Chinese so he took on a Chinese name — Ho Tung.

(Yeo, 12)[8]

Florence Yeo also identifies the maternal European ancestors of Lady Clara. Lady Clara, she says, was

> a second generation Eurasian, with both parents being Eurasians (her European blood was English and Scottish). Her grandfather was Lane, one of the founders of Lane and Crawford of Hong Kong. She was brought up, like Father, according to Chinese custom.
>
> (Yeo, 12)

After a seemingly endless series of vignettes of the Ho Tung clan members, Irene Cheng finally addresses the issue of her Eurasian background. At this point, her tone sounds somewhat hesitant, which she attributes to her failing memory:

> Yet with regard to certain aspects of the family, my knowledge is hazy even though we were very close. One of the reasons for this is because there were some things that were never mentioned. Father and Lady Margaret were first generation Eurasians while Mamma, whose parents were both first generation Eurasians, was second generation. The Eurasian community, which tended to intermarry, was rather isolated. The Chinese community did not respect them, and the British did not accept them. The British who married into Asia did not normally live with their Chinese families, so it was an embarrassing situation for Father and those of his generation. He did not like to talk about it and, in the main, I continue to respect his wishes to this day.
>
> (1997, 43)

The Eurasian heritage of Sir Robert became a kind of taboo in the family and Cheng, in her memoir, decides to support this unspoken pact of reticence. As if to justify her filial complicity, Cheng relates an incident in her father's early life not long after he graduated from Queen's College:

> Father later applied for a post with the Chinese Maritime Customs in Guangzhou. They wanted people who could read, write and speak both Chinese and English. When the applicants all lined up outside, there were obviously many who were older and perhaps wiser than Father — erudite scholars and other learned people. There were even some who did not like Father because he was Eurasian. His hair was

not pure black so it was easy to see that he was not pure Chinese.
One of them said: 'You don't stand a chance. Why do you even
bother?'

(1997, 44)

According to Cheng, her father never really seemed to have got over this
insult. In the 1930s, when he was not chosen by the Nanjing government
to join the Chinese delegation to London, he saw that as directly attributable
to his Eurasianness.

Unlike Joyce Symons and Peter Hall, who trace their own European
heritage with a detective's thrill for clues, Irene Cheng politely refuses to
disclose or address her Eurasian heritage to the reader, hoping that the reader
will share her delicacy in dismissing the subject. Perhaps Cheng, like Symons,
is also unable to verify the identity of her European ancestors.[9] Symons
accepts the unverifiable. Cheng cannot. The subject of the Ho Tung Eurasian
origin inevitably becomes a gaping silence and gnawing absence that haunts
the narrator and her autobiographical text.

Cheng's taciturnity about her European heritage is in dramatic contrast
to her zealous celebration of her Chinese heritage and connections —
something her more Westernized sisters had refused to acknowledge.

As discussed above, the large Ho Tung family that Jean Gittins has
depicted in her texts is based more or less on a Western family model. Despite
the large number of children, visiting cousins, nannies, amahs, *muitsai*,
coolies, and chairbearers, it is still easily recognizable as a family unit based
on the Western understanding of a family. So far as Gittins is concerned,
Lady Clara is her only mother and Sir Robert's only wife. There is absolutely
no mention at all of Lady Margaret, Sir Robert's first or '*kit fat*' [*jie fa*] wife,
nor is there any reference to the concubine. There is also no mention of the
adopted son of Sir Robert and Lady Margaret, or of Mary, the daughter of
the concubine who was of the same age as Daisy. Gittins says, 'we were a
large family — by no means a rarity in the east ... My parents had ten
children ...' (1969, 9).

Florence Yeo, the youngest of the Ho Tung girls, mentions that 'she
was born at the tail end of a large family of eleven' (Yeo, 7). Evidently,
Florence Yeo has included her half-sister Mary in her count. However, like
Jean Gittins, Florence Yeo never mentions the existence of Lady Margaret

or the concubine Ah Jeh in her memoir. The closest she came to referring to the existence of Lady Margaret is when she describes how in 1941 her brother Eddie with his four children had been trapped in Hong Kong while on a visit to celebrate Father's diamond wedding anniversary (71), when only ten pages before (61), she has already mentioned that her mother had died in 1938. Yeo does not clarify why Sir Robert was celebrating a diamond wedding anniversary and who was he celebrating with, when Lady Clara had passed away three years before.

Plate 9   The Ho Tung children, around 1910, from Irene Cheng, *Intercultural Reminiscences*, courtesy of The David C. Lam Institute for East-West Studies, Hong Kong Baptist University.

Jean Gittins says that her parents had ten children. Florence Yeo says eleven (Yeo, 7). Irene Cheng says, 'we ended by having in the family eight girls and four boys, one of whom was adopted' (1976, 18). The narrator, obviously, has deliberately included both the adopted one and the one by the concubine. In fact, she has included in *Clara* a chart of *her* version of the Ho Tung family tree, which includes Lady Margaret and the concubine and their respective adopted and biological children (1976, 201). In *Clara*, Cheng has also included the Ho Tung group picture where all the women were in ceremonial gown celebrating the Diamond anniversary of Sir Robert and his first wife Lady Margaret on 2 December 1941, a few days before the Japanese invasion of Hong Kong. Gittins has simply omitted this Diamond anniversary in her narrative in spite of the prestigious presence of grand colonial personage like Sir Mark Young.

There is clearly a conscious effort on Cheng's part to include family members, acquired in the customary Chinese traditions, who were omitted in her sisters' memoirs. Cheng, as the ardent traditionalist and preserver of family customs, sees it her duty to acknowledge their existence in her personal narrative.

Without much ado in the first chapter, the narrator says:

> We had three parents: my father, Sir Robert Ho Tung; my mother, Lady Clara Ho Tung (nee Cheung), whom we were taught to call Mamma; and father's first wife, Lady Ho Tung or Lady Margaret (nee Mak), whom we called Mother ...
>
> (1997, 1)

Irene Cheng refers to Lady Clara as 'Mamma' and Lady Margaret as 'Mother', a term which Jean Gittins uses to refer to Lady Clara. In *Clara*, the narrator says:

> Mamma was about five feet six inches, which would be tall for a 'pure' Chinese,[10] but for a Eurasian it was average. Mother was shorter than Mamma, but of a heavier build, so some people referred to her as the 'stouter Madame' and Mamma as the 'slimmer Madame'.
>
> (1976, 11)

Plate 10 Ho Tung family celebration in 1930, from Irene Cheng, *Intercultural Reminiscences*, courtesy of The David C. Lam Institute for East-West Studies, Hong Kong Baptist University.

Plate 11   **Lady Margaret in Chinese ceremonial gown, courtesy of Form Asia Books Limited.**

Cheng explains that her father married Lady Margaret in 1881, but she remained childless. Different solutions were sought to rectify the situation. Not having any offspring was deemed to be the worst kind of unfilial behavior. As a temporary remedy, the 5-year-old son of Ho Tung's younger brother Ho Fook was adopted into the Ho Tung branch, and his uncle and aunt became his parents. Eventually, a concubine named Chau was taken. The narrator goes into great length to explain the legitimacy of the taking in of a concubine, how it was according to the Laws of the Qing Dynasty, which at that time were officially recognized in Hong Kong. The concubine became a secondary spouse ('*tsip*') [*qie*] to the husband, and a subsidiary mother ('*shu mu*') to any children of the wife ('*tsai*') [*qi*]. The Ho Tung children were taught to call her Ah Jeh (Elder Sister). The concubine, however, remained childless at first. Lady Margaret undertook a more drastic measure, as it was her 'moral duty' (Cheng, 1976, 10) to ensure that Ho Tung must have children of his own. Instead of taking another *tsip* or secondary spouse, she decided to take in another '*p'ing ts'ai*' [*ping qi*] or equal wife. So Lady Margaret sought her aunt's permission to allow her daughter to marry Ho Tung. Lady Margaret promised to treat the equal wife as a sister, with absolute equality. The letter setting out the promises is included in her 1976 text. 'My two mothers continued to call each other Elder Cousin and Young Cousin with Father known to them as Second Young Master, in accepted Chinese style' (Cheng, 1997, 3).

This harmonious relationship between Sir Robert, Lady Clara and Lady Margaret remained a source of awkwardness for Cheng in her dealing with the Western community in Hong Kong and elsewhere.

In the Foreword to *Clara*, Governor Grantham, whom the narrator in *Reminiscences* calls 'Uncle Alex' (1997, 310), seems quite at a loss as to the appropriate way to identify Lady Clara in her relationship to Ho Tung and Lady Margaret. In eulogizing the extensive charitable works of the Ho Tungs which include the Hong Kong University women's hostel, Grantham explains rather cumbersomely how the hostel which 'bears the name of Lady Ho Tung Hall, and was founded by her [Lady Clara's] husband in memory of her cousin (referred to in *Clara* as 'Mother') (1976, vii)'. In the somewhat delicate situation, Grantham obviously finds it more appropriate to identify Lady Clara through her relationship to Lady Ho Tung (Lady Margaret) as cousins, rather than co-wives of Ho Tung.

As if to normalize the situation, the narrator sees it necessary to occasionally assure her readers that:

> For many westerners it may not be easy to imagine a situation in which a man had two wives and a concubine alive at the same time, all getting on amicably with one another, including the children born of different mothers. Yet to us this seemed quite natural.
>
> (1976, 41)

Ironically, despite the attempts by the narrator in *Clara* to normalize and naturalize the situation, the narrator in *Reminiscences* recalls how as a member of The Hong Kong Council of Women in the late 1940s, she had energetically fought against the practice of keeping concubines. Having 'grown up in a family where my father had two legal wives and a concubine, so I could, within reason, understand the man's, the woman's and the children's points of view … the various women's organizations of which I was a part had collected much evidence of the suffering experienced by families …' (1997, 319). This slip and change of tone on her personal views towards the concubinage system betrays Cheng's own ambivalence and awkwardness towards the incompatibility of the Ho Tung family system with modernity.

Cheng, in reconstructing her life as a Ho Tung, has meticulously included important family figures that were conspicuously absent in the life stories of her two sisters. Among others are: Lady Margaret (the matriarch which plays an extremely important role in the Ho Tung family); the adopted brother; Miss Katie, Ho Tung's nurse[11]; Ah Jeh the concubine (a marginal and tragic Chinese figure within the large Eurasian family, presented with much sympathy, and whose death was not known to her husband until two years later); and Ah Jeh's daughter Mary, (a figure briefly mentioned in Yeo's memoir).

⊱━◈━◦━◈━⊰

The Ho Tung family portrait drawn by Cheng is based very much on a Confucian (if not feudalistic) model. Despite Cheng's attempts to characterize the Confucian ethos, in Western terms, as being equivalent to a dedicated Humanist of the late nineteenth or early twentieth centuries, or a Stoic in Classical Rome (1976, 179), what she has unintentionally depicted in her narrative is a kind of Confucianism that stresses the strict adherence to rituals and practices. Her rigorous observance and austere obedience to Confucian rituals and ancestor worship pervades all her writing. Gittins, too, recalls the Ho Tung ancestor worship rituals at home, but with none of the enthusiasm found in Cheng. She remembers that it was a custom 'observed in our household' since 'Mother', that was Lady Clara, was 'a devout Buddhist' (1969, 31). For Gittins, the Buddhist rituals were something that she, as a daughter of Lady Clara, had no alternative but to comply with. In contrast, Cheng's memory of her childhood days is filled with ardor for the Confucian rituals and Chinese festivities.

Young Irene never seemed to be bothered by the kind of isolation felt by young Jean, nor does she remember any racial discrimination from other European children in the Peak neighbourhood. One obvious explanation is that she never felt the need to become part of the European Community on the Peak.

Here, perhaps, it is important to juxtapose the two sisters' views towards their residential status on the Peak. As discussed in the Gittins chapter, the narrator sees their ability to live on the Peak as a rare privilege granted to a Eurasian family. She clearly feels an exuberant sense of pride that her family was able to live in this exclusive residential district and a consciousness of their position in the colonial social hierarchy. Contrastingly, for Irene Cheng, the Ho Tung residence on the Peak is described with a somewhat apologetic tone. Instead of seeing it as a rare privilege obtained from the colonial authorities, she describes it as a result of their family having found the 'loophole' in the racist colonial ordinance. Cheng the narrator is obviously trying to perceive the matter not only from the point of view of the privileged, the included, and the initiated, but from the point of view of the excluded, the other. In dwelling on the memory of the 'loophole' situation, her narrative suddenly assumes the tone of a resistant rhetoric expressing her sense of indignation towards the pre-war colonial racialism and separatism:

> Although our family had found the 'loophole' in the ordinance that enabled us to reside on the Peak, many other Chinese families could not help feeling discriminated against. A similar racial prejudice angered those who were denied membership in the Hong Kong Club or stewardship of the Jockey Club. Although racing days always attracted tens of thousands of Chinese patrons, it was to be many decades before this irksome anomaly was righted. It took the Battle of Hong Kong during World War II, to finally convince the British and other Westerners that both the Chinese and the Eurasian communities were ready to fight and die side by side with all others to defend Hong Kong.
>
> (1997, 40)

Yet within the same page, her tone of indignation quickly shifts back to the privileged elitist rhetoric as she recalls the house numbers on the Peak:

> I believe the numbering started with the road up Victoria Peak, just next to the Upper Peak Tram Station, where the then Governor and his wife lived in a house called Mountain Lodge. When I was a child it was occupied by Sir Henry and Lady Blake, who were afterwards succeeded by Sir Henry May and his wife, both of whom I knew personally. Lady May was friendly to all the local school children, especially those of us who were members of her Ministering Children's League.
>
> (1997, 40)

The Bakhtinian double-voicing is commonplace in Cheng's narrative. There are moments of shifts during which Cheng quite genuinely enjoyed the attention bestowed upon her by the colonial rulers. Yet, they are often followed by an involuntary rebound towards a resistant rhetoric, lashing back in another direction.

The tram ride on Hong Kong's funicular railway occupies quite an important position in the sisters' memory of their childhood. Both sisters remember how conspicuous the Ho Tung girls were on the tram. But their reasons were quite different. Gittins believes that their conspicuousness was due to their ill-fitted western attire that made them so different from everyone else (1969, 29). Cheng says that they stood out simply because 'there were no other Chinese girls travelling daily on the tram, we were probably quite conspicuous' (1997, 79). From Cheng's point of view, they were conspicuous because they were 'Chinese'. From Gittins's point of view, their conspicuousness had nothing to do with race (they were a de facto part of the Peak community). They were merely betrayed by their quaint Western outfits.

The childhood that Cheng depicted was principally and predominantly Chinese, with everything regulated by the lunar calendar. Her process of getting familiar with Western knowledge, practices and other 'Western fare' (1997, 233) is often accidental, such as her discovery from her locket that she was born on 21 October 1904. Prior to this discovery, she recalls that she only knew that her birthday was on the 13th day of the ninth month (10). Cheng relishes the Chinese myths and classics taught by Master Chiu and recalls vivid detail the Chinese operas they performed, in particular the *Song of the Lute* where Daisy played the role of the grandmother scolding the son (57). Jean Gittins recalls with fondness their English governesses and the Western plays staged at home under their direction — particularly *Sleeping Beauty* where she herself was the Lilac Fairy (18).

Young Irene entered DGS in 1914 when she was 10 years old. Young Jean was in DGS between 1917 and 1923. Both sisters recall warmly the mixed community of the school. Gittins seems intent to emphasize the Eurasian and European origin of the school. In explaining the history of DGS, she says,

> It was known at that time as the Diocesan School and Orphanage, having been established by the Church Missionary Society for European and Eurasian girls.
>
> (1969, 27)

For Gittins, DGS had been established for 'European and Eurasian girls'. Symons, as we saw earlier, is very much in line with Gittins in her memory of DGS. Symons recalls that the demographics of DGS in the mid-1920s as having about 150 students with *just a few Chinese* among a crowd of Eurasians, Portuguese, Indians and expatriates (1996, 9). Cheng, however, represents a DGS community as one which included 'of course many Chinese and Eurasian girls as well'. The ideological inflection in the memory of the three DGS alumni is clearly in operation. Gittins and Symons remember DGS as a predominantly non-Chinese school with a just a small minority of Chinese. Cheng, on the other hand, remembers the school as one with a large majority of Chinese. Cheng says:

> In our class we had two Portuguese, two Indian, one Danish, several English, and of course many Chinese and Eurasian girls as well, and we all lived happily together in a truly international atmosphere. We did not talk much about our backgrounds …
>
> (1997, 84)

Cheng's concept of a 'truly international atmosphere' seems to be one where everyone's ethnic differences are not to be distinguished and not to be discussed openly as a form of courtesy. In *Clara*, Cheng says, 'the fact that many of the girls were of mixed parentage did not bother anyone; in fact, the atmosphere in the school was such that we never considered such matters' (1976, 77). For her, the norm of not talking and not considering about one's ethnic background seems to be the ideal environment for Eurasians — which for her began in DGS.

As can be seen, the home and school environment of the Ho Tung girls was not always compatible. At home, they were immersed in rigorous Confucian codes of behaviour. At school, the cultural sensitivies and national identification encouraged were fundamentally Western and modern. Hong Kong was never really directly involved in the First World War. But as DGS students, their sense of duty towards the Allied cause was instilled in them. The narrator remembers how 'each of us had to sew a flannelette shirt for the soldiers'. The students were often reminded of how 'the poor soldier waiting over there in France' was 'waiting for his other sock' (1997, 82).

Like many school children in Britain and throughout the empire who were encouraged to do their bit for the war effort, the Hong Kong Eurasian girls were also doing their part. But their training, apart from being a national identification with Britain or rather the Empire as an Allied Power, can also be seen as a form of class identification. The girls were getting practice in the kind of charitable work assumed to be part of the duties of the women of the privileged class in England or Europe. Girls growing up in the British elite class during this period were trained in charitable gestures, like Mrs Ramsay in *To the Lighthouse*, knitting her stocking for the lighthouse-keeper's boy.

There were instances where Cheng's early allegiance as a British subject was also instilled and demonstrated at home. According to the Editors' Introduction, we were told of Cheng's recollection of the death of King Edward VII in 1910. At the age of six, she and her sisters wore black hair ribbons and were dressed in somber clothing. It was a serious event for a young child because the whole family was in mourning, and that day they went to church to attend a memorial service (Cheng, 1997, xvi).[12]

As their education in DGS came to an end, the English education of the two older Ho Tung girls (Eva and Irene) also came to a halt.

> ... Eva and I had taken the Hong Kong Senior Local Examination, which was then the highest academic goal for girls in Hong Kong. Having reached this point, some girls took commercial courses that would qualify them for secretarial or clerical posts; others undertook nursing training or studied to become primary school teachers.
>
> (1997, 92)

But none of the three avenues seemed suitable for the daughters of Lady Clara. A decision was made by their mother that the girls should attend Sheung Fu, a traditional Chinese *si-shu*, where a relative, Diana Ho,[13] was studying. The girls found themselves switched abruptly from a genteel Victorian context to a rigid Confucian academia. The discipline was rigorous, as Cheng recalls, but the place did not evoke in her any form of embarrassing and alienating feeling so vividly described in the memoirs of Gittins and Yeo. The Sheung Fu narrative provides for Cheng another opportunity for a literary guide to the Chinese classical curriculum.

This reversion from a British education in DGS, which was based on what English students would learn 'back home', (1997, 77) to a traditional Chinese *si-shu*, marks Lady Clara's attempts to prevent her Eurasian daughters from getting too Westernized. Sheung Fu became a kind of balancing or diluting agent to reconnect the Ho Tung girls with their Chinese heritage.

⊳—۱ ٭⊱·٭·O·٭⊰٭ ۱—⊲

During the summer of 1921, Eddie, who was a student at HKU, learned from the Registrar that there would be a change in its admission policy towards females. Cheng recalls that a few years before 1921, DGS had asked HKU if it would be willing to let Anna Braun, a very bright Eurasian student of German and Chinese extraction, to attend as an external student. But the request had been refused, and nobody else tried or dared to say anything about the Ho Tung girls entering. Eddie came home one day and told his sisters, 'If you girls want to go to university, now is your chance' (1997, 105).

Since its inception in 1912 and up till 1922, the University of Hong Kong had remained an all-male university.[14] In 1921, E. A. Irving was serving as HKU's first registrar. His daughter, Rachel Irving, having previously obtained a Social Science Certificate at Bedford College, London, wanted to complete her education at HKU. The university at first refused her application, so the matter was referred to the attorney-general. On 23 June 1921, the Senate resolved to admit Miss Irving to the third-year arts course. During that autumn in 1921, while Eva[15] was still in Beijing with her parents, the narrator says:

> I entered as the first local girl to join the university, enrolling in the first-year arts course. Apart from Rachel Irving and myself there was only one other female student enrolled at the university that first term, Miss Lai Po-Chuen,[16] who was studying medicine. The effect we created can be imagined. We were three women students among a total enrollment of about 300 or just one percent of the total.

> (1997, 105)

The racial demographic of the first three female undergraduates was also satisfyingly symbolic in its representation: a British, a Eurasian and a Chinese. The following term, Eva Ho Tung and an English girl from Changsha joined the University. The in-take of female undergraduates had been such a progressive move for the institution that the authorities, according to Cheng, had quite forgotten to provide them with basic amenities such as a female restroom.

><+>-o-<+><

During their period at HKU, Lady Clara was often tied up in her charity work and travelling, and the Ho Tung girls had to take turns looking after the household. Jean served her turn in 1927. But apparently she was much less involved than Irene. 'Although I was in charge, this was nominal because things were really run by our staff of good and trusted servants. All I had to do was to sign the orders for money ...' (Gittins, 1969, 54). Irene's turn to take charge of the household was in 1925. To her, taking charge means more than just disbursing salaries. She was in effect the ritual secretary for the family:

> ... As Mamma's housekeeper, I was responsible for the remembrance of all the anniversary memorial days that we celebrated. I reminded and supervised all the staff at the Peak house to arrange for appropriate offerings for the anniversaries of the births and deaths of the Chang family ancestors. I also had to remind my siblings that they should visit Idlewild to pay their respects on Ho ancestral anniversaries.
>
> (Cheng, 1997, 125)

However, it had not been all that easy for Irene, for her other siblings apparently did not share her faithfulness towards family rituals:

> Once, when Jean and Grace were away at a beach party, I suddenly remembered that they had forgotten it was an anniversary day. Fortunately, I was able to get word to them to get up to Idlewild in time for the family dinner, as otherwise Lady Margaret would have been highly displeased at their lack of respect.
>
> (125)

Irene and Jean seemed to exist in totally different spheres of cultural sensitivity within the same Ho Tung household. Irene was like a dutiful young priestess of the family, while Jean was the happy carefree Eurasian girl who was eager to liberate herself from these anachronistic rituals at every opportunity.

><+>-o-<+><

Irene completed her final examinations at HKU despite the havoc caused by the general strike of 1925. The year 1926 marks the beginning of Irene's life away from the Confucian extended family. After graduating from university, she was sent to China as a companion to Lady Clara's god-daughter to spend the summer in Beijing. For the first time, Irene was on her own, as she recalls with much pride:

> This trip was one of the highlights of my life. It was a wonderful experience that I valued greatly, in the same way young people in England treasured their Grand Tour of Europe at a similar period in their lives.
>
> (1997, 127)

As if to 'write back' against the European tradition, Cheng sees her China trip as a kind of rite of initiation into Chinese heritage and refinement, in the way that sons of English aristocrats had been sent to continental Europe as an initiation into the refinement of European culture and heritage.

Her 1926 trip to North China was for Irene not only an introduction into the gentility of Chinese elite habits and thinking but, more importantly, the trip had become a kind of a watershed in her own construction of her Chinese identity. Before this grand tour, her Chineseness was defined largely as an identification with China as a culture and a tradition. This visit had allowed her to identify with China the place, its history and its people — more specifically the Chinese elites in the capital.

Beijing in 1926 was torn by swaggering warlords, unabated corruption and rancid poverty, but none of this was able to affect in any way the spell that the city cast on Irene. In the Chinese capital, just as young English elites were initiated into polished European society, young Irene was received into the illustrious circle of the Liangs. The narrator lavishly recalls how old Mr Liang was one of the famous '120', a group of students selected by the Ching Imperial government in the nineteenth century to go to the United States 'when they were still boys wearing pigtails' (1997, 128). One of the sons of old Mr Liang was a former prime minister turned financier. They lived in an old Chinese 'fortress of its day, with courtyard after courtyard' (132). For Cheng, the Liangs symbolized the privileged literati, the mandarinate, and the scholar-official class in old China. They were different from the Hong Kong Chinese bourgeoisie. They were not tainted by the compradore culture. They were not treaty port cosmopolitans or the hybrids in the International Concessions. For Cheng, the Liangs became metonymic of the old Chinese refinement and purity, free from any colonial mediation, yet in their traditionalism, they thrived in a kind of Chinese modernity with their overseas experience.

It was on this trip that Irene Cheng met her future husband H. H. Cheng, a brother of one of the Mrs Liangs, and a descendant of one of the three daughters of Imperial Commissioner Lin Tse-hsu. Lin's destruction of 22,000 chests of opium surrendered by the British traders in Canton in 1839 was seen as a heroic act against the humiliation wrought upon China by foreign imperialism. This connection with the Chinese national hero is meticulously recounted. But for the more critical reader, Irene Cheng's ecstatic enthusiasm about H. H. Cheng's connection to Commissioner Lin seems somewhat ironical considering the fact that her own father was a leading comprador of Jardines — a firm known for its proliferating opium trade in the nineteenth century.

Perhaps as another of Lady Clara's strategies to balance her children's cultural education, not long after Irene's return from China, she was sent to England and Europe with her sister Eva and Lady Clara. They sailed via the Indian Ocean and the Arabian Sea into the Red Sea to Suez before reaching the Mediterranean. Then they travelled overland through Europe before crossing the English Channel. Although the narrator named her China trip 'the Grand Tour of China', she refers to her trip to Europe and England as her 'Postgraduate Travels'. This shift in terms clearly relegates the importance of her European trip to below that of her China trip.

Her European travel experience is remembered and translated by the narrator in terms of her China experience. The snow-capped mountains in Chur, Switzerland reminded her of the light snow she experienced in Beijing (1997, 148). Soochow quickly came to mind when Irene saw Venice. The translation of these landscapes works in quite the opposite direction for Jean Gittins, for whom 'the arch bridges in Soochow bring to the mind of the traveler memories of Venice' (Gittins, 80). One sister translates places in the East through her impression of places in the West, while the other sister translates the West through the East. Each has a mental map that reflected and reconstituted the priorities of her own sense of identity.

Irene stayed in England with Lady Clara and attended some courses at the London Day Training College for a Secondary Teachers' Diploma Course. Her academic ambition, however, was cut short. Just before she was about to seek the examination for the diploma, a cable from Hong Kong demanded that Lady Clara should hurry back for the wedding of Robbie, who had returned from his training at Woolwich Military Academy. The wedding of a son was of such important magnitude for the family that Lady Clara could not afford to let her daughter stay in England alone.

Dejected, the filial daughter returned to Hong Kong with her mother and her half-completed diploma. Her parents were unable to see her unconventional priority of giving precedence to her own professional ambition. Ho Tung reminded her that she was then "'of suitable marriageable age" — I was almost 24 — and that if I went off for a few more years of study I might be "leaving it too late for marriage"' 'for girls of our upbringing' (1997, 161; 1976, 86).

Continuous written and oral appeals to the patriarch amid tearful protestations from her two mothers were made. It was not until many tantalizing attempts that the restraining Confucian codes were temporarily relaxed. Permission to leave home for studies abroad was granted. The young aspiring educationalist had by now decided that China and not Hong Kong was the place where she would to devote herself in the work of education. She enrolled at the Teacher's College of Columbia University at New York where courses were more compatible for teaching in China (1997, 155).

During her one-year stay in New York, Irene met two elderly ladies at a luncheon who were members of the Board of Trustees of the American Foundation for Lingnan University.[17] A wire from Lingnan was received a few months later inviting her to teach at the university. At 26 years old, the new postgraduate wired back 'Accept, subject to parents' approval' (172).

Irene's struggles to negotiate a balance between Confucianism and modern individualism, filial loyalty and personal aspirations, Western practice and Chinese theories continued to pull her in different directions. Her experiences in China in the 1930s, which will be discussed in the second part of this chapter, further complicated her already decentred subjectivity by her awakening to a nascent Chinese nationalism — a political loyalty which she, growing up in the Hong Kong compradore culture, had never before experienced.

Weighing Loyalties

It is almost biological ... I had to live by what was imprinted in my cells, remaining averse to and suspicious of high-flown abstractions, but totally engaged to that smell and savour and warmth, that feel of the tide, blood, heat, which is for me the people of China. With others, exultant ideologies may have priority, but it has never been so with me ... .

(Han Suyin, 1980b, 315)

The individual's announcement of an identity is always hostage to others' social constructions.

(Lim, 1994, xvii)

B eginning in the late 1920s and until after the war, Irene was spending most of her time outside the Confucian extended family network. It was during this period that she developed more consciously than ever an avidly strong Chinese identity — a Chinese identity that, far from being weakened by her absence from the East, had in fact been dramatically strengthened in her years of working and studying abroad in the West. With this newly appreciated Chinese identity, we also see an awakening to a growing sense of Chinese nationalism, a development that did not always co-exist harmoniously with her Confucian beliefs, or her loyalty as a British subject. This section examines the changes in the ideological configuration embedded in the narrative of this segment of Cheng's life from the late 1920s, and particularly, how she dealt with her new sense of Chinese patriotism in conjunction with her profound allegiance to her Confucian beliefs, her loyalty as a British subject, and how this intermittent patriotic feeling became dormant and then re-awakened, changing and affecting at every turn her perception of her own identity.

Cheng's own articulations of her Chineseness and Chinese national sentiments had undergone different nuances and changes and are marked by a kind of fluidity quite characteristic of some Hong Kong Chinese of her generation, particularly those who later went into diaspora. In the early part of her narrative, China was perceived as a culture rather than as a state. Her Chineseness was based strictly on her embracing Chinese culture, traditions and practices — a model of Chinese identity described by Tu Wei-ming which is based on a 'a lived reality' (1994, 1). Being Chinese, as a result, is as much an attainment as a given. China, for Cheng and many of the Chinese outside of the Mainland, functions as a 'civilization-state' rather than a geopolitical entity (viii, 18). So, in spite of the fact that Cheng was not born in China, had not physically grown up in China, and had never lived in China but in the colony of Hong Kong, she was still able to forge a relatively stable Chinese identity.

Her perception of the Chinese capital cities of Beijing and Nanjing had always been one of deference and awe. Yet, at the same time, she herself was always conscious of her own position in the periphery in three senses: coastal, colonial and Eurasian; in other words, born and raised as a British subject of mixed heritage from the colony of Hong Kong, away from the Chinese cultural and political centres. Her Chinese identity gained a political dimension in the early 1930s as she began to identify with Chinese nationalism, which was at that time fuelled by the encroaching Japanese aggression.

There is something in Cheng's Chinese nationalism that defies being grouped in the same category as a Chinese/Eurasian patriot like Han Suyin. Han Suyin's articulation of her own Chineseness is dramatically and overwhelmingly biological, transhistorical and essential to her very being. Metaphorically, she and her China are almost synonymous in her writings. She constantly refers to China, 'our own land' (Han, 1952, 261) and often invokes the collective peoples of China by saying, 'We are all Chinese together' (252). But under this intense patriotism, Han admits that 'at times, a wince, a twinge, from deep down within me reminded me that to many Chinese I was a Eurasian, and not always acceptable' (1968, 22). For Cheng, there is no such collective attention to 'we' or 'us'. The wince or twinge of being a Eurasian, if any, has been gently brushed aside. Perhaps conscious of her peripheral status as a Hong Kong British subject of mixed heritage, Cheng often refers to the Chinese as 'the Chinese' and Chinese patriotism as 'their patriotism'. Her omission of the first person plural pronoun suggests a kind of subtle detachment and perhaps a preference of staying on the periphery.

With her newly acquired postgraduate degree from the Teachers' College of Columbia University, Irene's entry into the 1930s was marked with exuberance and optimism in her devotion to education in China. Having obtained parental approval to work in China, Irene became a lecturer at the Department of Education at Lingnan University, Guangzhou.

Before the start of the spring term at Lingnan, Irene stayed briefly at her family home in Hong Kong. During this stay, she visited her alma mater to enquire of Florence's development. The narrator remembers a rather confrontational exchange on the Chinese language issue with Miss Sawyer, the principal of DGS. In her failed efforts to recall the details, she admits that 'I cannot remember the exact words that transpired between us' (Cheng, 1997, 174). (This admission of not being able to remember the exact exchange might appear to be an apology for her failing memory, but it could also be a claim of an autobiographical faithfulness and her refusal to fabricate the dialogue for narrative purpose.) Florence Yeo, however, quite vividly recalls the incident in her own memoir. Miss Sawyer drew herself up to her full height and bristled, 'Miss Ho-tung, we do not profess to teach Chinese in this school. If you wish your sister to learn Chinese, you had better take her away to another school' (Yeo, 26–27). With that, the matter was quickly settled between Irene and Lady Clara. Florence was to follow her sister up to Lingnan as an external student 'to catch up' on her Chinese. Lingnan became the place for the youngest Ho Tung to re-connect with her Chinese culture. The two Eurasian sisters travelled up the Pearl River to Guangzhou, Florence as a pre-matriculated student and Irene as a lecturer. In looking back at the hasty decision, the narrator says, 'I now very much regret that Mamma and I decided the matter without consulting Florence for her own reaction' (1997, 174).

Cheng confesses 'it was not until I read Florence's book, My Memories, written in later years and published in 1989, that I realized how miserable she had been during the months she spent with me at Lingnan University' (174). Cheng inserts extracts from Florence Yeo's memoir in *Reminiscences*, where she recalls her Lingnan experience:

> I was a little apprehensive about coming into an entirely Chinese community — the only Westerners were American missionary professors and lecturers in the University.
> There was a great problem welling up within me. At school in

Hong Kong, I was known to be Eurasian and not pure Chinese. But my family, especially Irene (who was determinedly hanging on to the fact that she was pure Chinese and nothing else) told me to say I was pure Chinese too. This puzzled and confused me and I felt it was dishonest. I found it difficult to mix with the other students, all of whom were of pure Chinese origin and I was continually teased about my appearance. I had light brown hair and brown eyes, my skin was fairer, whereas Chinese people have black hair and black eyes.

Chinese people can be very snobbish about race and I was made to feel an outcast. I wept through most of the first term and would hardly ever leave my sister's flat (I had to stay with her instead of in the girls' hostel, which made me even more 'different'). Lingnan was a disaster as far as I was concerned.

(Yeo, 28)

Florence could not accept her sister's insistence of their being 'pure Chinese'. But Irene saw their Chinese heritage (though only represented a partial ancestry) had the power to become totally defining so far as their ethnic identity was concerned. Florence saw this as deceptive and therefore dishonest. For Florence, Eurasianness had always signified a kind of visual prestige in pre-war Hong Kong; but in China, her Eurasianness suddenly became a visual stigma, a visible impurity and a biological adulteration. In this strongly Chinese environment, Florence's experience dramatically enacts Korgen's description of the ordeal of the bi-racial person who is in danger of having no identity or having a false identity — one in which only part of the racial heritage is acknowledged (Korgen, 5).

This is a case where an attempt to deny 'the difference' has the effect of highlighting it. It is not difficult to imagine how a bi-racial person who claims such racial purity would inevitably appear to others as overly race-conscious. In reflecting on her own Eurasian experience, Han Suyin argues that the need to insist on a pure racial identity (especially when the person's appearance does not seem to bear out the claim) often manifests a deep-seated racism or racial complex.

Han too writes about the embarrassment of claiming racial purity. During the 1930s in China, her husband Pao had insisted in front of his friends that Han was a pure Chinese. His intense race-consciousness, Han believes, was the result of the humiliating 'imprint of the West in Asia' which had triggered a reverse racial complex among the Chinese upper class (Han, 1968, 51). Han recalls how Pao's friends used to tease him:

'There is foreign blood in her, one can see that...'
'Not at all, she is pure Chinese,' retorted Pao. As if it was not written on my face that I was a Eurasian! I knew better now than to contradict him, but he would be furious with me, as if my face were my fault ...

(Han, 1968, 70)

Florence Yeo's situation at Lingnan is quite similar to that of Han Suyin. She found it difficult to insist on being pure Chinese when her physical attributes clearly did not conform to the Chinese ethnic norm. Irene's insistence on their racial purity might not reflect a reverse racial anxiety like that of Han's husband, but it certainly does reflect Irene's desire to deny the European Other in herself and her sister — a tendency which might have to do with the 'racial nationalism' (Xiao Liu, 203) prevailing at that time in China.

Cheng includes in her narrative that moment when the two elderly sisters finally talked about the anguish caused by the perceived racial differences:

About 60 years after the event, when I first read Florence's words, I was stunned. I had never fully realized how miserable I had made her. It was then 1990 and we were both in the twilight of our years, but I immediately telephoned Florence to apologise for having unintentionally caused her so much suffering back then. Of course, I had realised during the period 1930–32 that Florence was unhappy about certain things, but I thought that it was chiefly the exams she had to pass that concerned her. I had simply not realized that the racial question bothered her so much.

(1997, 175)

The narrator has politely navigated away from the 'racial question'. With all her regret for making her sister unhappy, she remains silent on why she had insisted on their being pure Chinese sixty years ago. Perhaps the event is too blurry in her memory. Or perhaps the subject is still too uncomfortable for her to probe into. But her silence on the subject of racial hybridity has again the effect of highlighting it.

Each of the Ho Tung sisters had her own strategy in dealing with her Eurasian heritage and visibility. Florence Yeo felt dishonest in claiming to be 'pure'. Irene Cheng believed in being 'pure'. Jean Gittins refused to tip the scale to either side in front of the Immigration Officer in Sydney and stood firmly within the intermediary space. Their cousin Diana Ho, as discussed in the second part of the Symons chapter, decided on a more practical way out: she simply went quietly to plead with Joyce Symons not to disturb the public perception of their racial identity since Joyce was British and she was Chinese (Symons, 51).

Irene's perception of herself and China had changed dramatically during her two years at Lingnan. Her Chineseness and Chinese identity, hitherto based upon social and cultural connections, now acquired a political dimension. She believed in the need to strengthen the country against foreign aggression. The feverish nationalistic sentiments that had seized the entire campus with General Man Chan San's [Ma Zhan Shan] hard-worn victory over the Japanese in North China had also had an effect on the Hong Kong Eurasian lecturer.[18] She participated in the fund-raising campaign for General Ma and encouraged one of her protégés to go into military training.

But like most things she aspired to in her life, this patriotic afflatus was soon to be countered by the deep-seated Confucianism that had dominated her existence for so long. Her intense filial and clan loyalty, that unassailably monolithic and prohibitive force in Irene's life, asserted itself at the most unexpected moments.

In late spring of 1932, Irene received a letter from Sir Robert, 'in which he said he was planning to go with Lady Margaret to Europe for their Golden Honeymoon. At the end he said: "It would be so nice if you could have gone with us"' (1997, 185). In spite of that odd third-conditional, the call of duty was clear and loud. How could she justify abandoning her students in the middle of a semester? 'I felt quite guilty leaving them, but I had to weigh my loyalties on both sides' (186). Cheng sought the advice of a colleague in Lingnan.

> We walked out on to the verandah just as the sun was setting, and
> almost simultaneously we both thought of a famous Chinese saying:
> 'When the sun has set, where will you be able to find it?'
>
> (185)

Irene immediately felt compelled to respond to her filial call. Her loyalty to
her parents was to take precedence over her loyalty to her students, her
educational aspirations for China and her burgeoning patriotism. Her
situation is very much as Bertrand Russell has described the Chinese of her
generation, where 'family feeling' is constantly militating against the growth
of public spirit (Russell, 40). For all these claims of filial piety, Irene was not
unaware of the possibility that by accompanying the elderly couple to Europe,
she might be able to persuade her father to allow her to stay for her doctoral
degree (1997, 186). So, it was by fulfilling her Confucian filial piety that
Irene could ease her way into the Western world of higher research and
studies. The clear antithesis between traditionalism and modernity becomes
blurred. Here, we see the collusion of different values, the apparent
Confucian filial loyalty collaborated happily with modern Western values
of individual desire and ambition.

The self-representation of Cheng in this part of her narrative is the figure
of the perfect Confucian daughter — the ever patient and respectful daughter
accompanying the aged father and his first wife (Lady Clara was not on the
trip) in a foreign land. They went by boat from Hong Kong, travelling via
the Suez Canal to England. In London, the Ho Tungs stayed at the Park
Lane Hotel. As she had previously escorted Lady Clara with her bound feet
around London three years before, she now escorted her other two parents
around the city. The trip had brought the daughter closer to Ho Tung and
Lady Margaret. 'We enjoyed the fun of doing things together and even
minor events took on a special meaning …' (Cheng, 1997, 190). It was
with a mixture of amusement and filial satisfaction that she recalls how the
old couple 'experienced some difficulty in negotiating the moving stairs' in
the tube trains (191).

The trip was concluded with Ho Tung presenting his daughter with a

Chinese poem. The autograph album where the poem was kept had long been lost, but the narrator distinctly remembers the free translation of the verses (the Chinese original of the poem is not included in *Reminiscences*):

> Fond of learning, industrious, and modest,
> Born intelligent, outstanding, glorifies my family.
> After studying and teaching you again pursue studies,
> You are indeed a hero, and your ambition deserves praise.
> This time studying in the English capital,
> When your studies have been complete you should return home quickly.
> Remember that your parents are advanced in age,
> Always bear in mind that you should consider both loyalty and filial affection.

(190)

The poem is heavily laden with the Confucian tenets subscribed by the Ho Tung family. Irene is praised as 'fond of learning, industrious and modest'. But perhaps the most satisfying line for Cheng is 'Born intelligent, outstanding, glorifies my family' (190). Her achievement is seen in the poem not as something personal but as a glory that she had brought to the Ho Tung family — a Confucian endorsement of her unconventional educational pursuit as a woman. The poem, however, ends with a strong Confucian injunction to return home.

Having faithfully performed her filial duty, Irene was allowed to stay behind to begin her PhD in London at the Institute of Education. Her five years in London marked a turbulent phase in Irene's emotional life where, among other things, her status as the daughter of Lady Clara was questioned and, in working with Eurasian youths, she was forced to confront her own Eurasianness.

As she began her life as a PhD student in London, Irene became involved with Dr M. K. Yue, a Hong Kong University medical graduate studying in Edinburgh, and a devout Christian from Fujian. There was, however, one concern on Irene's part — Dr Yue's family had arranged his engagement to a girl in Fujian eight years ago. Irene wrote an English letter, addressed to all three of her parents, seeking consent for her engagement to M. K. (194). Lady Clara was ill so Sir Robert did not consult her. The matter was handled by Sir Robert and Lady Margaret. The parental response was that they could not approve of her breaking up someone else's 'marriage' (194). Apparently, the two parents fully respected the contract of the arranged engagement entered into by Dr Yue's parents and the girl's family.

In any case, the relationship became sorely tested when Dr Yue, a staunch Christian, received a letter from his bishop, an Englishman, who was concerned that Irene's mother was not Sir Robert's first wife and 'wanted to know what her status really was' (195). Irene was furious about the bishop's question. It is a dramatic moment in which we can sense that the aged narrator, who has hitherto assumed the role of the detached memoirist faithfully reporting on the events and people in her life, suddenly re-lives that moment of indignation again. The autobiographical act in this instance is no longer a process of recording but a poignant re-living of that long past event. The long temporal gap seems to have suddenly shrunk. The narrating self re-enters and merges into the experiencing self. Normally, admitting the blurriness of her memory is quite common in her narrative, but here, the narrator specifically says: 'I remember saying angrily, "What does my mother's status have to do with him?"' (195) It is important to note that the narrative device in *Reminiscences* had mainly been very scrupulous (often laborious and sometimes confusing) recording of events and peoples in the reported speech. Dialogues and direct speech are rare. An assertion by the narrator of the exact words used and in direct speech signifies the impact the event had on the subject even after the lapse of sixty years.

The sensitive issue of illegitimacy was clearly implied in the bishop's questioning of her status. Cheng had deeply sympathized with Sir Robert in his coping with his own illegitimacy. Now she herself was being subjected to the same query about her legitimacy from an English minister who did not approve of Chinese marriage practices.

> It was indeed this letter from the Bishop of Putien and similar remarks made by others from time to time that led me much later to write the true story about my mother's marriage as a P'ing Chai (equal wife), which was fully in accordance with Chinese tradition and custom.
>
> (195)

Forty-one years later, her book *Clara Ho Tung: A Hong Kong Lady, Her Family and Her Times* (Chinese University, 1976) defends her mother's status and indirectly, her own status — a dual defense reiterated in her own memoir two decades later.

Meanwhile, Irene was conducting her research in juvenile delinquency for her PhD thesis. Her fieldwork involved working with British Eurasian youths in East London. Her choice had been inspired and conceived in 1928 when she and Lady Clara were invited by Chinese diplomatic and business circles to attend the Chinese Lunar New Year annual tea party with the Chinese community in London. Remembering the tea party, Cheng says,

> They also invited all the ethnic Chinese children residing in Chinatown and Soho. There were a couple of hundred of them, full of energy, and practically all of mixed race. I was told that only one of the [Chinese] men in East London had a Chinese wife. Most of the other fathers had been seamen, and they had to sign on to their ships in London. Many of them thus took English wives, whether or not they went through any form of marriage ceremony. However, they at least lived with their children and the children's mothers and supported them to the best of their ability.
>
> (1997, 198)

The word 'Eurasian' is never used to describe these children of mixed race. Cheng simply refers to them as 'ethnic Chinese children'. This is another instance where 'Eurasian' to her is synonymous with 'Chinese'.

The narrator shows particular respect for the Chinese fathers who, despite conditions during the Great Depression, 'did their best for the children, often spending their last penny on them' (198). The narrator never compares the condition of the London Eurasians to those early Hong Kong Eurasians of her father's generation, although from her descriptions of the early Hong Kong Eurasians (1976, xv; 1997, 43), one can find many similarities in the two cultures, particularly in their sense of marginality.

In her work with the young British Eurasians in Chinatown, Irene became a kind of Chinese presence and Chinese identity anchor for these Eurasian youths. She recalls how the Chinese fathers were eager that their children should know and understand China:

> During one of my visits to the family, Mr. Chang told his eldest daughter in broken English: 'Dolly, you no want go China. China nobody speak English. This lady come China. This lady speak English.'
>
> (1997, 202)

Irene was a living proof of Chinese modernity for the Eurasian youths, steering them to identify more closely with their Chinese heritage. Yet it is not clear whether Irene represented herself to the Eurasian youths as Chinese or as Eurasian. It is very likely that she represented herself as a Chinese as she did in Lingnan. The narrator does not mention any similarities between her own ethnic background and those of the British Eurasians. Nor does she compare her own Eurasian experience with those of the London youths. Neither the narrator nor the narrated Irene seem to see herself as anything other than a Chinese presence in the midst of a London Eurasian community. Though the narrator has not consciously admitted it, Irene Cheng must have found herself sharing much of the difficulties and ambivalence felt by these Eurasians. The difference, of course, is that for her it was her Europeanness that she found hard to accept, while for them, it was their Chineseness that was the problem.

Cheng describes with a kind of empathetic poignancy the plight of these young London Eurasians:

> If they found a job advertised, they probably would not even be called for an interview if they used their Chinese names on their applications. Sometimes they would try using their mother's maiden name, but if they were lucky enough to be called for an interview, their half-Chinese features would invariably give them away ... . In many cases they might not get the job because of the fierce competition, but they could not help feeling their Chinese blood put them at a disadvantage. This gave them a severe inferiority complex, and some of them were quite bitter and hated themselves for being part Chinese.
>
> (203)

This bitter sense of being part Chinese is certainly a familiar feature among Eurasian voices, particularly during the Second World War when many Eurasians failed to pass as whites in the port of Manila.

In her Chinatown-Eurasians narrative, Cheng also describes other academics, scholars and anthropologists working with her. Among them was Dr Y. K. Tao from Berlin University.

> Dr. Tao wrote his thesis on the anthropological aspects of children of mixed parentage. For his research he had taken samples of children of mixed Chinese and German race, the measurements of some of

their features, samples of their hair, and had done the same with some children of mixed heritage in Paris. He hoped later to obtain sample information from the children in East London's Chinatown.

(204)

The narrator describes the anthropological research on Eurasians in a very detached tone. Hybridity and Eurasianness become strictly objects of study. Her stance remains very much identified with that of the researchers, as if to precariously avoid slipping into the category of the research subject.

By the time the 'Chung Wah Club' was established for the Chinese and Eurasian youths around Limehouse and Pennifields in 1936 (1997, 339), Irene was in a state of nervous anxiety. With her heavy involvement with the social, psychological and anthropological research into mixed race children, in combination with her hectic schedule, her parents' and the English bishop's disapproval of her relationship with Dr Yue, and her conflict with Eva[19] (1997, 197) — all these had combined to cause her condition to worsen. At this point, the complexity and ambiguity of her own identity was heavily implicated in her problems, both at work and in her private life. Florence, who met her in London 1933, recalls:

Irene was a little changed. I felt, she couldn't stop talking … She was attempting too many projects. She was taking her higher degrees, as well as starting up a club in Chinatown for the young people of mixed parentage …

(Yeo, 44)

A sudden confession of her own inability to cope with her Eurasianness in 1933 dramatizes her hitherto detached manner of recording the events of her life, and is in direct opposition to her complicit reticence on the 'race question'. The long suppression of the issue suddenly bursts to the surface. As she painfully retrieves this part of her Eurasian experience, the reticent pact falls apart.

In 1933, Sir Robert unexpectedly came to London where Irene had to serve as his personal secretary. Sir Robert had hoped to join the Chinese delegation for an economic conference in London. However, soon after Dr T. V. Soong's (brother-in-law of Generalissimo Chiang) arrival in London, Sir Robert was told that the Nanjing government had not approved his appointment as a delegate. The narrator recalls how Sir Robert was much affected by his unsuccessful bid to join the conference:

> He felt that they had not accepted him because he was Eurasian. I realized that this was still a sore point with him and tried to cheer him up.

(1997, 209)

That evening the father's Eurasian quandary seemed to have an effect on the emotionally delicate daughter. The Eurasian issue was something which Irene herself had never really been able to resolve satisfactorily. After a long and exhausting meal with the Chinese delegation, father and daughter returned to Claridge's Hotel. Irene was too polite to tell Sir Robert that she wanted to rest. Their conversation changed from one topic to another, then for no apparent reason, Irene suddenly broke down sobbing. This marked the beginning of a nervous breakdown, which announced itself, appropriately enough, as she sat face to face with her Eurasian progenitor.

Irene was sent to a nursing home to the north of London where she had to take complete rest. At this point in her story, the narrator seems ready to abandon her earlier reserved manner in dealing with her Eurasian heritage. With an uncharacteristic candour she tells the reader:

> The psychological stress posed by my voluntary work with the young British Eurasians, combined with overwork and physical illness had become too much to cope with. This was partly because I had not yet come to terms with my own Eurasian background.

(212)

This sudden forthright confession had literally thrown all the earlier reticence and delicacy into pieces. Was she questioning the authenticity of her own 'Chineseness' in her capacity to help these London Eurasian youths to get in touch with their Chinese heritage? Or was she unable to reconcile that 'European' Other in her? But the brief confession leaves as quickly as it came. There is no outpouring of emotions, no inward reflective self-exploration, as if afraid that by probing further, it might invoke more pain than she could endure. The reflective self-scrutiny of autobiography gives way again to the historical record of memoir.

Irene was very much cut off from the outside world during her enforced rest. Visitors were denied for fear of upsetting her. Both Eva and Dr Yue were turned away. But she was allowed to receive letters from outside. A friend in Guangzhou sent her Chinese periodicals. But, the narrator recalls, 'I was too busy, too tired, or too lazy to read them' (1997, 55). These rolled-up Chinese periodicals were used as limbs for a doll that the patient was making for herself. Is this her way to distance herself from her earlier intense identification with China and the happenings in China? One day, Irene received a letter from a friend who had read in the newspaper that Ho Tung was hospitalized. Fearing that her father might be dying, the filial daughter anxiously appealed to the doctor, 'according to Chinese custom, children must be at the bedside when a parent passed away' (211). Here, the narrator seems to suggest it is in a sense her filial call that had cured her — the Confucian sense of filial duty had saved her from the nervous prostration, restoring her to a traditional Chinese order.

Whether or not it was her Confucian sense of duty that shook her out of her illness, Ho Tung did not die and Irene was released from the nursing home. The narrator confesses that she could not possibly continue her thesis based on her work with the British Eurasians. 'I decided to take some of the pressure off by changing to a more philosophical topic' (212). Is this another of her avoidance strategy to deal with her Eurasianness? Her new thesis was entitled 'Ancient and Modern Educational Theory in China'. Is this an admission that the Eurasian issue had contributed to making her ill, or that a return to the purely Chinese was the path back to well-being and equilibrium? Abandoning her research on the Eurasian youths, Irene sought security by immersing within Chinese theoretical confines. By late 1936, Irene finished her PhD oral defence and was preparing her return to the East.

⊱━━❖━━⊰

Irene's personal goal of devoting her work to education in China materialized as she secured a position with the Ministry of Education in Nanjing. Like her years in Lingnan, Irene's Nanjing experience had further inspired her loyalty for the war-torn China. In early 1937, the Japanese had already turned North China into a second Manchuria (Hsu, 78). Nanjing was now very much within their target. But Irene's ardour to serve China was undiminished and she continued to be drawn towards China — a feeling also shared by Han Suyin at this time in the 1930s. 'The Japanese invaded China, and this old biological stir took over: I could not stay in peace in Europe, studying, where there was war in China' (Han, 1980b, 315). Han Suyin returned to China in 1938. Irene Cheng returned to China in 1937.

Irene's faith in the Nanjing government remained strong. 'The Nationalist Government had moved there and seemed to be doing a good job of developing it into a new capital city for the country' (1997, 214). As Editor by Special Appointment, Irene started working for the Ministry of Education in Nanjing in March 1937 where she edited and translated booklets about education in China from Chinese to English (217). But more importantly she acted as an escort of foreign educational visitors to the leading schools and universities in Nanjing (218). She served as a kind of public relations officer for the Nanjing government — introducing the Chinese contexts to the West — consciously or unconsciously taking up again the role of a bridge figure.

Soon after Irene started working in Nanjing, the Japanese aggression in China worsened. The bombing of Nanjing began around the middle of August. Wealthy residents and officials had already evacuated their wives and children, while a large part of the population did not have the means to leave. Poorly prepared for war, the city did not even have any air raid shelters. Standing under a large tree during an air raid was probably the best protection they had. The narrator recalls how the young patriot arrived at her decision: 'All the same I was determined to stay. I argued that I had gone there to work, and it was now my moral duty to remain' (221).

Irene's zealous commitment to Nanjing and her dedication to education in China superceded all fears of the impending Japanese invasion. She participated in patriotic war work in Nanjing under Madame Chiang Kai-shek who was actively organising the women in Nanjing under the Chinese Women's National Association for Relief of the Officers and Soldiers of the Defensive War. Chinese women everywhere were urged to form their own local branch associations. 'As a matter of course, all of us women in Nanjing who had been invited to join the parent association did so and contributed whatever time and resources we could afford' (221). Cheng's reference to 'all of us women in Nanjing' illustrates how very strongly she identified with the people in Nanjing, despite the fact that she had only started working in Nanjing a few months before. There was a sense of moral heroism in her insistence on staying. Residing in a wartime capital in the midst of a defensive war is a perfect site for an identification and investment in 'resistance'. Yet her heroism was short-lived as her determination to stay began to waver.

Towards the end of 1937, the government had fled, and no Chinese authorities remained to protect the civilians when Japanese troops poured into the city bent on violent retribution (Fogel, 18).

Around the end of August 1937, H. H. Cheng, brother of one of the Mrs Liangs whom Irene met in her first Beijing visit in 1926, was in Nanjing. He repeatedly urged her to leave the city. 'I was quite confused and did not know what I should do. H. H. repeatedly tried to persuade me to leave, but I felt strongly that it was my moral duty to stay'. As if to alleviate the guilt she felt, the narrator recalls how H. H. described to her the normal practice among official circles in China at the time. 'Today you may see your friends and colleagues around; tomorrow they might have taken flight and not even told you they were going' (Cheng, 1997, 222). Eventually, after discussing the matter with her boss Dr Wang, Irene Cheng decided to leave, but not without a heavy conscience:

> Since I had not told my colleagues about my conversation with Dr Wang, they must have regarded me as a deserter.
>
> (223)

As a member of the Nanjing Ministry of Education, Irene saw herself as part of the disgraced government that had fled and abandoned the city. Particularly in view of what was to happen to Nanjing not long after she left, Cheng had become, in her own words, a 'deserter' (223).[20]

Accompanied by H. H., Irene went to the Yangtse Hotel near the river where a British flag was flown (222). The Union Jack had, in the midst of all the chaos in Nanjing, provided for the Eurasian British subject not only physical protection but psychological security as well. A British presence in the form of the Union Jack in a frantic Chinese city can be read as a strategic device symptomatic of choices in being Chinese and/or British. Irene in a way was exercising that strategic identity choice that in some way foreshadows the wartime manoeuvre of her sister Jean as well as many wartime Eurasians. The two sailed for Hankow and took the train to Guangzhou where they took the night boat back to Hong Kong.

Considering the horrors and atrocities inflicted on the fateful city soon after her departure, Irene's Nanjing period, though brief, serves as a vital and essential source in her construction of her Chinese identity from then on.

⊱───◦───⊰

The Hong Kong that Irene returned to had become a haven for those who had the means to flee China. Well-known ladies from China joined hands with the leading local Hong Kong ladies in relief efforts. The Hong Kong Chinese Women's Relief Association under Madame Sun Fo (daughter-in-law of Dr Sun) was formed. Lady Clara became the vice-president and Madame T. V. Soong the chairman (Cheng, 1997, 224).

Upon her return to Hong Kong, Irene found herself 'immediately roped in to serve as the English general secretary' to the Hong Kong Chinese Women's Relief Association (224). Lady Clara, she recalls, became heavily involved with the Hong Kong New Life Movement Association in support of the Chinese army. Perhaps sensitive to the ideology associated with the New Life Movement, the narrator does not mention the ideological tenets associated with this movement, but describes it as a purely army relief association. The political tenets of the New Life Movement and its associated 'Confucian' ideology were sometimes likened by many at the time to the ideological organs of Fascism in Germany.

⊱───◦───⊰

Irene, who was then 33 years old, decided to seek her parents' approval for her courtship with H. H. Cheng. H. H. was from North China, and did not belong to any of the ethnic socioeconomic categories from which other Ho Tung sons and daughters-in-law were drawn. Nor did he share any of the common alliance with the Eurasian compradore families like the Los or the Hungs, or the Westernized Eurasian families like the Gittins. And he was not a bright 'local boy' who had made his way through the colonial system like Yeo. Both his English and Cantonese were weak. From Irene's point of view, H. H. represents the untainted, unhybridized Chinese from the cultural centre of China. But from her parents' point of view, H. H. represents the Chinese from the provincial North who lacks the sophistication of the treaty port culture — a very marginalized figure within the Eurasian community.

Plate 12 Last photo of Lady Clara (second row, third from right) with the Ho Tung family, taken on Irene Cheng's birthday on October 1937 at Idlewild. Reprinted from *Intercultural Reminiscenses*, courtesy of The David C. Lam Institute for East-West Studies, Hong Kong Baptist University.

In many ways, the choice of spouses of the Eurasian women is an expression of their own ethnic identities. Joyce Symons and Jean Gittins both married Westernized Eurasians who never used any Chinese surnames. Vic, the eldest Ho Tung sister, according to Irene Cheng, being a very obedient Ho Tung daughter, married the choice of her parents, a Eurasian with a Chinese surname (Cheng, 1997, 89). Compared to the other Ho Tung sons-in-law, H. H. was an extremely undersirable suitor which potential alliance would never harmonize with the social and cultural sensitivities of the Ho Tungs." Lady Clara seemed to have a particular aversion for this man from North China:

> Mamma and I never discussed it face to face, but occasionally she would make some little remarks or facial expression if she saw H. H. with me. That made it quite clear to me that she did not approve of the match. It hurt me terribly that she was not pleased.

> (228)

Lady Clara died suddenly in January 1938 surrounded by the large family. Irene, needless to say, experienced spasms of remorse and guilt and felt that she and H. H. had unintentionally added the 'straw that broke the camel's back' (232).

As a way to assuage that painful sense of guilt and grief, Irene immersed herself in war work. The extensive war work that Irene was involved in was very different from those described in her sisters' memoirs. It had nothing to do with the Auxiliary Nursing Service (ANS) or the Voluntary Aid Detachment (VAD), which included many Europeans and Eurasian women. Florence Yeo was a member of the ANS and so was Joyce Symons's mother Lucy; and Tanya Lee served with the VAD. Cheng's elaboration on the Chinese relief associations and other local bodies like the Po Leung Kuk is another indication of her ethnic preference and political loyalty.

In 1940, having recently returned from Nanjing, Irene saw herself as nothing other than a Chinese, closely tied to the Mainland. At this point, her loyalty seemed to rest more with the Nanjing government than the local Hong Kong Chinese community and certainly not the colonial government. She did not look to the British to help her out, nor did she feel inclined to participate in any British-related war work. During the summer of 1940, as discussed in earlier chapters, the evacuation process in Hong

Kong was feverishly under way. Cheng makes no reference to the evacuation process, which had so pre-occupied the Eurasian community and takes up much important narrative space in the other Eurasian memoirs. Nor does she mention the dissatisfaction of the local Hong Kong Chinese community about the racialised evacuation scheme. Having dutifully observed the mourning period of 27 months for Lady Clara, Irene married H. H. in September 1940. There is no mention of any lavish banquet or traditional ceremonies — a clear sign that it was not a highly regarded alliance in the eyes of the Ho Tung family. The couple spent a few days on honeymoon at a hotel in Macau (238). Irene's eventual marriage to H. H. seems to constitute for her a kind of authentication of her Chineseness. H. H., who had descended from an unbroken elitist lineage from Imperial Commissioner Lin Tse-hsu, the Chinese anti-colonial hero of the nineteenth century, had in a way compensated for the hybrid descent and underlying illegitimacy that tinted the Ho Tung lineage.

Out of the three Ho Tung autobiographers, Irene Cheng is the only one who narrates in great detail the Diamond Anniversary of Sir Robert and Lady Margaret's wedding on 2 December 1941 — six days before the Japanese invasion of Hong Kong. It is an occasion that cannot be found in Jean Gittins's texts despite her detailed recounting of almost all of the family weddings. Florence Yeo, as we have seen, has mentioned it briefly but has not clarified with whom Sir Robert was celebrating. With much autoethnographic enthusiasm, and without foregoing another opportunity to educate her reader, Cheng describes at great length these traditional ceremonies and customs. Again, like most Ho Tung celebrations, it is more a colony-wide event than a family event. Gwen Dew, the American reporter who was stranded in Hong Kong, describes how

> A thousand guests were invited, from high-ranking Sir Mark Young, the Governor-General, to lowly me. Golden decorations filled the elaborate ballroom; champagne flowed as proverbially. The candle was burning at both ends in Hong Kong, but time was wearing thin — this lavish fête took place in the first week in December.

> (Dew, 16)

But if Irene Cheng describes it as a celebration of Chinese cultural continuity, Dew is more inclined to see it as signaling the end of a way of life — a way of life for the powerful and closely-knit Eurasian community as well as for the colonial elites.

Hostilities began less than a week later on the morning of 8 December 1941. Irene Cheng and Florence Yeo have both reconstructed in their respective memoirs the experience of the stranded Ho Tungs in the Peak and Idlewild during the days of fighting. Gittins glosses over it very quickly. Their inclusion and exclusion of the Ho Tung experience and their reconstruction of the events must not be read as accidental as they provide important pointers to these authors' own sense of social identity within and without the Ho Tung community.

The thought of returning to the Ho Tung family never seemed to have crossed Jean Gittins's mind. Once Billy Gittins was called to duty, she had decided to move into the university staff house — it is a decision that eventually leads to her voluntary internment with other British university staff. Irene Cheng saw herself as a Chinese and Florence Yeo regarded herself as a Eurasian, and they were a part of the large crowd of the unprotected Ho Tung refugees who had to leave the European reserve and find their way to the Chinese part of the town. The Ho Tung Peak residence (The Falls) was under heavy shelling and bombing. Irene, H. H. and their six-month-old infant were there. Eddie, his four children and his secretary Miss Webb were also there, for they had not yet returned to Shanghai after the Diamond Anniversary celebrations. There was a retired British nurse, Mrs Archer, who took charge of the Chang children whose parents were family friends working in Chungking. There were the two baby amahs and a couple of women servants in addition to an army of household staff. Florence, too, was there with her three children.

Both Irene Cheng and Florence Yeo recall the events in great length during those initial weeks of fighting: how the group had to move from the Peak to another semi-detached house billeted for them, how all fourteen of them piled into the little car of a Lingnan professor in order to reach Idlewild on Seymour Road (Cheng, 1997, 252–257; Yeo, 72); how each member of the group appealed to his or her own divine power, one to the Goddess of Mercy, one to Lady Clara, one to God and Jesus Christ, while another said Hail Marys (Cheng, 1997, 256; Yeo, 72); how Eddie was hit by a shell and lost his legs (Cheng, 1997, 258; Yeo, 71); how the Japanese commandeered Idlewild for their use alternately as a site of pleasure with young prostitutes (Cheng, 1997, 259; Yeo, 74) and as a parlor for a memorial service for Japanese officers killed in the fighting (Cheng, 1997, 259); how H. H. with his fluent Japanese saved the Ho Tung women from the harassment of the Japanese 'guests' (Cheng, 1997, 259; Yeo, 74).

Yet, the two war narratives remain very different in tone. Cheng's narrative is very much a story of a large family group who huddled together under the general protection of Lady Margaret and tried to share what little resources they had. Idlewild was the haven for the Ho Tung family, their relatives and friends in adversity. Yeo's narrative is more a story about the confusion, the distrust and the uncertainty of a motley group thrown together in time of war. She vividly recalls the pilfering in the large household by 'hangers-on' (Yeo, 74), the numerous relatives and servants, the crowded conditions in the basement with forty people having access to one toilet and a basin (72), the constant fear of living in the town house with the Japanese quartered on the top three floors, and most importantly her sense of being unwelcome. 'I felt unwanted and a burden in my Father's house' (76). She does not say by whom she felt unwanted and to whom she was a burden. Lady Margaret is not mentioned in Florence Yeo's story.

As can be expected, in Cheng's story the figure of Lady Margaret looms large as the head of the household under siege. The reader can feel the presence of the matriarch pervading the text as the narrator reverently refers to her benevolent authority. We feel how the dignity of this great lady was compromised as she was forced to move into the basement with her amah-companions. With the magnanimity and family piety expected of the Confucian gentry, Lady Margaret took responsibility for providing the Ho Tung refugees with shelter and food. Irene was consulted by Lady Margaret in her worry about how to feed all the people gathered there. The narrated Irene seems very much in control of the situation. Florence, on the other hand, appears to have felt like one of the unwelcome refugees, quite at the mercy of those in control. Cheng narrates from high up on the household hierarchy, while Yeo narrates from the lower rungs of the household hierarchy.

In Cheng's narrative, Lady Margaret became a benefactor not only to the motley Ho Tung group from the Peak, but also to the people in the neighbourhood. As the Japanese had turned off the water supply to Hong Kong Island, Idlewild survived because of a well in its courtyard, which seemed to have an inexhaustible supply of water. The narrator recalls how Lady Margaret allowed people from the neighbourhood to come and queue up for water:

> Each would be shouldering a pole with a pair of buckets usually Standard Oil Kerosene tins tied to each end with wire. There was a constant stream of these people coming and going all day long, so the side gates leading immediately to the inner courtyard were left open during daylight hours ... .
>
> (1997, 258)

Perhaps without consciously realizing it, Cheng has created a powerful symbol of the Ho Tung family head — in this case, Lady Margaret the matriarch — as the epitome of Confucian virtue, and the manifestation of moral goodness (*ren* and *yi*) of those in power. The matriarch had not only provided for her own clan members but also her dependent neighbours by allowing them to draw water from the well in Idlewild. In this instance, she had performed the moral duty pertaining to a good Confucian gentry lord. On another level, this moral goodness or generosity of the Ho Tung matriarch could also be read as symbolic of the Western Christian virtue of humanitarianism. Water represents a life-giving source in the Christian context. By sharing the water with not just their own clan members but with their neighbours, outsiders, and by extension, the people of Hong Kong, the Ho Tung matriarch (representing the Ho Tung clan) had expressed a boundless Christian universal compassion and humanitarianism. This story of the Ho Tung well, of course, serves as a very important reminder to the reader of the historical benevolence and munificence of the Ho Tungs to Hong Kong people, not only in times of peace and prosperity, but also in times of adversity.

The story of this life-giving well figures quite differently in Florence Yeo's memoir. The well is briefly referred to. But instead of possessing an inexhaustible supply of water meeting the needs of the Ho Tungs and the entire neighbourhood, Yeo recollects: 'as far as I can remember, there was a little spring in the main courtyard of the house. But, it was during the dry winter months and not much water came through' (73).

How should we explain the very different versions of the same story? Certainly we are dealing with two elderly women with imperfect recall of events long ago. But a more interesting factor here is the ideological inflection of memory. Here, I would again argue that their different cultural orientations and ethnic identifications would best explain their different perceptions, which affect their different ways of reconstructing their memory, and which in turn affect their respective ways of representing the family experience. Florence Yeo, like Jean Gittins, saw herself very much as a Eurasian. The family that she remembers was very much based on a Western bourgeois family model. Lady Margaret has never been acknowledged by Yeo as part of her family. Besides, Yeo never embraced the kind of rigorous Confucian filial piety that Irene Cheng had taken to heart. Even if she had, her very Western perception of her family would not require any absolute Confucian filial obedience to Lady Margaret. Consequently, Yeo's remembering and representation of the Ho Tung family experience during the war is very much affected by her own alienation from the matriarchal power embodied in Idlewild. Things and events associated with the matriarch, such as the story of the bountiful well, are subconsciously downplayed or forgotten, while in Cheng's memory they are emphasized and celebrated.

Putting together all the three war narratives of the sisters (or all four war narratives if we include the war narrative by the sisters' relative, Joyce Symons), their respective perception of the war also creates very dramatic contrasts of political loyalty. For Jean Gittins, Florence Yeo and Joyce Symons, the war remembered was very much between Japan and Britain. Their sympathies were clearly with Britain and the Allied countries. The heroic defense of the indefensible Hong Kong occupies a very important position in their personal narratives. Though Gittins herself was not involved in the battlefront, the defense of Hong Kong stays very much in the limelight. The role of the Hong Kong Eurasians Volunteers in the protection of the island plays a crucial part in the defining of their Eurasian identity – one that is intricately linked with privilege but also with sacrifice not fully appreciated by the Hong Kong society.

Cheng's narrative of the war does include briefly the Hong Kong war effort by the locals. She recalls how 'numerous young and middle-aged men and women volunteered and received varying degrees of military training so that should Hong Kong become involved, they could immediately join up and participate in its defense' (1997, 244). Yet, this is recalled with a kind of distance and detachment. For Cheng, the war in Hong Kong was more like an extension of the Sino-Japanese war theatre than a conflict specifically between Britain and Japan. Hong Kong was at the complete mercy of Japan as Nanjing was. As was the fate of many other Chinese cities, defence was quite out of the question.

Cheng's sense of her Chinese patriotism and loyalty as a British subject takes on an interestingly ambivalent turn as she narrates the warm benevolence of a Japanese officer friend of H. H. during the most difficult part of her life in occupied Hong Kong.

One morning in April 1942, after feeling unwell for a few days, H. H. died suddenly of kidney failure. In less than twenty months of marriage, Irene found herself a widow and a mother. Irene phoned the Japanese officer to inform him that H. H. had died. As he did not fully grasp the meaning of what she said, he came immediately to their house.

> When he found H. H. dead, he simply knelt down silently beside the body and must have said a prayer of some kind in Japanese. …
> As soon as he knew that I wanted to have H. H. cremated, he immediately set about making all the necessary arrangements with the Japanese crematorium. For the funeral he came wearing full military uniform, including his sword, and led the funeral procession.
>
> (1997, 267)

Despite the narrator's earlier distrust of the Japanese and her own husband's uneasiness with the Japanese, there is almost a sense of satisfaction in this open demonstration of Japanese friendship for H. H. Her description, of course, indicates how her husband's devotion and interpretation work for the Japanese was honoured, which might be important to emphasize since his acceptance into the Ho Tung family had not exactly been unanimous. But she does this at the cost of admitting to an image that would horrify a nationalist — the funeral procession led by a Japanese military officer! Yet, there was no resistance or flinching from this bestowing of Japanese military honour. How can this open Japanese honour reconcile with her Chinese patriotism, if not with her loyalty as a British subject? This Japanese friend remains anonymous throughout the memoir.[21] This could well be a memory lapse but could perhaps also be read as the narrator's strategy to distance herself from this unusual Japanese honour during the war.

After the death of H. H., like most Chinese during the Occupation who returned to their village of origin in China, Irene returned to the Cheng family in North China, of which she was a new member, where she worked in a Japanese-controlled mining company in Mukden until the end of the Second World War.

Many local Hong Kong residents returned to the city after the Japanese surrender — some to stay and some to visit. Joyce Symons returned in September 1945. Jean Gittins returned in August 1946. Irene Cheng came back to Hong Kong in September 1946. She did not share the sense of displacement so poignantly represented in Symons nor the sense of indignation recalled by Gittins (1969, 191–192). Perhaps, thinking back on the experience of the Ho Tung clan marooned at Idlewild, she felt a strong sense of elegiac mourning at the passing away of an old genteel world of bourgeois Hong Kong:

> Looking back I realise that the Japanese occupation of Hong Kong was a true turning point in the lives of my family and the whole Eurasian community. In some ways it no doubt brought us closer together, as we helped each other through the hardships caused by the war. However, it ultimately caused us to scatter and heralded the end of a gracious lifestyle that had its roots in the very social foundation of Hong Kong.
>
> (1997, 293)

The structure within the Ho Tung clan had also changed by the death of Lady Margaret during the Occupation. The choice of burial of Lady Margaret presented another interesting shift of Eurasian identity. Lady Margaret wanted to be buried in the Colonial Cemetery instead of the Chiu Yuen Eurasian Cemetery in Pokfulam, even though she herself had administered the Chiu Yuen Cemetery, the land of which Sir Robert had obtained from the Hong Kong government for use by the Eurasian community (292). Was it her final attempt to re-identify with her Scottish father Hector Coll Maclean, who was also buried in the Colonial Cemetery?[22] The narrator does not comment on this.

In the post-war decades, Irene served the education sector in Hong Kong in her capacity as member of several school boards, as an Education Department school inspector, and later as principal of Tai Shing School (under the Confucian Academy). In her initial post-war years, her loyalty to the Nanjing government was still evident as she continued to advise some of the vernacular schools to register with the Ministry in Nanjing (even though the colonial government was becoming extremely wary of these affiliations with Nanjing).[23] How can her loyalty to Nanjing be compatible with her colonial loyalty? This is perhaps another example of double loyalty, which is very much a decisive feature of the Hong Kong compradore culture — one based on collaborationism and nationalism. As Carroll says of Ho Kai, the first Chinese to serve on the Legislative Council, 'Ho's Chinese nationalism was formed as part of his colonial experience' (149).

It was during the 1950s and 1960s that Irene's Chinese patriotism seemed to have receded while her colonial loyalty came back to the foreground. Upon her retirement from the Education Department in 1961, she was awarded an OBE. This royal recognition of her work in education serves as another instance where colonial loyalty and Confucian duty can be celebrated simultaneously. Brimming with pride, the narrator gives an inventory of decorations her family had received — something which neither Jean Gittins nor Florence Yeo, even at the height of their colonial loyalty, had attempted.

> Of course, my family had already received signal honours from the Crown. Father was first awarded a Knight Bachelor by King George V in 1915 … My eldest sister Vic became an MBE, and her husband M. K. was knighted as Sir Man Kam Lo. Later in 1955 Father received a second Knighthood, this time becoming a KBE or Knight of the Order of the British Empire. It was probably the highest award that could have been given to a person who had not been a senior government official.
>
> (1997, 351)

Irene herself had lived up to the honour of the Ho Tung family. She elected to receive her honour from Queen Elizabeth in Buckingham Palace. An acute lucidity infuses the narrator's memory as she recalls the details in her meeting with the Queen (quite contrary to her earlier blurry memory of meeting Queen Mary[24] [wife of King George V] [191] and the rather token description of the young Queen in 1953 [341].)

> The Queen was seated on an elegant but simple chair placed on a dais about several steps higher than floor level … . When my turn came, as the Queen leaned forward to place the red ribbon over my neck, I asked her softly if she remembered giving my father his award in 1955. I reminded her that he had been in a wheelchair at the time. She assured me that she had not forgotten.
>
> (351)

Her recalling process leaps onto a new euphoric stage as she remembers how the Queen assured her that she had not forgotten her father Sir Robert. It is an exhilarating colonial moment and a Confucian one too.

Irene retired in 1967 and left Hong Kong for San Diego, US. For Hong Kong, 1967 was a year of riots, bombs, uncertainty and trouble spurred by anti-colonialism and anti-British sentiments. Many Hong Kong people, including Joyce Symons (1996, 62), agree that the first wave of post-war migration out of Hong Kong started in 1967. Irene Cheng, however, never makes any reference to the 1966 or 1967 riots. Her omission of the riots seems curious considering her position as a school principal of a vernacular school, since during that period, many schools were interrupted by the demonstration and riots. This may or may not have to do with a reluctance to allow her departure to be seen as a sign of loss of confidence and abandonment of Hong Kong — a sentiment quite familiar to many Hong Kong residents who left Hong Kong in the 1960s and later in the 1980s. Perhaps the prickly, bitter feeling of being a 'deserter' from Nanjing remained uncomfortably strong in her memory.

With her change in status from a Hong Kong British subject to a 'Chinese' in the diaspora, her sense of her Chinese identity had also changed. We feel a kind of boldness in her claiming China as a mother country and a new confidence on her own Chinese heritage. She says, 'The Chinese side of my personality was not simply a matter of genetics'. In articulating this renewed sense of Chineseness, she says:

> One way it manifested itself was the genuine concern I felt for the welfare of China and its people … Like many overseas Chinese, I do not profess to understand politics to any great extent, but I have

hopes for the future of what I consider to be my mother country and
the teeming millions who live within its borders.

(1997, 384)

The last two chapters of Cheng's memoirs are devoted entirely to the new
China, based on her series of trips to China between 1972 and 1985. Her
first China trip was taken in November 1972 — the same year that US
President Richard Nixon visited China and a year after China's entry to
the United Nations. This section of her memoir departs from the mode of
life-writing hitherto, and becomes a kind of expository defence of China.
In fact, during this period, there grew up something of a literary tradition of
figures from public or intellectual life 'reporting' on communist regimes
during the cold war decades. For example, Julia Kristeva wrote *About Chinese
Women* (1975) after her visit to the People's Republic of China in April
1974.

The narrator declares that her belief in the success of Communist China
does not spring from any political motives; she is speaking from a purely
humanitarian non-political perspective. Her devotion to China and her
insistence that there is no politics in her sentiments resonate much with
Han Suyin's formulation of her feelings for China: 'I love China, but China
to me means the Chinese people' (Han, 1980a, 191). Like Han, Cheng also
inclines to explain her patriotism with her avid devotion to the tide of the
'teeming millions'.

What Cheng now calls 'my mother country' had in fact undergone
much metamorphosis in her memoir. During her formative years, the notion
of China was closely entwined with the embracing of Chinese culture and
traditions. As we have seen, beginning in her Lingnan years, her idea of
China had changed and solidified politically as a modern geopolitical
republic. During the war, she saw China as a victim and captive nation
under its Japanese military master. But China, with its stubbornness, had
doggedly survived its conqueror: her own adaptability in adversity and loss
might be emblematic of China's will to survive. In the post-war decades in
Hong Kong, her notion of China seems to have resumed a cultural profile.
In the diaspora after 1967, there is an avid desire in Cheng to perceive
China as her 'mother country', both as culture and as a state. But also
operating within this part of her discourse is an undeniable racial sentiment

that transcends the cultural and the political — a sentiment that is based upon her racial and ethnic bond with the teeming millions of Chinese people within its geographical borders.

In her new China chapters, the narrator's earlier discourses on colonialism, ancestor worship and her loyalty to the Nanjing government, as well as the race question, seem to have been pushed and locked away into some remote compartment in her autobiographical consciousness. All her earlier temperateness and modesty seem to have been displaced by a determination to defend China from a negative Western perspective. The narrator is eager to present to the reader the new China after more than two decades of isolation — a China no longer torn by internal strife between warlords and civil war, a China no longer humiliated by foreign imperialism and Japanese militarism, a China that had been purged of all its earlier social ills and corruption, a new communist China who was still faithful to its Confucian principles, a China which was ready to educate the young, take care of the old, restore dignity to the downtrodden masses and, most importantly, a China in which communism was based on its innate Chinese essence. Cheng sees it her duty to act as an ambassador of goodwill, offering a glimpse behind the bamboo curtain to the West, based on her own eyewitness account. Consciously or unconsciously, Cheng is acting as a bridge figure again, the function her father and many Eurasian leaders before her had served between the colonial government and the Chinese populace. But this time, her intended bridge is much more extensive and ambitious in its desire to cross the gap between the critical and doubting Western world and the misunderstood and reticent Chinese world.

Cheng's description of the new China as 'more Chinese than Communist' (1997, 407) is also another classic instance where we see Cheng's need to distinguish and negotiate with different and sometimes antagonistic discourses that are crucial to her sense of identity. It is her strategy to give some order and cohesion to the endless parade of alternating and shifting identities of a much-decentred subjectivity. The arrangement into an order of precedence becomes an important paradigm to define who she is: more Chinese than Eurasian, more 'pure' than 'mixed', more national than colonial, and more mainland than coastal.

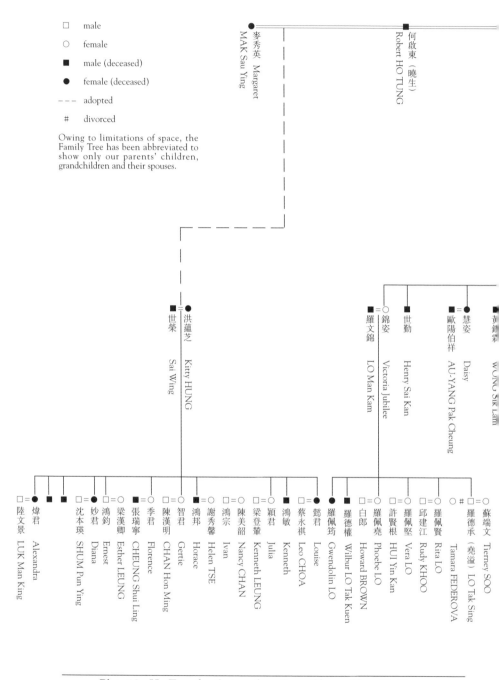

Plate 13   Ho Tung family tree, from Irene Cheng, *Clara Ho Tung:
A Hong Kong Lady, Her Family and Her Times*, by permission of
The Chinese University of Hong Kong

張靜蓉（蓮覺）
Clara CHEUNG
Ching Yung (Lin Kok)

周綺文
CHAU Yee Man

孝姿　Florence
楊國璋　YEO Kok Cheang
吉廷士　John GITTINS
堯姿　Grace
羅文浩　Horace LO
賀樂　Serg HOHLOV
文姿　Jean
吉廷士　William M. GITTINS
洪奇芬　Hesta HUNG
世禮　Sai Lai (Robert)
奇姿（艾齡）Irene
鄭湘先　CHENG Hsiang Hsien
嫻姿（綺華）Eva
世儉
Mordia O'SHEA
Edward Sai Kim

楊紫霞　Wendy YEO
麥約翰　John MACK
楊約翰　Daphne YEO
范羅弼　Robert VALLANCE
楊紫廉　
楊儀鳳　Yvonne METCALF
楊允誠　Richard YEO
羅佩嫻　Shirley LO
潘通理　Tony PAYNE
　Barbara GIBSON
　John GITTINS
　Elizabeth GITTINS
吉懿璧　Stewart DOERY
吉約翰　Min (Margaret)
勉君　KWAN Hau Ming
關孝明　Greta LO
羅　
鴻毅　June CHENG Ka Yuk
鄭家玉　Bobbie (Robert) H.N.
丹勵嘉　Walter Beech DANDLIKER
勵君　Mary
　Robert KETTERER
淑君　Toni (Sister Patricia)
　Ann CARLO
鴻卿　Joseph
麥　Mary McGINLEY
鴻憲　Paddy
佘　Patricia Ann SHEA
鴻章　Eric

Excerpt From *Intercultural Reminiscences*

Family

Plate 14 Dr Irene Cheng,
author of *Intercultural Reminiscences*,
courtesy of The David C. Lam Institute
for East-West Studies, Hong Kong
Baptist University.

It is no doubt natural that my earliest intercultural reminiscences related to my family and closest friends. Although we were Eurasians, ostensibly we were brought up in the Chinese tradition. We spoke Cantonese at home, honoured Chinese festivals, and lived according to the lunar calendar. Still, Hong Kong at the time was becoming cosmopolitan, and many Chinese families were accepting Western influences. Therefore Western dress and the English language were becoming more popular, particularly among the younger members of Chinese society in the territory. Looking back, I realise that these trends were preparing the new generation to play an increasingly active role in the international city that Hong Kong was becoming.

We had three parents: my father, Sir Robert Ho Tung; my mother, Lady Clara Ho Tung (née Cheung), whom we were taught to call Mamma; and father's first wife, Lady Ho Tung or Lady Margaret (née Mak), whom we called Mother. However, to avoid any confusion, I shall generally refer to Father's first wife as Lady Margaret. Father was born on December 23, 1862, the first year of Emperor Tung Chi's reign. Lady Margaret was born in 1865 and Mamma in 1875, the first year of Emperor Guang Shu's reign. Father married Lady Margaret in 1881, but she remained childless. This was probably because she had a uterine tumour that had been diagnosed in America quite early in her life. Surgery might have helped, but she refused to be operated upon. The tumour did not bother her most of the time, but during the final years of her life it caused her considerable suffering.

In traditional Chinese thinking it was a serious matter for Father not to have any offspring. As the saying goes: "There are three kinds of unfilial behaviour and, of these, the worst is to have no heir." Consequently, in accordance with recognised Chinese custom, Father's younger brother, Third Uncle Ho Fook, was obliged to allow his eldest son, Ho Wing (Ho Sai-wing), to be adopted into our branch of the family. From then on my family regarded him as the eldest son. He even had to call his own parents Uncle and Aunt. The transfer took place around 1889, when the boy was nominally seven by Chinese calculation, which meant that he was in the seventh lunar year of his life. However, because he was born only four days before Chinese New Year, he was really just over five years old.

Father and Lady Margaret still wanted to have children of their own, if possible, so Father took a concubine whose surname was Chau. This was also according to Chinese custom and fully approved by the Laws of the Qing Dynasty, which at that time were officially recognised in Hong Kong. The woman thus became a secondary spouse (tsip) to the husband, and a subsidiary mother (shu mu) to any children of the wife (tsai) born either before or after her entry into the family. These children would be taught to call her Ah Jeh (Elder Sister), which was the appropriate way of addressing the concubine of one's father. Father and Lady Margaret had naturally hoped that this concubine would bear him some children, preferably a son. But at first she, too, remained childless.

Although Mamma had been born in Hong Kong, her father took his family to Shanghai where he worked for the Chinese Maritime Customs. He was later transferred to Kiukiang, farther up the Yangtse River, to take charge of the customs office there. He died in 1892 after a short illness, and Mamma was thoroughly heartbroken. It was said that she mourned and missed him so much that for a long time she never left home. However, during this period, as there were many books around the house, she taught herself to read Chinese. Mamma's parents had actually sent her to school when she was younger, but she had not liked the regimen so they allowed her to stay home.

Burying the deceased in their native town is a traditional Chinese custom. Accordingly, one year after Grandfather's death, his widow, accompanied by Mamma and her nine-year-old younger brother Gai, brought his remains to Hong Kong so that he could be buried in his birthplace. Grandfather was the brother of Lady Margaret's mother, who had died long before. But since Chinese tend to keep in close contact with their relatives, Lady Margaret noticed that her younger cousin, Mamma, was "good, intelligent, and attractive" although quite shy. She decided to seek her aunt's permission to allow her daughter to marry Father as a P'ing Ts'ai (Equal Wife). Lady Margaret promised to treat Mamma as a sister, with absolute equality, and confirmed her verbal request with a letter to Mamma's mother.

After their arranged betrothal, Father and Mamma were married in Hong Kong in February 1895. The wedding was conducted in a full traditional Chinese ceremony, with Father wearing the double red sash and with a red sedan chair sent to fetch the bride. My two mothers continued to call each other Elder Cousin and Younger Cousin, with Father known to them as Second Young Master, in accepted Chinese style. Mamma often mentioned that she got on well with Father's mother, who treated her just like a daughter. However, her mother-in-law died a year after Mamma married Father.

My sister Victoria (Vic) was born in June 1897 when Father was already 35 years old. In those days 35 was regarded as being quite late for a Chinese person to have his first-born. Everyone was delighted, of course — Father, Mamma, and Lady Margaret — but especially our maternal Grandma whom we called P'aw P'aw, the correct Chinese form of address for this relative. Grandma and Vic were tremendously attached to each other, right up until Grandma's death in 1912. Vic remembers clearly that as a little girl, when they ventured forth in sedan chairs, she always preferred to sit in Grandma's chair if possible. When there was a large dinner party, Grandma would bring Vic along to sit with her and the other old ladies. They all liked Vic because she was so sweet and well behaved. Since all the grown-ups doted on her, Vic had a very happy childhood. She was named Victoria Jubilee because she was born in the Queen's Diamond Jubilee year. When we later studied English history, we learned the vivid story of how in 1837 Queen Victoria, still in her late teens, was called upon by the minister of state and told that she had become Queen. By 1897 Queen Victoria had reigned for 60 years and Hong Kong, by then a well-established British colony, enthusiastically participated in the celebrations.

Fifteen months after Vic's birth, my brother Henry was born. He was a bright, good-looking, and lovable child, and everyone idolised him. Unfortunately, he was not destined to live long. Chinese compare children who live only an exceedingly short life to the night-flowering ceres or epiphyllum blossom. These flowers are beautiful, exude a wonderful fragrance, and are admired by all who view them, but fade and die within a few hours.

In the late 1800's, attitudes and events within mainland China were destined to have a direct effect on the lives of Hong Kong Chinese families. China was still ruled by the Manchu Emperors of the Qing Dynasty, and people referred to their chronological years as the "n-th year in the reign of emperor so-and-so." In 1895 China, a huge country, lost the first Sino-Japanese War to her tiny island neighbour. Many Chinese scholars and statesmen were furious, and some demanded that China introduce reforms in order to strengthen itself. Among the most vociferous of the critics was a Cantonese scholar by the name of Kang Yu-wei, who sent many petitions on the subject to Emperor Guang Shu. The Emperor was genuinely impressed by these missives and on a number of occasions summoned Kang to visit him at court. Acting upon Kang's advice, the Emperor issued a whole series of edicts and introduced many changes, later known as the Hundred Days Reforms.

In Chinese history, these reforms are referred to by the name of the year (Wu Shu), according to the "60-year cycle." Unfortunately, when his aunt, the Dowager Empress, learned of the reforms she stopped them all and confined the Emperor to his quarters. Kang's six co-workers, including his own brother, were beheaded. Kang was more fortunate because the Emperor had immediately asked him to leave the imperial court and try to get help from abroad, and so the British authorities engineered Kang's escape to Shanghai. Father read about all this in the newspapers. With the assistance of the British Consul in Shanghai, he invited Kang together with his family and retinue to stay at Idlewild, our family home in Hong Kong. Accompanied by a few friends, Father met the vessel at quayside on its arrival from Shanghai. He greeted Kang who, for his own safety, spent the first week of his sojourn in Hong Kong at the police barracks. Afterwards he and his family moved to Idlewild, where they became guests of the family for a couple of weeks before moving on to Japan.

Before he left, Kang wrote in Chinese calligraphy a beautiful set of four small scrolls thanking my parents for their kindness and hospitality. The scrolls mentioned the good advice and assistance extended to him and also praised Father for his patriotism. Mamma often mentioned the Kang family visit, which coincided with the birth of Henry, who was just a week old at the time. During that time she became close friends with Kang's two eldest daughters, especially the younger one who was then not married. This girl later became a student at Columbia University in New York and was probably one of the first Chinese women to be enrolled at an American institution of higher education.

As fate would have it, the Kang family came into my life once again in 1942 when as a new widow with a dependent child I found myself in Beijing. An elderly lady who had allowed us to live in her home spoke of a good friend of hers, Madame Lo, who was formerly Kang Tung-bi, second daughter of the well-known reformer, Kang. I immediately recognised this to be Mamma's good friend of whom we had all heard so much as children. When

Madame Lo was made aware that I was in Beijing she immediately arranged a lunch for me and thereafter came regard me as her god-daughter.

At the close of the 19th century, on December 31, 1899, a second daughter, Daisy, was born to my parents. Since our family's lives were regulated by the Chinese lunar calendar instead of the Gregorian record of time, we always celebrated our birthdays accordingly. Thus Daisy's birth occurred on the 29th day of the 11th month. None of us children realised the significance of that date to Europeans, being the last day of the century as well as New Year's Eve according to the western calendar. I only realised this fact when writing my book on Mamma about 80 years later. In the larger editions of the Chinese Red Almanac, there is usually a section that gives the corresponding solar and lunar dates for each year, up to a total of 80 or 100 years. Mamma told us that soon after Daisy was born, Father came into the room and asked whether the child was a boy or a girl. When told it was a girl, he exclaimed: "Another girl!" Feeling that he was disappointed, Mamma replied: "You may expect that I shall be having many more girls, and if you don't want girls you had better not have any more children!" As was usual, they conversed together in Chinese.

Years later, I attended a lecture on mental health, one of a series run by the Tavistock Clinic in London. The psychiatrist noted that "the first daughter is forgiven for being a girl, but the second daughter is never forgiven." How true this was in Daisy's case, especially being born into a Chinese family where there is such heavy emphasis on male children and succession. Sad to say, Daisy was unfortunate in other ways as well. I believe she had adenoid problems when she was a baby. Doctors knew little about glandular troubles in those days, so nothing was done about it at the time. Some experts say that if Daisy's adenoids had been removed, it might have helped her general development. I have always felt sorry for her because in today's parlance she would have been classified as a "backward" child.

Excerpt From *Intercultural Reminiscences*

When Daisy was six months old she and Henry, who was then 20 months old, both developed pneumonia. He became very ill and died about a week later. Mamma was overcome by grief at the loss of her first-born son and eulogised his memory in many ways. On his tombstone of polished dark green marble, there is engraved a short poem in English, plus a carefully composed eulogy in Chinese. The English version is arranged like an eight-line stanza:

HENRY HO TUNG
BORN 28th SEPTEMBER 1898
DIED 15th MAY 1900
SAFELY SAFELY GATHERED IN
FAR FROM SORROW FAR FROM SIN
NO MORE CHILDISH GRIEFS OR FEARS
FOR THE LIFE SO YOUNG AND FAIR
NOW HATH PASSED FROM EARTHLY CARE

The Chinese version is a long, poetic eulogy entitled "Grieving the Loss of a Son" and written in customary Chinese style. It recounts that Henry was very special and died in the third year of his life in the early summer of Geng-tsi (1900). It describes in detail the many ways in which the small boy was missed and contains classical allusions which make it a masterpiece of Chinese literary composition. The poem concludes by stating that the tombstone had been erected by the family and, at the end, gives the family title: "Long Prospering Tang of the Ho Family" (Ho Cheong Yuen Tong). In the Ancestral Hall of the Buddhist Tung Lin Kok Yuen Temple in Happy Valley, built by Mamma with money given her by Father to celebrate his golden wedding with Lady Margaret, there is a beautiful oil painting of Henry positioned on the wall together with those of our grandparents.

Mamma told us that after Henry's death she was so upset that she could not take an interest in anything. She often talked about this phase of her life and wrote about it in the autobiographical notes at the end of her travelogue. She said that Father and Lady Margaret had already booked passage for a trip to the United States and thence to England and, in due course, set sail. Father frequently wrote and telegraphed Mamma in a bid to cheer her up. Mamma later said that her sisters-in-law, Mrs Ho Fook and Mrs Ho Kom-tong, as well as other relatives and friends all rallied to her side, but they did not succeed as she remained inconsolable over Henry's demise.

Finally, Mamma's doctor took firm control of the situation and told her: "Mrs Ho Tung, you may think you want to die, but you won't die. However, unless you pull yourself out of this state of mind you will have one of two illnesses. Either you will develop tuberculosis or have a nervous breakdown. You will have to choose between the two. " Mamma told us that the doctor's dire warning woke her up to the seriousness of her condition. She did not want to have either disease and so employed sheer will-power to pull herself together. Meanwhile, Father had succeeded in persuading her to join him and Lady Margaret in England and so, in the spring of 1901, she agreed to go. Mamma arranged to take Grandma along with her as well as the two little girls, Vic and Daisy. In addition, they were accompanied by brother Gai and the adopted son Wing, who were about the same age. A Chinese amah also embarked on the voyage to help look after the children. The trip was not a total success since Grandma was not keen on travelling and Daisy began to fret and cry a good deal. As a result, it was arranged for Grandma and the servant to return home to Hong Kong with Daisy. The young men also returned with them, while Vic and Mamma stayed on in England until autumn. Grandma lovingly supervised Daisy's care and remained exceedingly fond of her throughout her childhood. It was especially unfortunate for Daisy, who was only 12, when Grandma died in February 1912.

At the same time Daisy was born, Father's concubine was six months pregnant, and in March 1900 she gave birth to a daughter, Mary. During most of Mary's life before her marriage, she was generally referred to at home by her Chinese name, Shun Jee. As the Chinese classify a concubine's children with those of a wife, Mary became Third Young Mistress in the

Excerpt From *Intercultural Reminiscences*

family. Soon after Mary's birth, her mother contracted tuberculosis, a disease that was then quite prevalent in Hong Kong. Mary, however, continued to live with her mother until her death early in 1911. By then Mary was almost 11 years old, and Lady Margaret took her home to Idlewild, our house in Mid-Levels, where we had a live-in lady tutor and Chinese scholar, Miss Yim. Before moving up to the Peak, Vic, Daisy, and some of Lady Margaret's older servant-girls had all studied under Miss Yim. At Idlewild, Mary became chief student among the group of younger servants under Miss Yim's tutelage. Some of these girls learned a good deal from this unique opportunity to acquire an education, while others did not profit much from the experience. Mary later attended a Chinese primary school and then studied at the grant-aided St Stephen's Girls' College. She was also a classmate of ours at the Sheung Fu Girls' School from 1919 to 1920. Actually, her knowledge of Chinese was much better than ours, due in part to the foundation laid by Miss Yim and in part because St Stephen's taught Chinese as a prime subject. Diocesan Girls' School, where we studied, had not yet introduced Chinese into the curriculum.

Father was in his 41st year when, much to the delight of both parents, my brother Eddie was born in March 1902. I remember Mamma telling us when we were young how glad Father had been to have this precious son born to him. Eddie was indeed "Mamma's darling and Papa's joy" and thus they began building their hopes around him. Unfortunately, when Eddie was about six months old, during the eighth moon, he became extremely ill. Our parents, especially Mamma, were thoroughly alarmed. They later realised that he could not stand Hong Kong's hot, damp climate, so Mamma took him over to the Portuguese enclave of Macau where it was a little cooler. Even there, though, she noticed that while playing on the floor, Eddie would often rest his cheek on the large, cool Chinese earthenware tiles.

Mamma brought him back to Hong Kong the following year and on the anniversary of Henry's death (17th day of the fourth moon), Eddie again became seriously ill. Uncle and Auntie Ho Fook, who had brought up ten children of their own, kindly offered to take care of him in their home. As Mamma was by then in an advanced stage of pregnancy, she gladly accepted the offer and accompanied Eddie, together with some members of her staff, to the Ho Fook residence. Eddie was greatly attached to his mother and would hardly allow anyone else to look after him. Mamma said she was afraid Eddie might die if she left him to return home to Idlewild for the new baby's birth. But she was a woman of strong will who somehow delayed the new baby's arrival for more than a month. Eva was finally delivered in late July 1903. Now, I do not know whether this "delaying tactic" was scientifically possible, but Mamma often said Eddie owed Eva a great deal because of it, especially because as soon as she was able, she left Eva in the care of other people in order to take her precious, darling son to Japan for convalescence. Mamma told and retold us these stores of her life, so that although it had happened more than a year before I was born, I can visualise it all as part of our family history.

A few months after Eva was born, and no doubt following careful consultation with Father, a wet-nurse and an amah were hired to look after her under the supervision of P'aw P'aw and Lady Margaret. Mamma was preoccupied with Eddie, of course, and it was hoped that his health would steadily improve in the climate of Japan, where it was less tropical and much cooler than humid conditions encountered in Hong Kong during much of the year. Mamma used to tell us that even on board the boat taking them to Japan, Eddie would still not allow anyone else to carry him. On occasion some kind fellow-passenger would carry Mamma with the baby in her arms to help her move around the ship. The change of climate seemed to work wonders, so for a couple of years Mamma took Eddie to Japan during the summer and left Eva behind with the servants and relatives. Eddie's endless illnesses as a child explain much of the subsequent mutual attachment of mother and son during the rest of their lives.

Mamma, for her part, certainly thought that if she arranged for the infant Eva to be cared for, the baby would not suffer because of her prolonged absences. In those days neither Western nor Chinese ideas on child-rearing placed any great emphasis on the special bond that exists between mother and child. It was thought that an infant could not differentiate between the adults charged with looking after it. I had accepted these ideas all along, that is until the early 1950s when Dr Jeannie Stirrat, a mental health expert, explained that it was vital for a baby to have the constant care and attention of its natural mother, for otherwise it would feel "deprived."

Because Eddie could not stand the dank heat of Hong Kong summers, Mamma must have been happy when Father intimated that there was a group of three houses up for sale on Victoria Peak, an exclusive residential district at that time mainly reserved for Westerners. She naturally urged Father to buy them, because mean temperatures at the Peak were sometimes around 10 degrees lower than those at sea-level where the majority of the island's people lived. She felt the altitude would be better for the health of everyone, especially the children.

It was in October 1904, when Eddie was 31 months old and Eva just 15 months, that I arrived on the scene. In those days pregnant women were not advised to add calcium to their diet, and although Mamma most likely visited the family doctor regularly, her general health must have been considerably run down due to the strain caused by Eddie's long illness and the mere fact of having three children born in less than three years. Even with my sparse knowledge of general medical matters, I believe that as a child my teeth were deficient in calcium, so I frequently had to visit the dentist. Actually, my general health was always poor when I was young as I did not seem to have much resistance to illness.

In a lighter vein, when all of us children were around one month old, Lady Margaret gave each of us a gold chain with several pendants, the central one being a little gold locket with a small diamond inset. The pendant's outer cover was also engraved with the year, month, date, and time of our birth, according to both the solar and lunar calendars. Inside, there was space for a little enamelled photograph to be inserted. Mamma would send a baby picture of each of us to Vandyke's of London, a well-known firm of photographers. They placed an enamelled miniature of the photo on the right-hand side of the locket, leaving space on the left to be used later as each of us saw fit. The locket was suspended on the chain by a fixed ring, although there were other rings on which we hung extra tiny ornaments of jade, amber, coral, or other precious stones. We children really valued these chains, although when we were young they were kept with Mamma's jewellery and only taken out for us to wear on special occasions. My daughter now has my locket and chain with one of her own childhood photographs placed there opposite mine. I hope she will always keep it in her family, as it is one of my most treasured heirlooms.

All along I had known that my lunar birthday fell on the 13th day of the ninth month. However, it was from my locket that I later learned I had been born on October 21, 1904, during the 30th year of Emperor Guang Shu's reign in the Chinese Year of the Dragon. During the early years, much of our life was regulated by the lunar calendar, as would be expected in a family that lived according to Chinese custom. One of the most important decisions that had to be made was when I should start my education. According to custom this should begin with a ceremony called the commencement of education. An auspicious day is chosen by consulting the Chinese Red Almanac to determine exactly when to begin a child's schooling and development. Even the year must be an appropriate one, because it is said that the child would otherwise never be a successful student. Some lunar years have two seasonal dates, known as Lap Chun (meaning the establishment of spring, or spring begins), that always correspond to the solar dates of February 4th or 5th. These years are said to be specially suitable for ceremonies such as the commencement of education, or for weddings and the like. Auspicious years are those that have an intercalary month in them, such as a Chinese leap-year.

Although Eva and I went through the ceremony on the same day and she retained some vivid recollections of it, I do not remember a thing. As a young girl I wondered why I had suffered a memory lapse on such an important occasion. Years later, while studying my own copy of the almanac, I discovered that the lunar year extending from January 25, 1906, to February

12, 1907, was one with two Lap Chun days, whereas those that followed (the Blind Years) had none. It was believed that if children went through the ceremony during such a year, they would be doomed to being stupid and unsuccessful in their studies. Therefore it had been arranged for Eva and me to go through the ceremony some time towards the end of that lunar year. By then Eva was three and a half years of age, whereas I was just over two and still quite a baby. If we had not gone through the ceremony then, we would have had to wait for more than a year, by which time it would certainly have been too late for Eva. So we went through it together early in 1907. Consequently I have no recollection of the event at all, even though it was supposed to be one of the most important events of my young life.

In order to have such a ceremony performed, the family had to select a well-educated person to act as "teacher" for the occasion. My chosen teacher was Brother Ho Wing. The ceremony is normally held early in the morning, symbolic of industrious study, with the child generally carried piggyback to the school or school room. The child's face is covered with a large piece of red silk cloth so that nothing could be seen along the way that might be construed as an unlucky omen, such as a dog or cat. Chinese customs and folklore are full of symbolism and make use of anything considered propitious, the name of which sounds similar to the idea to be conveyed. For instance, there would be various items set out on a tray at the commencement of education ceremony. These would include onions (yeung ch'ung) to denote that the child would be intelligent (chung ming), celery (k'un choi) to signify industriousness (k'un lick), and so on. Non-verbal symbolism was also employed. Some Cantonese families would make a large pancake, wrap it in red paper, and then place it on a chair for the child to sit on. This represents hope that the child will stay in his seat to study instead of frequently running off or playing truant. Many other such symbolic practices were used to represent good learning habits.

There was, of course, a portrait of Confucius in the school room and upon entering, the child would have the covering on his head removed and be led to pay his respects to the Sage by "kowtowing." The infant would then also kowtow to his teacher, who might give him in return the ubiquitous red packet of "lucky money" and perhaps also say something meant to augur well for this education. The passages taught at these ceremonies would always be the beginning and ending of the *Three Character Classics*, which freely translated read as follows:

> Man's nature is originally good. In accordance with whatever environment he comes in contact with his habits become different. If he is not properly taught, his nature will deviate (from the proper path). The important thing in the method of education is concentration.
>
> When a child is young he learns, and when he comes to manhood he puts into practice what he has learned. Thus he can serve his superiors and his government well, and his influence will promote the welfare of the people. In this way he earns a good reputation that will reflect glory on his parents and on his ancestors who have gone ahead of him. He will set a good example for posterity and for his descendants.
>
> Others bequeath to their children much gold and wealth, but I only have this little Classic to teach mine: 'Diligence is useful, but play is useless. Avoid the latter and persevere in your studies.'

The teacher would explain the Confucian passages in simple language and the child would be asked to repeat them several times by rote. A little calligraphy would also be taught, using a writing book in which identical rows of simple characters had already been printed in large red type. The teacher, standing behind the child, would guide his hand to help him trace, in black ink, a few columns of printed characters. The ink is usually prepared from scrapings off an "ink stick" that are ground to a fine powder. The powder is then placed in a small dish and mixed with water to the correct consistency before being transferred to a stone slab to begin the calligraphic exercise. This symbolic ceremony would then end, having been limited to these first lessons in reading and writing.

Reprinted from Irene Cheng, *Intercultural Reminiscences* (Ch.1., pp. 1–13), by Irene Cheng, with the permission of David C. Lam Institute for East-West Studies, Hong Kong Baptist University.

Epilogue

After reading the lives of these Eurasian memoirists, what emerged is a wavering continuum of their varying self-definitions of their Hong Kong Eurasian heritage. At one end of the continuum, we see Joyce Symons representing her interpretation of her Hong Kong Eurasianness as more British, less Chinese, colonial, isolated and tied to mercantile/treaty-port history. Moving away from Symons and edging towards the middle, there is Jean Gittins, whose notion of her Eurasianness is based on an indeterminacy and undecidability, though at most times it tends to lean more towards Symons's direction of being British. Occasionally, the pull from her Chinese side can be felt as she wavers in her choice of identity. Overall, Jean Gittins seems adamant about not making any strong ultimate identity decision as if this undecidability were itself constitutive and definitive. She insists on a Eurasianness that cannot be calculated or divided, a metissage that will always be in the intermediate space, having strong ties to both sides. Finally, at the opposite end of the continuum, we have Irene Cheng whose self-definition of Eurasianness is concessionary and contingent, a biological accident in her Ho Tung Chineseness. Her expression of Hong Kong Eurasianness is, most of the times, synomonous with Chinese. The two words 'Chinese' and 'Eurasians' are interchangeable in her writings. Her choice of identity is based on her intense cultural identification with her Chinese heritage. And yet she occasionally acknowledges, and more often betrays, some of the psychological stress imposed upon her by this strong interpretation of her ethnicity, with its elements of partial denial.

Lastly, another issue that needs to be addressed is the explanation of the drastic difference in the two sisters' conception of Eurasianness. One can, of course, rely on the explanation based on the power dynamics and sibling order within the extended family. Irene is apparently the trusted older daughter whose ethnic and ideological configuration would tend to be closer to her parents. But how could we explain the other older siblings such as Eddie or Eva whose ideological and ethnic sentiments clearly do not resemble that of Irene or their parents? According to Irene Cheng's memoir, Eddie, the eldest son of the family, to the utter dismay of the three elderly parents, had secretly married an Irish lady he had fallen in love with while in England (1997, 120). Eva was a successful medical practitioner and had remained single and independent, a powerful sisterly figure in Cheng's memory who does not seem to share Irene's enthusiasm towards Chinese Confucian sensibilities. The explanations of sibling order and family power therefore do have their weaknesses. I would argue that perhaps, the role of one's individual existential choice could not be underestimated. No matter how hard stalwart defenders of social determinism have tried to prove the illusory nature of free individual choice, this difference between the sisters' conception of their Eurasianness and ethnic identity has pointed to the fact that within the forces of social determinism, human beings can, to some degree and at certain moments, fashion themselves at their own willful choice.

Of all the memoirists, Jean Gittins is perhaps the only one who acknowledges that her own identity process could be highly strategic, contingent and perhaps nebulous at times. Standing at the two extreme ends, we have Symons and Cheng, who tend to find themselves constantly defending and negotiating their personal notions of Eurasianness against the prescriptive definitions and casual prejudice of others, often enough in circumstances of personal anguish.

Most of us do assume the role of storytellers of our own lives at one stage or another. But being a Eurasian from the early twentieth century Hong Kong, the task becomes less simple, as the question of 'who am I?' always seems to intrude into one's life narrative. Am I more European than Chinese? More patriotic than colonial? More colonial than indigenous? It is the constant jostling of choices which marks the storytelling of these Eurasian authors much more demanding, much more poignant.

In many ways, these life narratives not only coincide temporally with those very turbulent phases of Hong Kong, as the city itself underwent a series of identity changes, but the city, too, like these Eurasian authors, had to cope with its own set of jostling choices in its quest for its historical identity.

Notes

INTRODUCTION

1. 'Eurasian' is originally a term for a person of mixed European and Indian blood, first used in the mid-1800s. It was adopted as being more euphemistic than 'half-caste' and more precise than 'East-Indian' (*Hobson-Jobson: The Anglo-Indian Dictionary*, 344)

2. These early colonial fears and worries are reflected in the works of race theorists such as Edward Long, Louis Agassis, and Count Gobineau. Edward Long wrote *Candid Reflections Upon the Judgement Lately Awarded by the Court of King's Bench, in Westminster-Hall, on What Is Commonly Called the Negro Cause, by a Planter* (London: Lowndes, 1772). Long describes interracial mixing as a 'venomous and dangerous ulcer'. Agassis sees race mixing as a 'sin against nature' and 'an incest in a civilized community'. Gobineau in his *Essay on the Inequality of Race* argues race mixture as a phenomenon that mingles growth with decay, life with death, desire with repulsion. As discussed in Young's *Colonial Desire*, Gobineau explains racial mixing as both a regeneration as well as degeneration (130).

CHAPTER 1

1. Memoirs had never been a very popular mode of writing in Hong Kong for political and cultural reasons. The popularity of memoirs only gathered pace in the 1990s, when Hong Kong experienced a kind of 'memoir boom' that resulted in a proliferation of memoirs in bookstores.

2. V. R. Gaikwad, *The Anglo-Indians: A Study in the Problems and Processes Involved in Emotional and Cultural Integration* (London: Asia Publishing House, 1967); Elizabeth P. Wittermans, 'The Eurasians of Indonesia,' *The Blending of Races: Marginality and Identity in World Perspective*, ed. N. P. Gist and A. G. Dworkin (New York & London:

John Wiley & Sons, 1972); C. H. Crabb, *Malaya's Eurasians — An Opinion* (Singapore: Eastern Universities Press Ltd. 1960).
3. Gusdorf, 36.

CHAPTER 2

1. The Oral History Project on Reminiscences of the War Experience in Hong Kong (Phase 2) was conducted by the Hong Kong Museum of History. The project collected personal accounts of war experience in Hong Kong during the Second World War.

2. E. J. Eitel, in the late 1890s, claims that the 'half-caste population in Hong Kong' were from the earliest days of the settlement almost exclusively the offspring of liaisons between European men and women of outcaste ethnic groups such as Tanka (*Europe in China*, 169). Lethbridge refutes the theory saying it was based on a 'myth' propagated by xenophobic Cantonese to account for the establishment of the Hong Kong Eurasian community. Carl Smith's study in late 1960s on the protected women seems, to some degree, support Eitel's theory. Smith says that the Tankas experienced certain restrictions within the traditional Chinese social structure. Custom precluded their intermarriage with the Cantonese and Hakka-speaking populations. The Tanka women did not have bound feet. Their opportunities for settlement on shore were limited. They were hence not as closely tied to Confucian ethics as other Chinese ethnic groups. Being a group marginal to the traditional Chinese society of the Puntis (Cantonese), they did not have the same social pressure in dealing with Europeans (C. T. Smith, *Chung Chi Bulletin*, 27). 'Living under the protection of a foreigner,' says Smith, 'could be a ladder to financial security, if not respectability, for some of the Tanka boat girls' (13).

3. Evidence from the Jardine's records shows that such 'irregularities' as cohabiting with these protected women or mistresses were indeed the norm. A notebook of Donald Matheson contains records of payments to mistresses of Jardine's employees and friends (W. K. Chan, 34).

4. The Diocesan Female Training School was the first school in Hong Kong to offer English education to Chinese and Eurasian girls (Sweeting, 248).

5. Eitel mentioned in 1889 how an important change had taken place among Eurasian girls, the offspring of illicit connections: instead of becoming concubines, they were commonly brought up respectably and married to Chinese husbands who themselves had received an English education in the local boys' schools (Sweeting, 248).

6. There were regulations that specifically applied to Chinese only, e.g. the Regulation of Chinese Ordinance 1856, the Regulation of Persons Ordinance 1916, etc.

7. Wordie, too, points out that clothing worn by Eurasians had been 'an indicator' which helped to delineate the Eurasian's conscious choice of being 'one' and not 'the other' (Wordie, *SCMP*, 6 August 1998).

CHAPTER 3

1. In Clavell's *Taipan* (1966), the story behind the character Gordon Chen, a Eurasian interpreter and comparadore, has similarities with the origins of Ho Tung; in Elegant's *Dynasty* (1977), the origins of the head of the Shekloong Eurasian clan also bears resemblances to early life of Ho Tung.
2. According to Peter Hall, when Ho Tung was born in Hong Kong in 1862, there was a Charles Henri Maurice Bosman in Hong Kong (1992, 181). But there was not any factual confirmation that Bosman was Ho Tung's father. None of the memoirs of his daughters make any reference to their European grandfather. However, Ho Tung did name his first-born son (who died in infancy) Henry.
3. Ho Tung had a very close relationship with his teacher. When Stewart died in 1889, he erected a tomb in memory of Stewart in the Colonial Cemetery, where he himself was also buried half a century later in a site not far away.
4. As Hui Po-keung says, many early Hong Kong merchants obtained their 'first tank of gold' (7) from the coolie trade — shipping their fellow countrymen as contracted labour to North America and Australia.
5. The first Chinese name that appears in the list of Directors of Jardine Matheson & Co. is 'G. Ho' in 1981 (Keswick, 265).

CHAPTER 5

1. The desire for a Eurasian settlement is well represented in the works of Singaporean Eurasian writer Rex Shelley. One of his Eurasian characters, Gus, in Japanese occupied Malaysia, says, 'I also want a country of our own … We will grow. Mixtures like us from all over Asia can come and live with us' (Shelley, 208).
2. Stoler's essay, 'Sexual Affronts and Racial Frontier' (1977) looks into the experience of Eurasians in Vietnam.
3. The one-dollar commemorative stamp issued in 1946 was designed by the Director of Postage, Wynne Jones, while he was interned in Stanley.
4. The TAC was one of those committees the government created that included members of the general public. It provided a forum where the 'consumers' could raise their complaints and suggestions (Miners, 1995, 107).
5. Elsie Elliot was headmistress of a school for the underprivileged in Kowloon City (Tu, 173). Morris, writing in the late 1980s, describes Elliot as having been for 30

years the voice of Hong Kong's liberal conscience, fearlessly championing the poor, defying authorities and exposing corruption (Morris, 1988, 100).

6. These were elected by members of two political parties, the Reform Club and Civic Association (Endacott, 309).

7. The Ward office was instituted in 1965. The urban area was divided into wards each with a ward office where Councillors would be available at fixed times to hear complaints and to give advice (Miners, 1995, 163).

8. It was not until 1985, after the Joint Declaration, that the government incorporated into the Legislative Council for the first time, members elected by newly established functional constituencies as well as members indirectly elected through District Board electoral colleges.

9. Umelco stands for 'Unofficial Members of Executive and Legislative Council'.

10. It is true that some civil servants, e.g. European police officers, were trained in Cantonese. But their Cantonese was often spoken with an accent. As a child, Symons spoke Cantonese before she learned to speak English. Hence, her Cantonese was equally fluent as that of any local Cantonese speaker.

11. The Executive Council in the 1970s consisted of four ex-officio members (the Chief Secretary, the Commander of the British Forces, the Financial Secretary and the Attorney-General) and eight Unofficials, many like Symons, still serving on the Legislative Council (1996, 83).

CHAPTER 6

1. Eakin describes Ernest Hemingway's Nick Adams in *In Our Time* (1925) as one who collides with history head-on.

2. For the purpose of easy reference, *Eastern Windows – Western Skies* shall be referred to as *Eastern Windows*.

3. Ozick in *The Shawl* (1980) writes about how Rosa sees her life after the Holocaust experience (58).

4. The number of Ho Tung siblings was at variance between Gittins's text and her sister Irene Cheng's text.

5. Sheila Rowbotham, as explained by Friedman, argues that women consciousness was split in two: the self as culturally defined and the self as different from cultural prescriptions. From this division, came a sense of dislocation and alienation (Rowbotham, *Woman's Consciousness*, 31; quoted in Friedman, 39).

6. The narrator explains this apparent inconsistency in her father's decision about ethnic identity and choice of residence as solely attributable to her mother's domestic desire. 'Someone had suggested to Mother that there was nothing to compare with

the health-giving value of the Peak air for growing children, and this being the case, she would not rest until she had us settled there' (1969, 12).

7. Another larger house next to this cluster called The Falls was later acquired in the 1920s.

8. Bolton argues that the Leland's 'comic' account of the Pidgin-English sing-song (1876) had 'contributed to the formation of a cultural imaginary of Chinese people at a time of growing anti-Chinese racism in United States and Britain' (Bolton, 2000, 35).

9. The Grose family is another Hong Kong Eurasian family related to the Halls/Sins and the Choas/Belilios. The Chinese family name of Grose is 'Ko' (Hall, 179).

10. J. S. Lockhart was the Colonial Secretary and Registrar General of Hong Kong at the turn of the century (Endacott, 1958, 262).

11. During the first four decades of the twentieth century, when modern education was developing rapidly in Hong Kong as well as in China, the number of *si-shu* continued to be quite popular (Luk, 119).

12. Han Suyin was in a similar situation as Jean Gittins in 1930 in Beijing. Though she was a speaker of colloquial Chinese, Han needed knowledge of classical Chinese to get into Yenching University. Being a Eurasian girl educated in the modern western school system, Han, like Gittins, subjected herself to the 'large dose of gothic verbiage' in what she calls the 'equivalent of Chaucerian English' (Han, 1966, 160) to a twentieth century English reader.

13. Apart from Grouser, the other two Chinese that have been given some narrative space are Master Chiu and Chan Bun, the houseboy they inherited from Mr C. W. Richard, former owner of The Chalet.

14. *The Hong Kong News* was the only English language newspaper during the Japanese occupation. The editor was Japanese and the staff members were mainly Chinese and Portuguese who had worked for the *South China Morning Post*. It became the mouthpiece of Japanese propaganda (Emerson, 4).

15. The Vice Chancellor gave permission for Gittins to stay on condition that two students would be permitted to stay with her (1969, 130). Two Russian students from Manchuria were selected: Sergei Hohlov (who later married Jean after the war) and Victor Zaitzev.

16. For the purpose of easy reference, *Stanley: Behind Barbed Wire* (1982) shall be referred to as '*Barbed Wire*'.

17. The last three sentences of this paragraph were slightly revised when they appeared in *Eastern Windows* as she remembers that initial 'life after' stage. In their revised form, they no longer had that psychological immediacy and rawness as they were first written in her short memoir in 1946 where they appeared in the beginning of her chapter of emotional and spiritual challenge.

18. As shall be discussed in Irene Cheng's chapter, Cheng's first part-autobiographical text, *Clara Ho Tung: A Hong Kong Lady Her Family and Her Times* (1976) also includes a brief history of Hong Kong, but it served more as a factual background and lacks the kind of connectedness and sense of historical continuity in relation to the personal narrative of the author, which is distinctly felt in Gittins's 1982 text.

19. According to Mabel Gittins's son, Peter Hall, they were interned because of their right of residence in Britain. George Hall, Mabel's husband, had lived in Britain for many years (Hall, 56).

20. As shall be discussed in a later chapter, unlike her other sisters' memoirs, Jean Gittins did not mention that the rest was needed as a result of the excitement from the celebrations of his Diamond Wedding Anniversary with Lady Margaret, Sir Robert's first wife, on 2 December 1941, six days before the invasion.

21. One possible reason that Jean had not joined the Idlewild crowd is that Idlewild was headed by Lady Margaret, the matriarch whom she has not acknowledged in any of her memoirs.

22. Norwegians were originally allowed to remain outside on condition that they did not escape when on parole. But after two escape attempts all Norwegians were interned in February 1943 (Endacott, 1978, 161; Lindsay, 1981, 36).

23. According to Brown, it was not until the professor's sense of humour came to his help that he burst into laughter. The businessman joined in. They shook hands and apologized. The shoe was carefully divided. This is an incident where it ended happily, but there were numerous other cases, where internees turned violently against each other in their daily scrounging and other routines.

24. *Death of Nelson* is based on the Battle of Trafalgar in 1805 between England and France. The hero, the British Vice Admiral Nelson, is shot at the height of the battle.

25. According to Lindsay, at the risk of annoying the Japanese, sometimes a group of internees would sing songs like 'There'll Always Be an England' and their voices would hearten the wretched prisoners inside the prison walls (Lindsay, 141).

26. Jean Gittins described how most internees felt that they had been let down during the fighting. Recriminations and bitterness towards the colonial government were common within the camp.

27. The Formosan guards were brought over by the Japanese. They were generally remembered as mean and gruff figures.

28. Jean Gittins was again one of those selected few who were called in to fill the administrative vacuum. On 3 September, with about twenty government servants, she left the camp to start working as a secretary in the newly revived colonial administration.

29. Jean Gittins is not the only Ho Tung who had this experience of Australia's anxiety in the 1940s towards non-European ethnicity. Florence Yeo, the youngest daughter, also had her share of the Australian paranoia. Florence and her sister Grace were both travelling to Australia during 1946; Grace to visit Jean, and Florence with her husband K. C. Yeo on recuperative leave. Florence recalls how after they reached Sydney Harbour, they queued up for permission to land: 'Grace was ahead of me. She was greeted politely and was welcomed into Australia. Then, I was next, with a Chinese husband. "Do you realise that you are allowed to stay in Australia for only six months? You must also report to the authorities if you stay any longer," he warned gruffly' (Yeo, 111). Grace apparently had been perceived as white and had no problem. Florence, with a Chinese husband, was perceived as Chinese. Unlike Jean Gittins, she was not given the benefit of a choice. The presence of a Chinese husband quickly eliminated her Europeanness.

CHAPTER 7

1. For purpose of easy reference, Irene Cheng's 1976 text shall be referred to as *Clara*.
2. For purpose of easy reference, Irene Cheng's 1997 text shall be referred to as *Reminiscences*.
3. By this time Cheng's youngest sister, Florence Yeo, had published her own memoir entitled *My Memories* (1990).
4. Lionnet describes Hurton's autobiography as a form of 'autoethnography', 95).
5. Irene Cheng does not acknowledge any conflicts or address the existence of conflicts between the more Westernized Eurasians and the more Chinese Eurasians — an issue which both Symons and Gittins are painfully aware of.
6. Many feminist critics such as Joy Hotton argue that 'The presentation of the self as related rather than single and isolate is ... the most distinctive and consistent difference between male and female life-writing' (quoted in Eakin, 48). Eakin, however, sees that relational identity applies not only to women but to men's life writing as well. Relational identity, for Eakin, crosses the gender divide.
7. Her father was 'sworn brothers' with several others well-known Hong Kong Eurasians (1976, 26) such as Sin Tak Fan (alias Stephen Hall, great-grandfather of Peter Hall), and Chan Kai Ming (alias George Bartou Tyson, maternal grand-uncle of Joyce Symons) (Symons, 1966a, v).
8. Though Florence Yeo is willing to reveal that Ho Tung's father was of Dutch descent, she never identifies his name, which is commonly believed to be 'Bosman' (Hall, 181).
9. Though by 1990, Cheng had Florence Yeo's book to refer to, there is a possibility that she might not agree with Yeo's version of their European ancestor's identities.

10. Cheng's preoccupation with the notion of 'pure' Chinese is recalled by her youngest sister Florence Yeo in _My Memories_, which shall be discussed in the second part of this chapter, 'Weighing Loyalties'.

11. Miss Katie, Ho Tung's nurse, a lady of mixed descent, had a son by Ho Tung, which none of the sisters had included in their count of the Ho Tung children (Courtauld & Holdsworth, 33; Hall, 181; _Next Magazine_ No. 506, 19 November 1999, 109). Cheng does not mention the relationship between Miss Katie and her father.

12. This incident does not appear in the narrative.

13. Diana was the daughter of Cheng's adopted brother Ho Wing (nephew of Ho Tung) and Kitty Anderson, the younger sister of Charles Anderson. This is the same Diana who was to ask Symons not to reveal their relationship, as Symons was 'British' and she herself was 'Chinese'.

14. Sweeting attributes the eventual change of this policy to a response by the colonial university 'to the increased feminism in China and Hong Kong stimulated especially amongst educated classes during the "May Fourth" period' (1990, 348).

15. Eva was one year older than Irene Cheng. And all three of the Ho Tung autobiographers unanimously agree on her brilliant academic achievement. She became a medical doctor and remained single. During the Second World War, she worked for the Red Cross in China.

16. Lai Po-Chuen was probably from the Mainland, since Cheng calls herself the first local girl to join the University.

17. Lingnan was first established in 1893 with Rev. B. C. Henry of the Canton Presbyterian Mission as its president. It was he who had presented the idea of the college to the Presbyterian Board of Foreign Missions in America in 1885 (Corbett, 21). Cheng joined Lingnan during the administration of its first Chinese president W. K. Chung (1927–1937).

18. When the open seizure of Manchuria began in 1931, Chiang Kai Shek ordered the Young Marshal Zhang Xueliang, the warlord of Manchuria, to withdraw without serious resistance. To many Chinese at that time, the Nanjing government represents a combination of 'nonresistance, noncompromise and nondirect negotiation' (Hsu, 550). The regional victory of Ma Chan Shan helped to inspire much hope and patriotism amid the prevailing sense of indignation.

19. Irene Cheng has admitted that although she worshipped Eva as a hero when they were young, they had grown apart and while she was staying at Eva's flat in London, they occasionally got on each other's nerves (1997, 197, 207).

20. When Shanghai finally fell in November, the Japanese turned to Nanjing, with the goal of retribution. Nanjing was to be made an example to prove Japan's dominance (Fogel, 17). The result was an unprovoked and unconscionable attempt to exterminate the Chinese spirit (Eykholt, 11). Over 300,000 civilians and prisoners

of war were killed in late 1937 and early 1938. The Nanjing Massacre became a metonym for Japanese behavior in China (Fogel, 17). Ian Buruma has suggested that the Nanjing Massacre has become profoundly entwined with and even emblematic of contemporary Chinese identity (Buruma, 7; Fogel, 2, 9).

21. The narrator says that many years later after the war, she found this Japanese again in Japan. 'He brought his wife and daughter to see me. I was glad when he told me that he had resigned from military life and was making a living by establishing a factory that made chalk to be used for chalk boards … I am sorry I have again lost touch with this Japanese friend' (1997, 267).

22. Both Sir Robert (who was to die in 1956) and Lady Margaret were buried in the Colonial Cemetery, a two-minute walk from Hector Maclean's grave.

23. After the Nationalist Party established the new central government in Nanjing, it required all overseas Chinese schools to register in China and to follow certain guidelines of the Nanjing government, if they wanted their credentials to be recognized and their students to be eligible for university admission in China (Luk, 2000, 47)

24. On this occasion of meeting Queen Mary in 1932, the narrator only seems able to recall the long sweeping sequined gown and the pear-shaped diamond earrings she herself wore on that day.

Glossary

Romanizations as in Text	Mandarin	Chinese characters
chat gu neuhng	*qi gu niang*	七姑娘
kit fat	*jie fa*	姑髮
tsap chung	*za zhong*	雜種
da luen chung	—	打亂種
tsap ba lang	—	—
boon tong fan	—	半唐番
wun hyut yih	*hun xue ir*	混血兒
chin jia	*qin jia*	親家
Ma Chan Shan	*Ma Zhan Shan*	馬占山
muitsai	—	妹仔
Ah Jeh	—	阿姐
tsip	*qie*	妾
shu mu	*shu mu*	庶母
tsai	*qi*	妻
p'ing ts'ai	*ping qi*	平妻
si shu	*si shu*	私塾
mien po	*mian pao*	棉袍
lap chun	*li ch'un*	立春
ren	*ren*	仁
yi	*yi*	義

Note: Romanizations in the text are a mixture of Cantonese (not orthodox) and Mandarin pinyin.

Bibliography

Alabaster, C. G. 'Some Observations on Race Mixture in Hong Kong.' *Eugenics Review* 11(1920): 247–48.

Anderson, Benedict. *Imagined Communities*. London: Verso, [1983] 1991.

Baxter, George. *Personal Experience During the Siege of Hong Kong, December 8th–25th*. Hong Kong: United Press Association, 194–.

Bickley, Gillian. *The Golden Needle*. Hong Kong: Baptist University, the David C. Lam Institute for East-West Studies, 1997.

Biographical Dictionary of Republican China, s.v. 'Ho Tung'. Ed. H. Boorman. New York and London: Columbia University Press, 1968.

Birch, A. and Cole, M. *Captive Christmas: The Battle of Hong Kong, December 1941*. Hong Kong, Singapore, Kuala Lumpur: Heinemann Asia, 1979.

Blyth, S. and Wotherspoon, Ian. *Hong Kong Remembers*. Oxford, New York: Oxford University Press, 1996.

Bolton, Kingsley. 'Language and Hybridization: Pidgin Tales From the China Coast.' *Interventions*. Vol. 1. London: Routledge, 2000.

Bottrall, Margaret. *Every Man a Phoenix: Studies in Seventeenth-Century Autobiography*. London: John Murray, 1958.

Braga, Jose Pedro. *The Portuguese in Hongkong and China*. Macau: Fundacao Macau, 1998.

Brooke, Charles. *Ten Years in Sarawak*, 2 Vols. London: Tinsley, 1866.

Brown, Wenzell. *Hong Kong Aftermath*. Sydney: Smith & Durrell, 1943.

Buruma, Ian. "The Afterlife of Anne Frank." *New York Review of Books* 45.3 (19 February 1998): 7.

Carroll, J. M. *Empires' Edge: The Making of the Hong Kong Chinese Bourgeoisie*. Ph.D. Dissertation. Harvard University, 1998.

Chan, Ming K. 'Review of Jung-fang Tsai's *Hong Kong in Chinese History: Community and Social Unrest in the British Colony, 1842-1913*.' *China International* 2.1(Spring 1995): 257–58.

Chan, Wai Kwan. *The Making of Hong Kong Society: Three Studies of Class Formation in Early Hong Kong*. Oxford: Clarendon Press, 1991.

Chang, Diana. *The Frontiers of Love*. 1956. Seattle and London: University of Washington Press, 1994.

Cheng, Christine. *Macau: A Cultural Janus*. Hong Kong: Hong Kong University Press, 1999.

Cheng, Irene. *Clara Ho Tung: A Hong Kong Lady, Her Family and Her Times*. Hong Kong: Chinese University of Hong Kong, 1976.

———. *Intercultural Reminiscences*. Edited by Frank Murdock and Ian Watson, with introduction. Hong Kong: Baptist University, 1997.

Chow Kai-wing. 'Imagining Boundaries of Blood: Zhang Binglin and the Invention of the Chinese Race in Modern China.' Procedures of Conference on Racial Identities in East Asia, 25–26 November 1994. Hong Kong: Division of Social Science, Hong Kong University of Science and Technology.

Corbett, C. H. *Lingnan University: A Short History Based Primarily on the Records of the University's American Trustees*. New York: Trustees of Lingnan University, 1963.

Courtauld, C. and Holdsworth, M. *The Hong Kong Story*. Hong Kong: Oxford University Press, 1997.

Clemons, E. W. 'Japanese Race Propaganda During World War II'. Procedures of Conference on Racial Identities in East Asia, 25–26 November 1994. Hong Kong: Division of Social Science, Hong Kong University of Science and Technology.

Dikötter, Frank. *The Discourse of Race in Modern China*. Hong Kong: Hong Kong University Press, 1992.

Dew, Gwen. *Prisoner of the Japs*. New York: Alfred A. Knopf, 1943.

Eakin, John Paul. *Fictions in Autobiography: Studies in the Art of Self-Invention*. New Jersey: Princeton University Press, 1985.

———. *Touching the World: Reference in Autobiography*. New Jersey: Princeton University, 1992.

———. *How Our Lives Become Stories — Making Selves*. Ithaca, NY: Cornell University Press, 1999.

Eitel, E. J. *Europe in China*. Reprint. Hong Kong: Oxford University Press, 1983.

Emerson, G. C. 'Stanley Internment Camp, Hong Kong, 1942–45: A Study of Civilian Internment During the Second World War'. M.Phil. Thesis. Hong Kong University, December 1973.

Endacott, G. B. *A History of Hong Kong*. Hong Kong: Oxford University Press. 1964.

———. *Hong Kong Eclipse*. Hong Kong: Oxford University Press, 1978.

Eykholt, Mark. 'Aggression, Victimization and Chinese Historiography of the Nanjing Massacre.' In *The Nanjing Massacre: In History and Historiography*, ed. Joshua Fogel. Berkeley: University of California Press, 2000.

Fanon, Frantz. *Black Skin White Masks*. Trans. C. L. Markmann. London: Pluto Press, 1967.

Feldwick, W., ed. *Present Day Impressions of the Far East and Prominent Chinese at Home and Abroad: The History, People, Commerce, Industries and Resources of China, Hongkong, Indo-China, Malaya and Netherlands India*. London: Globe Encyclopaedia, 1917.

Fogel, J. A. *The Nanjing Massacre in History and Historiography*. Berkeley and London: University of California Press, 2000.

Friedman, Susan. 'Women's Autobiographical Selves: Theory and Practice.' *The Private Self: Theory and Practice of Women's Autobiographical Writing*, ed. Shari Benstock. Chapel Hill: University of North Caroline Press, 1988.

Gibbon, Edward. *Memoirs of My Life*. Ed. G. A. Bonnard. London: Nelson, 1966.

Gillingham, Paul. *At the Peak: Hong Kong Between the Wars*. Hong Kong: Macmillan, 1983.

Gittins, Jean. *I Was at Stanley*. Hong Kong: Ye Olde Printerie, Ltd., 1945.

———. *Eastern Windows — Western Skies*. Hong Kong: South China Morning Post, 1969

———. *Stanley: Behind Barbed Wire*. Hong Kong University Press, 1982.

———. *A Stranger No More*. South Yarra, Victoria, Australia: n.p., 1987.

Gandt, Robert L. *Season of Storms: The Siege of Hongkong 1941*. Hong Kong: South China Morning Post, 1982.

Gornick, Vivian. 'Why Memoir Now?' *Women's Review of Books*. July 1996.

Gosano, Eddie. *Hong Kong Farewell*. Special Limited Edition. Sandown Park, UK: Greg England, 1997.

Gramsci, A. *Selections From the Prison Notebooks*. Ed. Q. Hoare and G. N. Smith. London: Lawrence and Wishart, 1971.

Grantham, A. *Via Ports: From Hong Kong to Hong Kong*. Hong Kong: Hong Kong University Press, 1965.

Great Britain Public Record Office, Colonial Office (CO). General Correspondence, Hong Kong. CO 129/342 on Eurasian Girls and The Diocesan Female Training School.

———. General Correspondence, Hong Kong. CO 129/392 4/12/12, memo from May to Harcourt on the absence of mixed marriage.

———. General Correspondence, Hong Kong. CO 129/462 on Appointment of Chinese Legislative Council Members.

———. General Correspondence, Hong Kong. CO 129/590/1, Evacuation From Hong Kong.

———. General Correspondence, Hong Kong. CO 537/1651 on KMT Infiltration of Hong Kong.

Gusdorf, Georges. 'Conditions and Limits of Autobiography.' Trans. James Olney. *Autobiography: Essays Theoretical and Critical*, ed. James Olney. New Jersey: Princeton University Press, 1980.

Hahn, Emily. *Hong Kong Holiday*. New York: Doubleday, 1946.

———. *China to Me: A Partial Autobiography*. Philadelphia: The Blakiston Co., 1944; London: Virago Press, 1987.

Hall, Peter. *In the Web*. Heswall, Wirral, England: n.p., 1992.

Hall, Stuart. 'Introduction: Who Needs "Identity"?' In *Questions of Cultural Identity*, ed. Stuart Hall and Paul du Gay. London: Sage Publication, 1996.

Han Suyin. *A Many-Splendoured Thing*. London: Arrow Books, [1952] 1992.

———. *The Crippled Tree*. London: Jonathan Cape, 1965.

———. *A Mortal Flower*. London: Jonathan Cape, 1966.

———. *Birdless Summer*. London: Jonathan Cape, 1968.

———. *My House Has Two Doors*. London: Triad Grafton Books, 1980a.

———. *Phoenix Harvest*. London: Triad Panther, 1980b.

Higginbotham, E. B. 'African-American Woman's History and the Metalanguage of Race.' *Revising the Word and the World: Essays in Feminist Literary Criticism*, ed. A. Clark, et. al. Chicago: University of Chicago, 1993.

Ho, Eric Peter. *The Welfare League: The Sixty Years: 1930–1990*. Hong Kong: The Welfare League, 1990.

Hobson-Jobson: The Anglo-Indian Dictionary, s.v. 'Eurasian'. Ed. Henry Yule and A. C. Burnell. Ware, UK: Wordsworth, 1996.

Hoe, Susanna. *Chinese Footprints: Exploring Women's History in China, Hong Kong and Macau*. Hong Kong: Roundhouse Publications, 1996.

Hong Kong Hansard 1940. Minutes of Legislative Council Meeting dated 25 July 1940.

Hsu, I. C. Y. *The Rise of Modern China*. Fifth Ed. New York: Oxford University Press, 1995.

Hui, P. K. 'Comprador Politics and Middleman Capitalism.' In *Hong Kong's History: State and Society Under Colonial Rule*, ed. Ngo Tak-Wing. London and New York: Routledge, 1999.

Keswick, Maggie. *The Thistle and the Jade*. Hong Kong: Mandarin Publishers Limited, 1982.

King, Frank, et al. *The Hongkong Bank Between the Wars and the Bank Interned 1919–1945*. Cambridge: Cambridge University Press, 1988.

King, Nicola. *Memory, Narrative, Identity: Remembering the Self*. Edinburgh: Edinburgh University Press, 2000.

Kipling, R. *From Sea to Sea*. New York: Scribners, 1906.

———. *Plain Tales From the Hills*. London and New York: Penguin, 1987.

Ko, T. K. and Wordie, Jason. *Ruins of War: A Guide to Hong Kong's Battlefields and Wartime Sites.* Hong Kong: Joint Publishing, 1996.

Korgen, Kathleen O. *From Black to Biracial.* Westport, Connecticut: Praeger, 1998.

Lamson, Herbert. 'The Eurasian in Shanghai.' *American Journal of Sociology* 41.5 (March 1936): 642–48.

Langford, R. Interview with Kenneth Andrew. *Next Magazine*, 4 December 1998.

Law, Edward. 'To the Eurasians Lads Who Fell in the Battle of Hong Kong, December 8th to 25th 1941.' Program to *Face* with Veronica Needa. MacAulay Studio, Hong Kong Arts Centre, 7 December 1998.

Lee, Tanya. *Child of the East Wind: An Autobiography.* Port Macquarie, Australia: Persimmon Publications, 1992.

Lethbridge, H. J. 'The Best of Both Worlds.' *Far Eastern Economic Review* 62.41 (10 October 1968).

———. 'Caste, Class and Race in Hong Kong Before the Japanese Occupation.' *Hong Kong: Stability and Change.* Hong Kong: Oxford University Press, 1978.

Li Shu-fan. *Hong Kong Surgeon.* Hong Kong: The Li Shu Fan Medical Foundation Ltd. 1964.

Lim, Shirley G. L. Introduction to *The Frontiers of Love*, by Diana Chang. [1956]. Seattle and London: University of Washington Press, 1994.

Lindsay, Oliver. *At the Going Down of the Sun: Hong Kong and South-East Asia 1941–* London: Hamish Hamilton, 1981.

Ling, Amy. 'Chinese American Women Writers: The Tradition Behind Maxine Hong Kingston.' *Maxine Hong Kingston's The Woman Warrior: A Casebook*, ed. Sau-Ling Cynthia Wong. New York: Oxford University Press, 1999.

Lionnet, Françoise. *Autobiographical Voices: Race, Gender, Self-Portraiture.* Ithaca and London: Cornell University Press, 1989.

Loomba, Ania. *Colonialism/Postcolonialism.* London and New York: Routledge, 1998.

Luk, Bernard. 'Lu Tzu-Chün and Ch'en Jung-Kun: Two Exemplary Figures in the *Ssu-shu* Education of Pre-war Urban Hong Kong.' *From Village to City: Studies in the Traditional Roots of Hong Kong Society*, ed. David Faure, James Hayes, and Alan Birch. Hong Kong: Centre of Asian Studies, University of Hong Kong, 1984.

Luk, Hung-kay. *A History of Education in Hong Kong.* Report submitted to Lord Wilson Heritage Trust, 2000.

Matthews, Clifford. Interview by Jason Wordie. In 'Oral History Project on Reminiscences of the War Experience in Hong Kong (Phase 2).' Hong Kong: Hong Kong Museum of History, 14 November 1996.

McCall, G. J. and Simmons, J. L. *Identities and Interactions.* New York: Free Press, [1966] 1978.

McGivering, Jill. *Macao Remembers*. Hong Kong: Oxford University Press, 1999.

Miners, Norman. *Hong Kong Under Imperial Rule 1912–1941*. Hong Kong: Oxford University Press, 1987.

————. *The Government and Politics of Hong Kong*. Hong Kong and London: Oxford University Press, [1975] 1995, Fifth ed.

Mo, Timothy. *The Monkey King*. London: Vintage, 1993.

Moise, E. E. *The Present and the Past: Modern China — A History*. London and New York: Longman, 1994.

Morris, Jan. *Hong Kong: Epilogue to an Empire*. London: Penguin Books, 1988.

————. Foreword to *Hong Kong: The Colony that Never Was*, by Alan Birch. Hong Kong: Guidebook Co., 1991.

Olney, James. *Metaphors of Self: The Meaning of Autobiography*. New Jersey: Princeton University Press, 1972.

————. Ed. *Autobiography: Essays Theoretical and Critical*. New Jersey: Princeton University Press, 1980.

————. Ed. *Studies in Autobiography*. New York and Oxford: Oxford University Press, 1988.

Omi, Michael and Howard Winant. *Racial Formation in the United States From the 1960s to the 1980s*. New York and London: Routledge and Kegan Paul, 1986.

Park, R. E. 'Human Migration and the Marginal Man.' *American Journal of Sociology* 33 (1928): 881-93.

————. *Race and Culture*. Illinois: The Free Press, 1950, p. 376.

————. Introduction to *The Marginal Man*, by E. V. Stonequist. New York: Russell & Russell, [1937] 1961.

Pascal, Roy. *Design and Truth in Autobiography*. Cambridge, MA: Harvard University Press, 1960.

Poy, Vivienne. *Building Bridges: The Life & Times of Richard Charles Lee — Hong Kong: 1905–1983*. Scarborough, Ontario, Canada: Calyan Publishing, 1998.

Reagon, B. J. 'My Black Mothers and Sisters or On Beginning a Cultural Autobiography.' *Feminist Studies* 8 (Spring 1982): 81–95.

Rowbotham, Sheila. *Woman's Consciousness, Man's World*. London: Penguin, 1973.

Russell, Bertrand. *The Problem of China*. London: Allen & Unwin, 1922.

Scott, Ian. *Political Change and the Crisis of Legitimacy in Hong Kong*. Hong Kong: Oxford University Press, 1989.

Shelley, Rex. *People of the Pear Tree*. Singapore: Time Book International, 1993.

Shields, Carol. *Stone Diaries*. London: Fourth Estate, 1994.

Sinn, Elizabeth. *Power and Charity: The Early History of the Tung Wah Hospital, Hong Kong*. Hong Kong: Oxford University Press, 1989.

Smith, Carl T. 'Ng Akew, One of Hong Kong's "Protected" Women.' *Chung Chi Bulletin* 46, 13–17 June 1969.

Smith, Sidonie. *Subjectivity, Identity and the Body: Women's Autobiographical Practices in the Twentieth Century*. Bloomington: Indiana University Press, 1993.

Spurr, Russell. *Excellency: The Governors of Hong Kong*. Hong Kong: FormAsia, 1995.

Stericker, John. 'Captive Colony: The Story of Stanley Camp, Hong Kong.' ts. Hong Kong Special Collection. Hong Kong University Main Library.

———. *A Tear for the Dragon*. London: Arthur Barker, 1958.

Stoler, Ann Laura. 'Sexual Affronts and Racial Frontiers.' *Tensions of Empire*, ed. F. Cooper and A. L. Stoler. Berkeley, Los Angeles and London: University of California Press, 1997.

Sui Sin Far [Edith Eaton]. *Mrs. Spring Fragrance and Other Writings*. Urbana and Chicago: University of Illinois Press, 1995.

Sweeting, Anthony. *The Social History of Education in Hong Kong: Notes and Sources*. Hong Kong: s.n., 1986.

———. *Education in Hong Kong: Pre 1841 to 1941 — Fact & Opinion*. Hong Kong: Hong Kong University Press, 1990.

———. 'Hong Kong Education Within Historical Process.' In *Education and Society in Hong Kong: Toward One Country and Two Systems*, ed. G. A. Postiglione. Hong Kong: Hong Kong University Press, 1992.

———. *A Phoenix Transformed: The Reconstruction of Education in Post-War Hong Kong*. Hong Kong: Hong Kong University Press, 1993.

Symons, J. 'HKU, Macao and the DGS.' *Dispersal and Renewal: Hong Kong University During the War Years*. Hong Kong: Hong Kong University, 1998.

Symons, J. C. *Looking at the Stars*. Hong Kong: Pegasus Books, 1996a.

———. Interview by Jason Wordie. In 'Oral History Project on Reminiscences of the War Experience in Hong Kong (Phase 2)'. Hong Kong Museum of History, 18 November 1996b.

Tang, James T. H. 'World War to Cold War: Hong Kong's Future and Anglo-Chinese Transactions, 1941–55.' *Precarious Balance: Hong Kong Between China and Britain, 1842–1992*, ed. Ming K. Chan. Hong Kong: Hong Kong University Press, 1994.

Tu, Elsie. *An Autobiography*. Hong Kong: Longman, 1988.

Tu, Wei-Ming, ed. *The Living Tree: The Changing Meaning of Being Chinese Today*. California: Standard University Press, 1994.

Vines, Stephen. *Hong Kong: China's New Colony*. London: Aurum Press, 1998.

Wang, Gungwu. 'Marginal Nationalism in the East Asian Region.' Seminar organised by the History Department, University of Hong Kong, 2 May 2001.

Waters, Dan. *Faces of Hong Kong: An Old Hand's Reflections*. Singapore: Prentice-Hall, 1995.

Welsh, Frank. A History of Hong Kong. London: HarperCollins, 1993.

Wesley-Smith, P. "Anti-Chinese Legislation in Hong Kong". In Precarious Balance: Hong Kong Between China and Britain, 1842–1991, ed. Ming K. Chan. Hong Kong: Hong Kong University Press, 1994.

White, Barbara-Sue. Hong Kong: Somewhere Between Heaven and Earth. Hong Kong: Oxford University Press, 1996.

Wong, Sau-Ling Cynthia. 'Autobiography as Guided Chinatown Tour? Maxine Hong Kingston's The Woman Warrior and the Chinese American Autobiograph Controversy.' In Maxine Hong Kingston's The Woman Warrior: A Casebook, ed. Sau-Ling Cynthia Wong. New York: Oxford University Press, 1999.

Wong, Soak Koon. 'Reading Two Women's Narratives: Sold for Silver and The White Moon Faces.' In Texts and Contexts: Interactions Between Literature and Culture in South East Asia, ed. Luisa Mallari-Hall and Lily Tope. Quezon City: University of Philippines Press, 1999.

Woo Mo-Han. A Hong Kong Story Before 1997. Cremorne, Australia: Jeff Toghill, 1997.

Wordie, Jason.'Umbrellas for a Few: An Examination of the 1940 Civilian Evacuation.' B.A. dissertation. Hong Kong University, 1997.

———. 'Making a Life Between Cultures.' South China Morning Post, 6 August 1998.

———. 'The 1940 War Evacuation Plan Only Deemed Those of "Pure European" Descent.' South China Morning Post, 9 August 1998.

———. 'A Controversial Icon of Her Time: Emily Hahn Was an Extraordinary Woman — Defiant, Decadent and Outrageous.' South China Morning Post, 14 November 1998.

Wright, Arnold, and H. A. Cartwright, eds. Twentieth Century Impressions of Hong Kong, Shanghai and Other Treaty Ports of China: Their History, People, Commerce, Industries and Resources. London: Lloyds, 1908.

Xiao, Liu. 'On Racial Identity and Nationalism in Modern China.' Procedures of Conference on Racial Identities in East Asia, 25–26 November 1994. Hong Kong: Division of Social Science, Hong Kong University of Science and Technology.

Yeo, Florence. My Memories. Pittsburgh, PA: n.p., 1989.

Young, Robert J. C. Colonial Desire: Hybridity in Theory, Culture and Race. London and New York: Routledge, 1995.

Zuss, Mark. Subject Present: Life-writings and Strategies of Representation. New York: Peter Lang Publishing, 1999.

Index

Grose, Kathleen, 120–21
Grouser, 131
Gusdorf, Georges, 37, 46, 77

Hahn, Emily, 57, 67, 68, 96, 132–33, 145
Hall, George, 122, 147
Hall, Peter, 50, 51, 127, 194
Hall, Rev. R. O., 83
Hall, Stuart, 111
Han Suyin, 18, 21, 45, 49, 210–11, 213–14, 224, 238
Harcourt, Sir Cecil, 29, 73, 77, 80
Heathrow, 99-100
Hegel, 116
Hennessy, John Pope, 15
historical destinies, 50, 76
historical determinism, 186
Ho Kai, 236
Ho, Stanley, 70, 71
Holhov, Sergei, 109, 159
Hong Kong Chinese Women's Relief Association, 226
Hong Kong New Life Movement Association, 226
Hong Kong News, 136, 159
Hong Kong Volunteer Defence Corps (HKVDC), 61, 65
household hierarchy, 231
Huxley, T. H., 17

identity anchor, 219
identity hierarchy, 121
ideological configuration, 210, 258
ideological discourses, 187
ideological inflection, 203, 233
inter-ethnic, 186
intra-ethnic, 127, 130
intra-lexically, 118

intra-sententially, 118
Irving, E. A., 205

Jamesian stigma, 71
Jardine Matheson, 28, 51, 127
Jardine ship, 74
Jardines (the family), 124
Jardines (the firm), 208
Jews, 100
jus soli, 123

Kadoorie, Lord, 101
Kai Tak Bund, 56, 65
Kashima Maru, 123
Kempe, Margery, 38
Keswicks, the, 124
'Kidnapped', 16
King George V School, 28, 79
King, Nicole, 51
King, Professor Gordon, 108, 132, 136, 145, 147
King's Park, 146
Kipling, 16, 54, 131
Korgen, Kathleen, 213
Kotewall, Robert, 24–25

Lamson, Herbert, 57
Lee, Hysan, 17
Lee, Harold, 17
Lee, Richard Charles, 17
Lee, Tanya, 143, 157–58
Li, Ellen, 95
Li Shu-fan, 65, 77
Light and Pass Ordinance, 14
'likes of you, the', 62, 63
Limehouse, 221
Lin Tse-hsu, 184, 208, 229
Lindsay, Colonel, 101